LAST BOHEMIAN

The Life and Times of

Jonathan David Batchelor

Part 1

JULIA ANTOINETTE ROSENSTEIN

LAST BOHEMIAN:

THE LIFE AND TIMES OF

JONATHAN DAVID BATCHELOR

by Julia Antoinette Rosenstein

Studio of Books LLC
5900 Balcones Drive Suite 100
Austin, Texas 78731
www.studioofbooks.org
Hotline: (254) 800-1183

Ordering Information:
Special discounts are available on quantity purchases by corporations, associations, and others. For details, contact the publisher at the address above.

Printed in the United States of America.

ISBN-13: Softcover: 978-1-968491-32-1
          eBook: 978-1-968491-33-8

Library of Congress Control Number: 2025915450

LAST BOHEMIAN:

The Life and Times of

JONATHAN DAVID BATCHELOR

ACKNOWLEDGEMENTS AND DEDICATION

Dedicated to all of Jonathan's children:
Egl Batchelor, Tara Batchelor, Maya Batchelor Herbert, Thornton Gilmore, Myra Gilmore Pacheco, Auria Gilmore Rouleaux, Kimberly Kollmeyer, and Pamela Lorence.

Special acknowledgements
Thank you for your assistance:

Beverly Shea, Deborah Waller, Rosemary Waller, Elena Tyrrell, Virginia Menge, Roberta Llewellyn, Ron White, Cheryl Parent, Wendy Avelino, Gini Menge, Heddy and David Schneller, Allison Blankenship, Tara Batchelor, Kimberly Kollmeyer, Kathy Myers, Regina Molina, and Sean White.

Introduction

I called it my 'cocoon.' Smack dab center of the large, three-story edifice I called, and still do call, Jonathan's house, my room had one curtainless window, feet from a non-view dirt hill strewn with chaparral. The left side of my early morning bed brought peaceful recollections of my deceased soul-friend, Jonathan Batchelor; the right side of the bed had been his space. Steadfast on my back, his gentle mattress permeated my lifeblood and gave to me blessed emotions of love, happiness, contentment. He had been good to me and I missed him. Lucky to be with him for eighteen years, I now longed to see him again. Since I could not, I did the next best thing; I recollected. Gazing over old, distressed-wooden walls of my bedchamber, I was nourished with thought. The mattress below me had been given in exchange for a painting. Or so I was told. In his entire life, the artist never bought a single piece of furniture; most of his household belongings came either from years of benevolent patrons foisting cast offs in exchange for paintings or the bartering that was typical of old time Canyon residents.

Previous page: *Self Portrait* by Jonathan Batchelor, late 1980s. Although I am saddened that many paintings burned, the loss of this one is especially poignant because it was a favorite. I hung it in the bedroom after his death, so I could say goodnight/good morning to him. When I see this image, I see the very tiny start of a smile and a twinkle in his eye. When painting in his studio, he offtimes donned an old, worn, blue sweatshirt. He wore it that day along with his gold wire-rimmed glasses. In his 70s, his fiery red hair had dimmed to chestnut. His background fill colors were typically any color he chanced to have on his palette. Because he was painting himself in his studio, wood veneer hues from reddish-brown walls prevail. Behind him was a generous, expansive window without screen, that on hot summer days, we flung open welcoming typical Canyon humid aromas.

Half dozing in the dark envelope, I presently heard a tremendous unmistakable boom. I looked at the clock: not much more than 5 a.m. Marginally annoyed, I could only think, "What did the cats knock over now?" I considered overcoming my boudoir torpor to climb steps and find out what the cats did, but I was just too cozysnug beneath Jonathan's blankets. Presently, I realized the fallen object had made a much bigger racket than any bric-a-brac could possibly have made. "What fell over? One of his sculptures?" But they were all too substantial for the cats to overturn. I had better check it out.

Those who need rigid routine and struggle with aberrations can understand my perplexed bewilderment when I walked outside and spotted a narrow ribbon of flame on the corrugated-metal roof. My thoughts traveled years back when a small fire had ignited inside the foyer of this very same house. "Always tend a fire," Jonathan had instructed as he doused the small flames. Typical Jonathan dichotomy. Prone to anxieties, he was also cool as a cucumber, unruffled, and not disposed to panicking. He was no longer alive but well I remembered those instructions. Grabbing the hose hanging outside the second story landing, I turned on the water and…. nothing. Jonathan was gone. I had no set of instructions this time.

No water. Such is the hazard of living in idyllic Canyon, California. During the dry months, one never knew when our ancient pipelines might have a blockage of cyanophyte, the orange-hued blue-green algae that thrived in our natural water system. The spring that fed our house was a wonderfully resplendent, icy cool, raging font of crystal clear, mineral-laden liquid in the winter, and a trickle of refreshment in the summer that had to be tended, loved, and treated with kid gloves, almost as carefully as one might tend a stove when preparing a large meal for a party. And best of all, the water was natural, untreated with any chemical. The healthiest water in the world, Jonathan would say. Wherever we drove, we always carried bottles of Canyon water. Outside of his morning tea or occasional alcohol, Jonathan refused to down anything else.

The community labeled our water system 'Batchelor's Spring' and for good reason. In 1949, when first living in Canyon, long before I made my entry into this world, Jonathan was annoyed by the spring's erratic liquid flow that sometimes disappeared entirely. When he asked a nearby resident why, Jonathan was advised nothing could be done. But the disbelieving artist had to see for himself. Resolutely, he explored the spring, cistern, pipes, and valves, and was surprised to find maintenance was almost non-existent: the spring was tended only when faucets were empty. Creative and resourceful, Jonathan built a 'dam' for the spring using a 4 X 4 with a generous hole drilled through the center for a pipeline. The old pipe, which had been prone to falling out of the spring, now had stability all the way down to the cistern, some fifteen or so feet downhill.

The beauty of Jonathan's water system is that it functioned by gravity. From the spring, situated in a wash far above Jonathan's house, the pipeline descended a rather steep rock-strewn stream bed to an outlet valve before ascending back up the next hill to the first connected house. From that house it again rushed downhill to the second linked house, and finally, via pressure, back uphill to Batchelor's. It was, for all intents and purposes, a gigantic siphon.

For years he and I tended the spring, the source of our drinking, bathing and cooking water. For years, while Jonathan was alive, we were spoiled. Twice each week in the summer, our artesian well was tended and cyanophyte bailed out with a beat-up-old cooking pot.

Those duties were split with our then next-door neighbor, Beverly Shea-Schurr. Every 3-4 days, he or she would hike up to the spring and tend the source, followed by draining and cleaning the orange-yellow liquid in a cement cistern, which preceded opening the outlet valve. This large valve, at the bottom of the wash, was allowed to fully discharge a raging torrent of orange water till it ran crystal clear. Once all algae dispersed, it was just a matter of days before the bright orange bloom had to be tended again. Maintenance dropped to once a week in the winter when a violent rush disallowed algae blooms.

During Jonathan's waning years, after Beverly had moved, care of our water system fell to me, my roommate Tammy Maxon, and on occasion my other neighbor, Paul Tarushka; the old system of twice a week in summer, once a week in winter, became less routine. We had plenty of water throughout my first fifteen years in Canyon and rarely ran out, even in the driest of months, but without the teamwork of Shea-Schurr/Batchelor, the guaranteed supply of water became more erratic. Therefore, I was not entirely surprised when the modest water tank next to the second story landing of Canyon house lacked water.

My entire life I have been slow to respond, and this crucial moment was no exception. Dazed, I did not connect the fire on the roof with "my house is going to burn down." Muddled, I did the only thing that came to mind, which was to dial 911; I dialed from the landline on the middle floor. "My house in Canyon is on fire," I reported. And before anything further could be said, the line was cut. I was puzzled. "Oh," my autistic brain reasoned, "It must be the fire. Duh." The fire up above in the art studio must have been raging, but in my mind it was still a small rill on the roof. I did not know what to do. Why, I now reflect and ask, did I not grab paintings and throw them out into the night? Why did I not grab my 'babies', sleeping peacefully on my bed? I had a rabbit in one cage, a male calico kitten I had been bottle-feeding in another, and yet a third kitten brought to life when I found it beside the trail desiccated and near death. I return to that moment and I am pained, distressed, ashamed. Why did I not understand the house was going to burn completely? I have read that autistic people learn by rote. But how does one learn how to deal with a house fire by rote?

My bedroom was located in the midst of the middle floor toward the west end of the house and I wandered, stupefied and perplexed, in and out of the west side of the house. Next thing I knew, one of my tenants, Ron White, burst through my bedroom door from the east end of the house where his room was located, told me the house was on fire, and to get out. He then ran back to his room to grab his computer and fled from an eastern door. Years later I find myself troubled that I hadn't thought to run to his room to awaken him. It's as if there was a disconnect somewhere in my slow-moving brain. Ron only roused because my hefty orange cat, Mr. Moto, made a huge, spectacular, diagonal leap from an open window midst the top floor to the roof of the annex, where Ron's room was located. The cat made a perfect landing on the annex metal roof and the noise was substantial; Ron woke up. Furthermore, neither did it occur to me to run downstairs to awaken my other tenant, Mike. Asleep on the bottom floor, Mike woke up due to my Staffordshire terrier, Emily. My animals did what I could not do; they saved two lives.

Good judgment is, for me, a conundrum; I have not one iota of intuitive insight. In all my eighteen years with Jonathan, I gratefully lived in his shadow and allowed, with acknowledged relief, for him to take the helm in both our lives. Everything was about Jonathan and it could not have been any other way for me, or for him. At that moment, I needed his insight.

Furthermore, nothing in my upbringing could have prepared me for the loss of Canyon home. After Jonathan's death I had been working on his biography, going through his archives, picking out choice short stories he had written, singling out the best photographs, rereading letters to and from his parent/friends. I had slowly, during our eighteen years together, filed all manner of correspondence. Jonathan David Batchelor was not one to discard anything written on paper. He lived in that house for over half a century; paperwork tended to accumulate in whatever room he happened to be using for letter writing or stashing correspondence and bills. When the area he was using became too jam-packed with papers, he would simply move his letter writing/journal keeping/bill paying to another part of the house; and it was thus that I teasingly referred to myself as his "archive-ologist" because as I uncovered different paper piles and filed them away, I was moving back through the years of his life, all the way to his first marriage and earlier. Furthermore, he saved a draft of every single letter he ever wrote, this because as a young man, he was accused of writing something he hadn't, and was thus hungry to have copies of everything. Unearthed first drafts, covered by ancient bills, were not in any particular order, but they did represent points in time and I was able to piece together events in his life, some mundane, others dramatic. Archiving his correspondence was good for me and I was good at it; I was imbued with a sense of history by my mother, who was a history major in college, and never let us forget how important it is.

To say I was stung over the loss of his archives is an understatement. They were vast, what with letters dating to the 1930s. As I filed his letters, I brought them to him for clarification; what was happening in his life to cause him to write this, or why did a certain person write that? There were also handwritten journals dating to his teenage years, the 1920s. Artists tend to be keen observers of life and Jonathan was no exception; he had an almost obsessive need to pen his interpretations, opinions, ideas; he wrote almost every single day that I lived with him. His hand-written logs filled books and notebooks and I typed almost every single one of them. It took me years.

Filing personal versions of those who had written him gave me a peek into the zenith of his life, which was 1950s-1970s. Of utmost importance were letters/notes from his wives, Dorothy Dickinson Batchelor (wife number one), Ona McNamee Batchelor (wife number two), Sigrid Stovner Batchelor (wife number three), and finally Joyce Kollmeyer Batchelor (wife number four). I should also mention Patricia Starr Gilmore, never his wife, but who lovingly bore three of his children.

Not only did I archive letters; I leafed-through vintage 1920 union magazines, read small-scale self-published poetry broadsides from the beatnik era (picked up at various Bay Area poetry readings from 1940s-1950s), perused George Sterling poetry books and enjoyed special modest gift books self-published by family friend and astrologer Gavin Arthur. Jonathan's library had many first editions; I read all of those, mostly Jack London and Edgar Allan Poe, handed over to him in exchange for paintings. I especially treasured going through endless stacks of old National Geographics, Look, and Life magazines dating to the 1940s; they satisfied my penchant for studying old advertisements and magazine photos. Every room in that house had bookshelves, sometimes with books shelved behind other books in front, and I was in literary bliss.

The night Jonathan's house was reduced to ashes, nippy draughts of air (and thank goodness it was cool and moist, a rarity for the month of August, or the entire community conceivably could have burned) lifted paper scraps to the ridge of our hill where snowing fragments overwhelmed residents, including Jonathan's good friend, Barry Smith. Barry later expressed, "When I saw all those pieces of paper raining down, I said to myself, well, that must be Batchelor's house going (burning)."

Among the archives I created, I had made a special file for writings from the Endymion Society, a poetry group founded by Jonathan that was actually much more than verse; members read not only poems but excerpts from various and assorted prose, essays or promising novels in the making. Works of the Endymion Society also included paintings and photography; all the arts were encouraged and Endymion members were not to be taken lightly. This was a group of titan creativity. Everyone in the group refined his/her own craft and no words can describe my private images of wonderful magical readings with a softly lit, yellow globe-lamp illuminating the circle of narrators, sipping and/or gulping Jonathan's home-made zinfandel, 'Red Spider' (high alcoholic content, he used to brag). With few lights but many candles, the studio was overall cast in dusky shadow: sporadically hung spider plants filled obscure recesses with indescribably bizarre shadows cast on walls. Only one overhead yellow lamp and a strongly lit 100-gallon aquarium set against an inner bearing wall cast the only illumination on those precious pieces of binder paper, typing paper, notepad or even napkin jottings. Grouped in a small circle adjacent the tropical fish tank they would read, argue, joke and jostle into the wee hours of the morning. Jonathan was many years older than I, but his stamina never ceased to amaze me. I never made it through the night and was in bed, located on the bottom floor of our three-story home, by 3 a.m. Sometimes I awakened at 6 and could still hear roaring from the top floor. I was never surprised to find people asleep or passed out in the studio or even outside when the weather was warm. To this day the Endymion Society still exists in the hearts and minds of all those who participated. Jonathan's oldest son, mathematician and poet Egl Tarn Batchelor, carries on the spirit.

Amongst the most precious mailings lost in the fire were, of course, family letters, especially correspondence to and from his father (or pater familias, as Jonathan used to refer to him). For the most part, Thomas Leon Batchelor had been a single parent to his last and youngest child, Jonathan. The two were very close. Over the course of years, Jonathan, the young idealistic dreamer, had penned dozens of lyrical letters to his father. He typically addressed him as 'O Genie,' and often used words like thee and thou, and referred to his letters as missives or epistles. He rarely wrote of worldly events, but preferred a more poetic prose, writing of the earth, beauty, and art. One missive to his father included his ambitions alongside a blueprint he imagined for his future art studio. Curiously, I once asked Jonathan why he had referred to his father as a genie. "Because," the artist softly responded, "I thought he was so wise, I thought he could move mountains, I thought he could do anything."

The man with the obsession to write sheets of prose did not write to his mother. If he could have written her, he would have. But he believed she would not understand his letters. The latter part of her life was spent in a downward spiral of mental illness; before Jonathan was five, she had to be institutionalized, leaving Thomas without wife and Jonathan without mother. Although the adult Jonathan did visit her in a sanitarium, she never recognized him as her son and when he did visit, she called him her special friend.

Jonathan's mother, Kathryn Gano Batchelor, was also an artist. I am sorry the fire consumed the few paintings of hers we had. But as luck would have it, Jonathan did give to daughter Tara, a painting of Kathryn's. The painting is precise down to the itty-bitty details; a basket lay on its side, flowers spilling; the tiniest and most well-defined bees alight on basket and flowers. From his mother he inherited a love of nature and art; from Thomas, Jonathan inherited a soft heart and storytelling capability. From both parents, he inherited a passionate love of music.

Wine glass adjacent wine spattered poem.
Photograph by Sean White.

PERIPATETIC FATHER

Jonathan's pet descriptive word for his father was peripatetic. Thomas Leon Batchelor (b. April 1872) and his older brother John S. (b.1867), were raised in the pioneering town of Woodland, California. The boys' parents, Captain John Thomas Batchelor and the Sephardic Jewess Blanca Mende de Merez, had met and fallen in love while the captain was passing through New Orleans. The two eventually settled in Woodland, California, northwest of Sacramento, which by the 1870s was a small settlement with a population of about 1,600 and complete with schools, churches and a railroad stop; by the 1880s the community could claim telegraph operators, a telephone service, and streetlamps. Fairly close to the Sacramento River, the Woodland home provided for Captain Batchelor a means to earn a living through captaining steamboats or skippering the occasional scow schooner (small barges with sails that continually plied the waters from Sacramento/Stockton to San Francisco, and vice versa). They carried agricultural products down river and returned with gravel, salt, sand or fertilizer. The hay delivered to San Francisco literally fueled the city's growth; it fed drayage horses.

Previous page: Captain John Thomas Batchelor and his wife, Blanca Mende de Merez. Original renderings charcoal on paper from around 1860, victims of the fire.

Captain John Thomas Batchelor continued his river livelihood until woefully shot to death by an outlaw. Jonathan's rendition provided the captain joined a search party to pursue a gang of thugs; the outlaws, well forward of the squad, situated for a surprise ambush. The trapped posse met with a barrage of bullets and several of the law-abiding men were shot off their horses, including John Thomas.

With two young boys to care for, the widow Blanca Mende de Merez accepted an offer of marriage to Jacob Olhahn, a local Woodland grocer and widower, who was taken in by her striking Spanish features. He was indifferent to her Judaism and although Blanca was never particularly religious, the Sephardic Jewess did stick to her roots by acknowledging Jewish holidays and baking traditional holiday treats. I can only speculate she may have spoken Ladino for she was certainly educated and did hand down to her son Thomas two bibles, both written in Hebrew script. Although Thomas never learned to speak Hebrew, the bibles unquestionably meant something to him, because he kept and carried them close to his heart the rest of his life, finally handing them, before his death, to Jonathan.

Blanca, John Thomas Batchelor, and also Jacob Olhahn, were all adequately literate and although her sons never finished high school, Blanca, who was well educated, made sure the boys learned how to read and write. Assisting with Olhahn's store worked to the boys' advantage: both children developed a keen sense of industry from their stepfather. As adults, the brothers sustained middle-class sensibilities of cultivated entrepreneurship; John Batchelor was ultimately able to purchase a house and maintain a secure life; not so Thomas. Due to no fault of his own, a middle-aged Thomas Batchelor saw his existence unravel because of one unlucky event after another.

Despite Thomas' eventual ill-fated experiences, the one thing that anchored him throughout his life was music. As a child, with encouragement from his parents and one particular elementary schoolteacher, he devoted much time learning the trombone and developed a boundless passion for classical music. Not just the trombone, but also euphonium, French horn, and violin. His entire adult life was spent seeking orchestras to join; dance music gave him an income. But music was not his only hunger: as a youngster he had learned how to roll cigarettes; for the remainder of his life he would never be far from two favorite vices, tobacco and red wine.

When John and Thomas were older teens, the family moved to a ranch in Eastern Washington where Jacob had some land. It can be noted that despite no high school diplomas, growing up with an educated Sephardic Jewish mother could only mean one thing: a push toward education. In that simpler era, knowing how to read, write, and work numbers was all it took to carry one through life. Studious Thomas, who read voraciously, was governed by both love of music and enthusiasm for wide-open spaces. He had a soft spot for animals, particularly for horses, and loved the freedom of a racing gallop. Coming of age in Woodland, California and then experiencing wide-ranging sagebrush pastureland in Eastern Washington gave to him the opportunity to spend hours in the saddle. As an adult, he was always able to earn money working for various drayage and/or mail firms that existed in his day. Although too late for the Pony Express, work was still to be had as a teamster and he had just the right physique sought by horse services. They required strong men who were of slight build, lithe and lean. Jonathan, too, was always thin, and for years I teased him about it. He would thump on his chest where his prominent sternum was bumpy and chuckle about his "manly washboard chest." Lightheartedly he roared, "You should have seen my dad. He was skinnier than I am!" To Thomas' dying day, he never learned to drive an automobile and deplored the day when horses became an anachronism.

There they lived until Jacob passed; then it was to Cle Elum, Washington, where Blanca spent her remaining years. Her grown boys chose divergent paths; the more practical John migrated to California where he met and married Selma Swanson. A painting contractor, he settled in Santa Rosa and then Berkeley, California where they raised three boys and a girl; Lester, Clarence, Frank and Esther. The more impractical but lively Thomas cared for his mother till she passed, and then entered the roving world of music making and vaudeville.

At this point I would like to say in 1995, Jonathan sat down at his computer (which he learned how to use at the age of 80!) and typed his family history. The above two paragraphs were stretched into some sixty pages. The liberties Jonathan took to create various personalities of his ancestors and also his imaginary dialogues are priceless. A prolific and astounding writer, he jotted witticisms and reflections practically every day, and indeed, including the day he died. Instead of imposing his ancestral version in the midst of this biography, I decided to include it in the appendix. As typical per Jonathan, he chose the very doctrinaire name *A Compendious History of the Batchelor Family Descended from Captain John*. He very carefully made copies for all his children and included as the frontispiece the two images of Captain John Thomas Batchelor and Blanca Mende de Merez. On the last page of the biography, he made sure to include a photograph of the last self-portrait he ever painted, *Self Portrait in a Brown Hat*, 1993 (see book cover). All three portraits perished in the house fire.

My responsibility as a researcher is to verify facts. That is not always easy to do, especially when researching the deceased. I did, however, find Ancestry.com to be more than a resourceful tool. Through their website I located Thomas Leon Batchelor's 1930 United States census, and there was the information I sought; "Thomas' father's birthplace: England. Mother's birthplace: Spain." So far so good. To confuse the issue, Thomas married twice throughout his life, and both wives were named Katherine. For clarity's sake, I'll spell his first wife's name as Kathryn. She preferred it that way. Jonathan conveyed many a time that his mother (Kathryn Gano) was the daughter of Irish immigrants. And so it goes. On the 1930 census, Kathryn's/Katherine's parents are listed as Irish immigrants. But which wife was Thomas referring to? Kathryn was institutionalized by then and he may have been indicating his second wife.

Jonathan was proud of his Irish roots; indeed, he certainly looked the part with his shock of gleaming ruddy hair. Gleefully the loquacious redhead expressed to any passing ear the saga of his grandparents, bragging of his sea captain grandfather and the New Orleans Jewish beauty his grandfather courted and married. Curiously, I probed the 1920 census. Leave no research stone unturned was my thought. I was flummoxed, however, when Thomas, who filled out the census, listed his father's birthplace as Missouri, his mother's as

Kentucky. Furthermore, Kathryn's parents' origins, also filled out by Thomas, were listed as Ohio for father, Pennsylvania for mother. The surname Gano is considered either Italian or French in origin; but that would not preclude her parents emigrating from Ireland. Why did Thomas list her birthplace as the Midwest?

I was left baffled with only one desire: the 1910 census beckoned. I could hardly believe my eyes. Now both of Thomas' parent's birthplaces were listed as Kentucky and Kathryn's parents both supposedly came from Iowa. I fared no better with the 1900 census, where Thomas' father hailed from Indiana, his mother from Kentucky. Kathryn's parents were from Ohio and Pennsylvania. At least her parents' origins matched the 1920 census.

I thought to check the census reports of Thomas' brother, John; I fared no better. His 1910 census indicated the father to be from Indiana, the mother, Kentucky. His 1920 census indicated both parents from Missouri. It appeared that Jonathan Batchelor, a legendary storyteller, was descended from a long line of myth makers, albeit with the best of intentions.

I have given much thought to these discrepancies. My first thought was that Thomas might have been distancing himself from his immigrant history while protecting Kathryn by hiding the truth of her Irish ancestry if, indeed, her parents were immigrants. Irish immigrants were not treated well at the turn of the century; most walked from ship deck to almshouse and lived in tenement poverty. Irish culture, dress and brogue were made fun of: The Irish were discouraged from finding gainful employment and scorned in newspapers through political cartoons. The dailies freely used vernacular slang for all immigrants including words like coolie, coon, ape, wop, paddy and dago. Immigrants were snubbed and distrusted. Not only that, but the most popular vaudeville shows included some mimicry of Jewish, Irish and black culture. And surely as a vaudeville performer, Thomas must have seen/heard some appalling discrimination in his travels. And if Kathryn were truly the daughter of Irish immigrants, he may have tried to diminish her past. Perhaps John Batchelor had similar misgivings. From 1900 onward he lived in California; in 1905 the Asian Exclusion League was formed, dedicated to excluding Asian immigrants. The Exclusion League was a part of America's shameful past; I can only imagine how prevailing attitudes must have affected every person married to an immigrant. Although John's wife, Selma, was not Asian, she was an immigrant from Sweden. I find it somewhat ironic that John Batchelor finally settled in Berkeley, named after an immigrant, George Berkeley, an 18th-century Irish philosopher and bishop.

Then I turned to the person of Thomas Leon Batchelor. A man of the theater. A man who was famous for making people laugh and indeed, in 1940 as Thomas lay dying in Oakland California's Highland Hospital, he became something of a legend as he kept the nurses roaring with his rapid-fire quips. What an amazing, exceptional, human being. In the 1980s Jonathan's still-living older cousins told me that Thomas was selfless, compassionate and devoted to making those around him laugh until they had tears. I heard it said the old vaudevillian was kind, considerate, and outspoken on the appalling mistreatment of Native Americans, emphatically pointed out to Jonathan. That is a powerful statement coming from a man who was raised in pioneering California.

We, all of us, live our own ordinary lives. There is nothing wrong with a conventional existence provided one is content with life, and fulfilled with love and laughter. I also, personally, do not link embellishment/storytelling with negativity providing it does not hurt anyone. According to Jonathan, the raconteur Thomas was forever acting on and off stage, and I can only speculate there was no difference for the actor. And what is wrong with one's living room becoming a stage? Through the years, as father fostered an existence with son, the child absorbed his father's theatrics, witticisms, jokes. The father consistently and constantly consigned his household to laughter through his observations.

Jonathan adored his father; the two frequently lived together even as Jonathan was forging his young adult life. I can easily visualize the animated and ebullient Thomas peppering his life's story, aggrandizement here, enhancement there. I can picture the admiring look on young Jonathan's face and certainly his father could not have missed it, thus he recounted fabulous tales from his experiences including riding with the Pony Express. Never mind that the Pony Express ceased to exist ten years before Thomas' birth.

And the love-bound son could only glow with pride at his father's history: it is easy to speculate that Thomas must have soaked up the veneration. Scholarly from a young age and with a good memory, Jonathan was well equipped to recollect much of his father's ripostes. During our many parties at Canyon, after Jonathan had a drink or two, or three, a cockney accent would effortlessly pour from him as some of his father's anecdotes replayed to new audiences. I can still hear Jonathan's voice reciting:

> "She was poor, but she was honest,
> Though she came from 'umble stock
> And an honest 'eart was beating
> Beneath her tattered frock.
> It's the same the whole world over,
> It's the poor what gets the blame
> It's the rich what gets the pleasure
> Ain't it all a bloomin' shame."
> Or this one: "I lost 'arf a crown yesterday."
> "Did y' 'ave a 'ole in yer pocket?"
> "No, the bloke wot dropped it 'eard it fall."

It is easy to surmise that Thomas' recapped history may have been a tad embroidered. When he filled out the 1930 census, Jonathan was just out of high school, not yet fully on his own, residing with his father. Although Thomas was still earning money as a musician, he was also leaving vaudeville behind and perhaps he valued a good audience.

Assuming the 1930 census correct, Thomas would have been a mature sixty-year-old and perhaps wanted his son to know the truth of his Jewish history, of Captain John Thomas Batchelor and his lovely Sephardic wife, Blanca Mende de Merez. Although World War II had not yet transpired, certainly there were dreadful forebodings via newspaper articles describing mistreatment of Jews in Europe, and in those days, everyone read newspapers, including Thomas Leon, who loved to read as much as his son. He kept his religious beliefs close to his heart, professed not to be particularly religious, yet treasured two Old Testaments scripted in Hebrew with no English translation that his mother left him. He also named his youngest Jonathan David, after the Biblical Jonathan and David. He never let his son forget that Jonathan and David were best friends, and to treasure the name. Thomas may have been more religious than he let on and wished for his son to recognize their Jewish ancestry.

After his mother's passing in Cle Elum, actor, storyteller, and musician Thomas Leon set his sights on the Pantages vaudeville circuit. Alexander Pantages, of Seattle, had opened any number of vaudeville houses on the west coast including one in Tacoma, and had plans to extend his circuit all the way to the Mississippi River. Thomas figured if nothing else, he could play any one of his brass instruments. However, in truth, he wanted to perform on stage. Of his many gifts, he was blessed with a persuasive, glib tongue. A raconteur from birth, he had the uncanny ability to memorize dialogue and handily mimicked any number of foreign accents he may have heard in passing: Chinese, Russian, French, Irish and Scottish brogues, and of course, Yiddish. He was an unabashed sponge, soaking up human behavior and memorizing events that were theater-worthy. He was born to entertain and he was hired as both musician and comedian; binary skills made him a valuable employee. Adopting 'Tom Batch' as his stage name, he began a life of travel. He not only worked for the Pantages circuit, but he also traveled for a time with the Orpheum and in that manner was able to see the country.

Photographs on the following page: Thomas Batchelor in vaudeville costume. On the left he is a mad conductor. On the right he plays the quintessential Irish rogue. He loved to play the buffoon and effect hilarity. Photographs were taken at the turn of the century Tacoma, Washington. Photographer unknown.

Next page: The orchestral musician Thomas Batchelor. wearing his best suit, including tails. Always dressed nicely, this was his array for symphonic playing. Right: In formal band uniform playing fanfare trumpet. Jonathan absorbed his father's intense love of classical music and eventually began playing his father's violin. Regaling his son with anecdotes of travels, Thomas enjoyed retelling of the evening he watched Gustav Mahler conduct the New York Philharmonic.

Multi-tasker musician-entertainer 'Tom Batch' traveled by rail, coach, buggy; he spent months on the road, seldom returning home, which was now Tacoma, Washington. While in Tacoma he supplemented his income by playing in the local community band. Prior to radios or televisions, towns and cities typically funded community entertainment by hiring musicians to play in urban parks, sometimes in a bandstand, band shell, or gazebo. Rural or city townsfolk gathered with picnic lunches on blankets and brought chairs, played cards, read the latest newspaper or renewed friendships while listening. The pianist for Tacoma's town concert band, auburn-haired, blue-eyed Kathryn Gano, local musician and piano teacher, caught his eye.

Thomas was smitten. Beautiful and gifted, sensitive, creative, she not only played piano, she sketched, painted with oils, and was well educated. Jonathan was never certain of her birthdate or age (although according to the 1900 U.S. census, she was born in 1879, and if that is correct, she was eight years younger than Thomas), and although Jonathan only lived with her until he was five, for the rest of his life he waxed poetic about her (and in general revered motherhood) and never ceased speaking of her loveliness. Both father and son adored Kathryn and as an adult Jonathan handily made several drawings of her from old photographs. One he framed and kept on his desk.

The enamored couple readily wed August 14 of 1897. When Kathryn met her future husband, she already had a three-year-old (or five-year-old, depending on which census one is examining), Ralph Elliott, of whom Thomas willingly adopted (Kathryn, however, did not change Ralph's last name of Elliott to Batchelor, which was a bone of contention with Thomas. However be it may, Thomas chose not to make an issue of it, although he cautioned Jonathan, years later, to insist on a name change if he, Jonathan, ever adopted a child. Kathryn and Thomas rarely, if ever, had any open disagreements.) Adopting Ralph was never a question. And just like his adoptive father, Ralph displayed a keen interest in the trombone. Enveloping his stepson beneath his benevolent wing, not only did he teach Ralph how to play, but when Ralph was older, they developed father/son slapstick skits and made a good comedy duo.

Portraits of Mr. and Mrs. Thomas Batchelor. Typical for their era, they may be wedding photos, but I'm not sure.

There was good money to be made in entertainment; Thomas handily supported Kathryn and their growing brood. Their firstborn, Leon Edgar, or 'Lynn' as he preferred to be called, was born in 1898 (or 1899, depending on what document one is examining) that would someday mature into a handsome, blonde wine-quaffing party boy. The second baby, a girl, Blanche Demeris (named after Blanca de Merez), was brought into the world in 1902. Throughout her life, with her auburn-brunette hair and blue eyes, she was considered a regal beauty.

Both the Pantages and then Orpheum Circuits kept Thomas away from home for lengthy periods of time, sometimes months, but Kathryn had immediate family in Tacoma to assist if she needed help. That said, Kathryn was herself very competent and able to maintain her household, even with three children. Characteristic of her generation, she cooked all meals, darned all socks, embroidered, tatted lace, sewed the family's clothing, and on top of all that continued to play and teach piano. Furthermore, she was a time-wizard who was able to conjure space and time for oil painting; and although adopting the name Batchelor, she preferred to sign her paintings 'Kathryn Gano'.

Kathryn Batchelor was a mainstream turn-of-the-century housewife, enjoying fruits of the industrial revolution. Mass production brought prices down and almost everybody who could read ordered from their Montgomery Ward or Sears catalogs. People who bought radios developed a more worldly view, although women still could not vote. Be that as it may, they bobbed their hair, wore large hats with feathers, slipped into high-buttoned shoes, and raised the hemline in order to step into a rare car or onto trolleys. Henry Ford cranked out the first inexpensive cars and Americans became obsessed with taking their Sunday drives. Although the automobile was still backstage to horses, men took to motoring with their goggles, caps and dusters with a speed limit of twenty miles-per-hour. Many men, that is, except Thomas, who preferred traveling by horse and buggy when not taking a train or trolley. His love for beautiful equines never diminished across his entire lifespan. Shortly after the turn of the century, when Zane Grey started publishing his books with frontier themes, Thomas became a Zane Grey fanatic, and left an entire collection of Zane Grey books with his passing.

American urban society was evolving with extra leisure time and Thomas and Kathryn made their living from that niche. Today's modern families are lucky if they are able to sit down and eat meals together, let alone spend time with each other in the evening. At the turn of the 20th century, families commonly gathered in the evening and had sing-a-longs. The center of action was the piano, and most people commonly owned one; if no one could tickle the ivories, player pianos were used. Tin pan alley was in full vogue and millions of copies of sheet music were sold across the country from vendors or dime stores. Barbershop quartets became a common feature on Saturday nights.

Technologically, the two major advancements in the field of entertainment were the radio and hand-cranked Victor-victrola, forerunner of the record player. The Victor-victrola opened up a world of music for everyone, including opera, band music of John Phillip Sousa, and the songs of Irving Berlin, George M. Cohan or Scott Joplin.

A 'talking machine', forerunner of the record player.

Technological advances were not limited to audio. One of the most popular fads of nascent twentieth century was the penny arcade. One dropped a penny into a slot, put his eyes to the viewer, and enjoyed a short film clip, which was customarily naughty. Next came the nickelodeons where one could enjoy a short moving picture projected on a screen. Enormously popular, thousands were installed across the country.

Sometime between 1900 and 1910 the Batchelors moved from Tacoma to Ukiah, California. I can only speculate as to why they moved; perhaps Thomas tired of the uncaring/gray Northwest winters; perhaps he remembered California's pleasant weather and scenery. More than that, I suspect he was following older brother John, who had moved with wife and children to Santa Rosa, California. For Thomas the musician, there was only one prevailing criterion for every community he chose to live; a bandstand, dance hall, or entertainment facility (vaudeville halls now doubled as movie theaters or arcades). Most resorts had dance bands (which were considered orchestras if they had one or two violinists) and sometimes a smaller band or piano to accompany silent films. Ukiah was not only famous for its bubbling hot springs, but was also hop-and-a-skip by rail to either San Francisco or the myriad resorts that lined the Russian River.

Legendary Russian River resorts, such as Rio Nido, Guerneville, Monte Rio, Healdsburg, were immensely popular; they had their own railway lines direct from San Rafael, where San Franciscans disembarked from ferries. Cloud-wrapped in the summer, San Franciscans fled fog and cold for sun, beaches and warmth along the Russian River. Not only did travelers have multiple hotels to choose from, they had their pick of recreational activities which included boat rides, fishing, croqueting, billiards, canoeing, inner tubing, rafting, swimming, and roller skating. Separate resorts provided huge dining halls, big band music, enormous dance pavilions, and sometimes even water pageants. Water taxis zipped from one resort to the next. It can easily be said that Thomas fell in love with the Russian River and environs, as years into the future he would eventually retire there.

I have no idea when the Batchelors moved from Tacoma to Ukiah; I have only the United States federal census to verify their whereabouts. But this I do know: early in the 20th century, the federal highway system did not exist. The passage from Tacoma through Oregon to Ukiah more than likely would have been done on the Pacific Ocean; Thomas Batchelor loved the water, and I can only speculate their passage may have been made via coastal waterways. Considering they lived in the busy port town of Tacoma, travel by sea makes the most sense to me. At that time, rural shoreline cities in Oregon thrived despite being isolated (no major roads or railroad connections). For them, the ocean was their life and means of existence. A routine round of packet ships made their way between Puget Sound to Astoria/ Portland. A second set of steamers made regular round trips between Portland/Astoria and the Oregonian ports of Tillamook, Florence, North Bend, and Bandon (Indeed, the steamer *Patsy* was named after her ports: Portland, Astoria, Tillamook, Siuslaw and Yaquina). A third set of gasoline schooners made their rounds between Coos Bay, Bandon and San Francisco. Indeed, when Jonathan affectionately reminisced about his father, he chatted about inheriting his father's passion for water. Assuming Thomas and family traveled by steamer, they would have disembarked at Bandon for several days, allowing the steamer to load timber, coal, and natural products before shoving off for San Francisco (many giant, old growth northern trees were sacrificed to build San Francisco, Oakland, Berkeley, Richmond, and other cities). Once the steamer was loaded it was off to San Francisco where the family would have boarded a ferry to Petaluma, from whence they caught the Northwestern Pacific commuter train. First stop: Santa Rosa for a stay with John and Selma Batchelor. Ukiah proper was some sixty miles further along.

I found two references to Mr. Batchelor from that period of time. First was a blurb in the local Ukiah news-sheet. It appears that Tom Batchelor and neighbor Henry Keller traveled to Willits to furnish music for an upcoming Christmas Ball. I found a second reference in the *San Francisco Chronicle* regarding a show at the city's Orpheum Theater, where he soloed, playing the trombone. So, although he was an established musician in Ukiah, he was still on the local vaudeville entertainment path.

The 1910 United States census mentions Thomas (age 38), Kathryn (age 33, spelled Katherine on the census), Ralph (age 14),

Leon Edgar (age 11), and Blanche Demeris (age 8); Jonathan David had yet to make his appearance in the world. I think it interesting to note that Thomas listed his occupation as "professional cigar maker" and landlord. In that kinder and slower era, anyone with a commercial spirit could easily set up his own trade. Megalopolis corporations were nascent and robotic technologies had yet to displace laborers; a middle-class style of life was very obtainable. Ever business minded, the musician always purchased a family home and the fact that he became a landlord doesn't surprise me. Dynamic and energetic, he was a sparkling entrepreneur who wore many hats in order to earn a good living to support his family.

In 1912, both John and Thomas Batchelor rearranged their lives. John moved south and bought a house in the East Bay city of Berkeley, California. Thomas had cast his eye on a northerly relocation to Bandon, Oregon. I can only conjecture as to why. Perhaps he missed living by the water. Perhaps on his first ocean bound trip, when he disembarked at Bandon, he liked what he found. Perhaps it was the music, for Bandon had a concert band that was well known across the United States, no small feat, considering the only way to disseminate news was through newspapers, and at that, sometimes information arrived weeks after the fact.

Although it was windswept, rugged, and remote, Bandon was a tourist destination especially in the warmer months of the year when people, from nearby and afar, habitually camped on local beaches, a surprising fact, considering how out-of-the-way it was. A history published online by the Bandon Historical Museum informs of three ways to reach the town in 1915: "1) Take the steamer *Elizabeth* from San Francisco, 2) Take either *The Alliance* or *Breakwater* from Portland to Marshfield (now Coos Bay), then take a train south to Coquille at 9 o'clock (a.m.) connecting with the Coquille River Boat, and that would land you at noon the same day at Bandon and 3) Overstage from Roseburg to Myrtle Point, from which place you take the river boat to Bandon as before."

> Next page: Old postcard of Coquille waterfront, taken before 1895. Found online, the postcard is considered public domain, photographer unknown.

Local twice-weekly *Bandon Recorder* headlined "The Grand Orchestra" to herald the arrival of Thomas the musician. Smack dab in the middle of page one: "Manager Sellmer (of the Grand Theatre) takes pleasure in announcing to the many patrons of the Grand that he has secured the services of Mr. T. L. Batchelor, an excellent trombone player. This will give the Grand Orchestra, under the leadership of Prof. Kausrud, five splendid musicians, capable of executing the most difficult of overtures and other high-class numbers. Special musical features will be offered regularly at the Grand. Watch for their announcements." That was printed March 26, 1912. And sure enough, the next edition of the periodical (March 29) headlined: "Special Musical Program at the Grand". "Sunday night March 31, the Grand orchestra will play a special overture entitled "Poet and Peasant" between the first and second show. A splendid bill of pictures will be offered. If you enjoy good music and high-class pictures you will not be disappointed. Come and see this extra good program. Admission 10¢ and 5¢." Robustly, The Bandon Recorder supported its two theaters (The Orpheum and Grand) and with almost every issue publicized previews for both facilities. In their friendly competition, they tried to outdo each other with majestic and lavish proclamations.

The Batchelor children thrived in Bandon. Blanche Demeris would have been ten when she moved there and was fond of recalling

Bandon's beaches and grassy swales as a very pleasant place for her to play. Her older brothers more-than-likely grew up in Bandon; when they moved there, Ralph would have been 16, Lynn 13. Because his mother played the piano, it would be difficult to guess which parent influenced Ralph the most musically. (I can't help but wonder if she brought a piano with her, or purchased one after landing in Bandon. That is a long way for a piano to travel!) Needless to say, Ralph, just like his father, became an excellent trombone player.

Pictured is Ralph, dressed in concert band finery, clowning around with Thomas decked out for vaudeville.

Somewhere along the line, Jonathan David came into existence: without a birth certificate, nobody accurately knew when or where he was born. As an adult educator teaching in public schools, documentation was required as proof of existence. His evidence was a 1920 United States census that stated Thomas and Kathryn had one eight-year-old son living with them. (At that time, Kathryn was not living with them, but that will be discussed further on. Despite her difficulties, Thomas still loved her and she was, after all, the boy's mother). If born in Bandon, Jonathan's birth date was 1912. But Blanche always insisted he was eight years younger than she, which would put his birth date at 1910. For most of his adult life, Jonathan used 1911 as his birthdate, a nice compromise. However, if he were born in 1911, he would have been born in Ukiah, California. I did scour all three Ukiah publications from that period of time, and found no birth notice for him. To further complicate matters, I perused the 1920 United States census on Ancestry.com. The online census report indicates one son living at home, John D. Batchelor, six years of age, which puts his birth year at 1914. Well, we are all human; we all make mistakes. I looked at the report used by Jonathan the educator. It listed him as eight. Perhaps someone typed the incorrect number on Jonathan's hard copy, or maybe Thomas was inattentive with his details. After all, Thomas' birthdate appears as 1871, 1872, or 1873 in various places.

Furthermore, I have to make sense of Thomas the embellisher/ story teller repeatedly regaling to his son and other relatives that Jonathan was born at sea. I was curious. I really wanted to know if Kathryn was at sea traveling from Ukiah, or if I could find some evidence of a land birth. I set to scouring the Bandon Recorder; I examined every single issue all the way from 1910 through 1916. It was highly entertaining! I fell in love with quirky, idiosyncratic, turn-of-the-century Bandon and all the varied characters that lived there at that time. It's inevitable, in a small town like Bandon, that everybody gets mentioned in the paper at one time or another. Although numerous babies were born over the years, there was no mention of Jonathan.

Photo on the next page is Jonathan in a washbowl. That is Jonathan's handwriting in the caption, written when he was in his 80s. Notice the date. When he was older, the storyteller tended to push back his birthdate. If the photo was taken in Tacoma, then Kathryn may have been visiting her family. Could Jonathan's birth city be Tacoma? Photo courtesy Sean White.

Jonathan in washbowl
from 1910 photo
Tacoma, Washington

All I could do was try to construct a logical scenario out of clues; I gave my imagination free rein. Although Mr. Batchelor was hired in March of 1912 to play his trombone in Bandon, it is entirely possible he may have moved from Ukiah first, and sent for his family after the fact. I can only conjecture that perhaps he initially wanted to settle down, buy a home, and send for Kathryn. Kathryn, as countless people did in those days, devoted time to letter writing. Assuming a correspondence between husband and wife, he may have sent for her, and she could easily have traveled pregnant with her three children back over the Northwestern Pacific Railroad, back across the ferry from Petaluma to San Francisco, and thence to any number of steamers ready to depart for Bandon. There were quite a few gasoline schooners making the San Francisco to Bandon run, to name a few: *Fifield, Elizabeth, Ruby, Washcalore, Speedwell, Bandon, Brooklyn, Breakwater, Hugh Hogan, Arcata, Tillamook, Grace Dollar*, and *Yosemite*. She certainly had her pick of vessels.

Bandon, despite its small size, was a vital seagoing port with over three hundred vessels mooring each year. When traveling by sea, it is not always possible to dock at one's convenience. Indeed, the Bandon Recorder is chock full of harrowing news features of one packet or another grounded, or dashed about on a reef, or sadly, sometimes even sinking. Bandon had a rescue service, the forerunner of the coast guard, with one fast boat that could reach a wallowing steamer to give assistance. Some debacles were not as bad as they at first seemed, with the craft entirely restorable. Others were dreadful and breeches buoys had to be used to save lives. One odd disaster was the shipwreck of the *Santa Clara*, of which the *Bandon Recorder* published a series. On November 2, 1915, steamer *Santa Clara,* inbound to Coos Bay, grounded amidst rough weather. After capsizing on Bastendorf's Beach, somewhat north of Bandon, she was steadily pounded to pieces.

"Pirates Thrive on the Wreckage" headlined a column on November 9, 1915. "…There were liberal consignments of whiskey and cigars on board and these were free for the time being. Men, soused, inside and outside, walked the beach with their pockets full of smokes with Pebbleford in plenty and hilarity abounding. The pirates pitch their camp on the bluff overlooking the wreck with perhaps a blanket for a tent and a fire of driftwood to keep warm..." "… Flour was the pressing need of the day. There had been a large shipment aboard and in order to get at some of the other stuff that was thought to be worth taking the flour had to be unloaded first. This was done by dumping it over the sides of the vessel into the water or boats or arms of those who had waded out to receive it." To further compound salvage difficulties, some of the 'pirates' decided to extend an already sizable gash in the hold by burning the timbers that surrounded it. All they managed to do was set the boat afire and one of the oil filled tanks exploded sending flames two hundred feet into the air.

It was not uncommon to have reports advising Bandon of late steamers; just like the *Santa Clara*, some were kept from mooring due to inclement weather. The only choice for hapless ship caught in rough seas was to chug and tack against headwinds until the weather turned; crossing the bar in heavy gusts was suicide. It is entirely possible that Kathryn Batchelor may have been on one such steamer. That would place Jonathan's birth year as 1912. That would fit in with Thomas' hiring at the Grand Theater, and it would place Jonathan in Oregon during the measles/whooping cough epidemic of 1913. Over the years, he repeatedly told me his hearing loss, which afflicted him his entire life, was the result of infanthood pertussis. And indeed, one of the complications from whooping cough is hearing impairment.

I don't know where Jonathan's version of his birth comes from, whether it is something his father supplied, or something from Jonathan's own imagination. I am assuming it was initially Thomas' narrative, because Jonathan's older, at-that-time (1980s) still living cousins, recollected Thomas speaking of it. Jonathan's narrative had Kathryn living in Bandon and due to Thomas' absence while on the Pantages circuit, a pregnant Mrs. Batchelor arranged to be with her immediate family in Tacoma for the birth. According to this rendition, the gasoline schooner was caught by a storm outside Puget Sound and had to wait for calmer weather to steam home. Again, entirely plausible except that after 1912 Mr. Batchelor had a steady job with the Grand Theater that kept him in Bandon. He may have traveled, but it could not have been very far if he were to be seated with the Grand Orchestra at show time. It may have been that years later, Thomas Batchelor, ever the active raconteur, conflated his own history to explain his son's birth.

Jonathan also didn't seem to be able to reconcile his own birth history. "To begin with," he wrote in 1946, "I was born in a diminutive town on the coast of Oregon. The fact that the place had grown up out of utter wilderness is nothing remarkable. It had been for many years a lumbering camp. My father was not a lumberman; he was a trombone player and had an expedience for making people laugh.

"But enough of this rot. I will not begin an ordinary tale in such an ordinary way. The fact is I was born in a wild place during a wild time. The ocean is a wild place and the rocks among the sand bore witness to my birth. The old house in which this thing took place stood in the middle of a sort of garden in a cedar grove on a knoll overlooking the fog-bound ragged rocks which stand like grotesque colossi, their feet in the lashing sea, their arms filled impassively, peering eternally into the mists and salty spume of the Northwest Ocean." Stupendous and fantastic as this description is, it is also entirely Jonathan's fanciful visualization. Thomas Batchelor lived amid town, surrounded by modest homes. Cedars, verdant swales, and rocky streams were certainly within walking distance; they created an extraordinary playground for the Batchelor and neighboring children. The infant artist was too young to remember his early life but Blanche, possibly a decade older, did recall lush sloughs and childhood play of catching lizards and chasing birds. No ordinary man, Jonathan seemed determined to give himself a very unorthodox beginning.

In 1912, Bandon and three local cities (Coquille, Myrtle Point, and Marshfield) made a deal to create their own mini-vaudeville circuit for the purpose of improving local entertainment, both theatrical and picture shows. They called it the Big Four Amusement Circuit; I can't help but wonder if Thomas had any input into that decision. In this case, it is entirely possible he may have continued on the stage and forthwith returned to Bandon for other obligations. With or without the Big Four Amusement Circuit, he was a very busy man. The Grand Theatre conductor, Mr. Kausrud, offered his orchestra for picnics or special events. "Big Dance at Wigwam" was the front-page write up of June 28, 1912 (Jonathan's birthday was on June 29, year unknown). "There will be a big dance at the Wigwam on July 4th. Dancing will begin in the afternoon and a grand ball in the evening. Kausrud's orchestra will furnish music for the occasion, and all who attend are promised one of the best times of their lives. Tickets for the grand ball in the evening will be $1.00". (The Wigwam was a confection stand/social hall flanking the beach). A 1912 land-birth would have kept Thomas Batchelor hopping between musical commitments and a new baby.

Fourth of July celebrations were typically small-scale, but the 1913 July fourth gala was colossal. Spanning two days (third and fourth) it included competitive water sports, dances, a carnival, morning concerts, human/ horse/and bicycle races, greased pig, greased pole, baseball game, more band music in the afternoon, tight rope performer and an aerial exhibitionist. The city fathers had all their expenses, disbursements, and receipts printed in the July 11 Bandon Recorder. Mr. Kausrud's orchestra typically played for holiday balls, including Thanksgiving, Christmas, and the fourth of July. Of all the musicians, the highest pay went to Thomas and another musician, the piano player. They were paid $23.65 apiece, a princely sum in those days. Indeed, music was the major source of entertainment and instrumentalists, considered almost sacred, were very well paid.

Thomas Batchelor and his stepson Ralph Elliott. Ralph's age is unknown in this photo, but he matured in Bandon, started a business there and joined his father as an instrumentalist. Here, father and son wear their fine concert tails.

Among a listing of businesses that contributed to the July festivities fund was the "Batchelor Bar." His devotion to music was as intensely passionate as his dedication to red wine. Confident and capable, the energized trombone player easily wore any number of entrepreneurial hats. Bandon was a small town without cars;

everybody walked everywhere. I can easily picture him closing the bar and walking to his other obligations.

Without benefit of a kept journal or log, I can only assume the Batchelor's led a normal, middle-class existence. As I continued to scour the *Bandon Recorder*, I found a reference to Mrs. Batchelor, who had won a prize at the local Thimble Club get-together. Social clubs were popular before the proliferation of television and electronics; people mixed and went bowling or to lodge meetings both in the daytime and at night. The *Bandon Recorder* ran lists of local associations with every issue and advertised events open to the public. I was not surprised to read that Kathryn was a member of the Thimble Club. While I was in Canyon, I had the opportunity to examine some letters she had written to Blanche. The writing was neat, precise, tiny. I can only speculate her stitches were orderly, close and taut. As women did in those days, she also tatted doilies, embroidered her skirts and blouses with fine stitched embellishments, and darned everybody's socks. Old clothing was not thrown out; it was repaired or handed down.

"Ralph Elliott Hurt in Bicycle Accident" announced the *Bandon Recorder* in April 1914. Ralph would have been nineteen or twenty by then and, like his father, demonstrated a strong entrepreneurial nature. The following brief article portrays him as a business owner: "Ralph Elliott of the French Dry Cleaning and Pressing Works had the misfortune to get badly hurt yesterday. He was riding down the Edison Avenue hill on his bicycle and ran full tilt into a plank, which was lying across the sidewalk. Mr. Elliott was thrown some distance and so badly bruised that at first it was thought he was fatally injured. He is much better today, but it will be some time before he will be able to look after his business again. He was taken to the Bandon hospital, where he was found to be suffering from a couple of broken ribs and was otherwise badly bruised." It is interesting to note that years later, in Oakland, California, Ralph Elliott and half-brother Lynn Batchelor opened a dry-cleaning business together.

The newspaper also mentioned Thomas two more times in 1914. In August he set about to unionize local musicians, and in November it was noted he rode to Marshfield due to business affairs. The *Bandon Recorder* left no trifling stone unturned: if someone journeyed out of town, it was appropriately noted; if somebody traveled via steamer for business or to visit relatives, it too received notice with gusto; if someone had a whist party, well, that was notable too, along with the invited guests. Nothing was too inconsequential. In 1912 The *Bandon Recorder* ran an entire column that tickled my funny bone. The entire column was a public service announcement devoted to the proper procedure for voting on a cow ordinance. Indeed, small towns can be amusing.

"Vote On Cow Ordinance". "When you vote on the Cow Ordinance read your ballot at least twice. Be sure that you have voted the way you intended. It has frequently happened in previous elections on this same question that citizens have voted directly opposite to what they intended. This is true of both sides of the question. The circumstances are that the Common Council passed an Ordinance that provides in itself that livestock shall not run at large, and have referred that Ordinance to the voters for ratification or rejection. If you want cows to run at large, then vote against the Ordnance, and note "No." If you desire to exclude livestock, you should vote for ratification of the Ordinance and consequently vote "yes."

"Any voters not stopping to consider the question thing, "yes I want the cows to run at large" and consequently vote "yes," are thereby casting a ballot for the Ordinance contrary to their wishes. Others, desirous that cows should not run at large, answer the question negatively and vote "no," which in effect is against the Ordinance, and thereby helps to defeat what he desires to accomplish. Remember, you are not voting directly on the cows. Instead, you are voting on the Ordinance, which the council has submitted. After you have voted, look at your ballot twice, to see if you have voted the way you wish. If in doubt as to its effect, ask one of the election judges. They will tell you correctly. That is part of their business, and what they are there for. The voters are entitled to a clear understanding of the premises that the wish of the majority, what it may be, may prevail."

In 1914, there were an inordinate number of fires in the city, from residences to businesses and in fact the entire downtown burned to the ground in June. No Independence Day celebration that year! Sorrowfully, Thomas Batchelor was not exempt from such a calamity.

"Fire Destroys Residence Tuesday Night: A Defective Lamp and Lack of Adequate Fire Protection Results in Loss of Home for Thomas Batchelor", was the January 15, 1915 heading, midst the first page. "Fire, starting from the explosion of a large coal oil lamp completely destroyed the residence of Thomas Batchelor on Alabama Avenue, Tuesday evening. The fire started about ten o'clock, when Mr. Batchelor was going (down) to the bathroom in the basement of the house. He was carrying the lamp and as he was going down the stairs he noticed the flame was working into the oil vessel. Setting the lamp on the stairs, he turned to look for something to smother it with, but had no more than turned his back when the explosion occurred. Within a few moments the entire building was in flames, making it impossible to save any of the contents except the piano and a few chairs and light articles, which were taken through the windows in the front of the house.

"Owing to the fact that there are no hydrants in that part of the city, and also that the water pressure is insufficient were there any taps, all that could be done was to watch the fire work its way through the $3,000 worth of property. With the heavy wind that was blowing it is remarkable that the flames did not spread. Mr. Batchelor stated that his property was covered by insurance."

Heretofore Thomas Batchelor had led a pleasing bourgeois existence. From now on, although totally blameless, the musician's family life began to unravel. In addition to his house burning, the WCTU (Woman's Christian Temperance Union) in Bandon was having frequent meetings where banning liquor (including his favorite red wine) was discussed. Prohibition fever consumed not just the United States, but Oregon; regularly featured articles covering the 'wets' and 'drys' appeared in the *Bandon Recorder*. Four years before the 18th Amendment, Coos County voted to go dry. The January 4, 1916 *Bandon Recorder* headlined: "Bandon Goes Dry Quietly: Saloons Close at Midnight Dec. 31 without Unusual Demonstration". "I would give my hat, I would give my shoes, for one more drink, of Bandon BOOZE. So blithely hummed a man as he stepped along First Street Monday morning and landed like a shot from a 42-centimeter gun against a familiar door. But the door, instead of opening, remained closed and the man turned thoughtfully away.

"Promptly at midnight the saloons of Bandon closed and although there was some last hour celebration, it was by no means vociferous. No outbreaks occurred, and the police had a quiet time. There were a few street fights earlier in the evening but on the whole the passing of the saloon in Bandon was a quiet event. There was not near as large a crowd of outsiders in town as there was for the Christmas celebration.

"Not a great deal of liquor was left on the hands of the saloon keepers December 31st. Several of the saloons put up signs advertising two glasses of beer for a nickel and all did a large package business. In all directions men went carrying jugs and demijohns and many a cellar is equipped for a long siege. This week the men whom the people of the state have put out of business have been busy readjusting their affairs, cleaning up and making future plans. Some will try mining, some will start up in the line of soft drinks and others are undecided. In the meantime the citizens of Bandon are checking up balances to find something with which to meet the occupation tax and the business of the city proceeds as usual."

Thomas' home burning to the ground was one issue; he could always rent a place to live. And although shuttering the Batchelor Bar cut off a secondary source of income, nothing could have prepared him for his wife's deteriorating brain. I'm sure he must have been perplexed at Kathryn's unfounded suspicions, fearful mood swings, and offbeat thoughts. It is known that creative minds are sometimes borne from individuals who have or eventually develop mental illness. And just as there are diverse levels of autism, there are distinctive levels of schizophrenia, from mild to severe. Kathryn's schizophrenia must have started revealing itself in small ways. At first modest behavior changes more-than-likely would have been livable; the women she socialized with may have considered her eccentric. However, given time, some quirky behavior would have become noticeable and bizarre, leaving ill-fated Thomas feeling abandoned as the wonderful, sensitive woman he married transformed into someone he could not recognize.

Although schizophrenia manifests itself in young adults, it can also develop in middle age or even later. For women, typical onset is around 30. Kathryn would have been in her early 40s when institutionalized and although at one point Thomas did try to bring her home again, she had to be committed permanently when her form of insanity endangered his life. According to Jonathan, his father woke up one night to find Kathryn standing over him, scissors in hand.

As the disease progresses, some individuals may isolate themselves, shut down psychologically, or cease being attentive to their appearance. They may not pay attention to those in the home.

Jonathan remembered his formative years as being basically motherless. Although she was in the house, she may have been distant emotionally, leaving Jonathan without warm embraces. Yet the adult Jonathan was hugely affectionate, exuberantly hugging both men and women with abandon, including a sturdy backslap now and then, a behavior perhaps inherited from his outgoing, loving father.

Before Jonathan was of school age, Kathryn's symptoms had become embarrassingly observable. With full-blown paranoia, she would have ceased socializing and stayed in the house, seldom going out. Jonathan recollected his mother responding to voices in her head: neglecting household duties, she boiled water in pots, and then with arms extended, one pot in each hand, slowly she swung the pots in semi-circles about her torso while standing in the middle of the room. Using the pots of steaming hot water to keep the 'evil spirits' away, she addressed the voices in her head, and demanded they leave. Tragically, Kathryn had the most severe type of schizophrenia, rife with mistrust, delusions, and voices overcrowding her mind. As it were, kind-hearted Thomas would have kept their marriage together, but eventually it became obviously clear she couldn't stay.

Kathryn, who loved to write verse, wrote sweet modest poems about birds, bees, springtime, and the mountains but within her vicissitudes were also references to aliens from a different planet residing on earth. In her latter years, confined to an asylum in Auburn, California, she continued to write Blanche. She knew Blanche was her daughter, but never acknowledged Jonathan was her son. When he visited, she called him her special friend. Her correspondence to Blanche started off normally enough, but subsequently devolved into beautiful, precise geometric forms that disintegrated into dots surrounding no particular words. Penciled in longhand, tiny printed letters mingled with carefully drawn shapes/symbols, mixed with pencil dots as well as drawings of bees, butterflies, and flowers, all very miniscule, delicate, and lovely. Initiating her letters with verse and rhyme, after a brief sentence or two all deteriorated into something not recognizable. It can be said that Jonathan inherited the best that his mother had to offer. She was a master draftsman, and so he was too. She certainly could not have instructed him artistically, for she was already out of the home and institutionalized by the time he was five.

Below: Untitled pastel drawing by Kathryn Gano. Her signature spells "Kathown Gano." Image is courtesy of Cheryl Parent.

Detail from the pastel.

Untitled oil painting by Kathryn Gano. Scarlet roses tumble from the tipped basket while bees alight. Jonathan must have inherited his ardent love of roses from his mother.

For Thomas, the trifecta was burdensome. First Thomas' home was gone, then his business shuttered, and now his wife was changing into a person he did not fathom. Perhaps he thought a change of scenery would bring his wife to her former self. The musician/ actor left music behind as he, with a friend unknown, vacated the city-by-the-sea. He and the friend pooled resources and bought into a cigar and smoke shop in Wyoming (city unknown).

Uprooted, his children followed along although I can only speculate that Ralph did not. He was of age, played in the Bandon concert band, and had established his own dry-cleaning business. I can only conjecture that he may have stayed behind. Jonathan did not recall much about Wyoming, except that it was bitterly cold and he liked to play in the snow. But Wyoming was an illusory panacea. The cigar and smoke shop was robbed; Thomas was left gagged and bound to a chair. That was enough to set Thomas wandering again and he briefly moved the family to Utah. When Utah was not the answer, it was back to sunny California. The family moved to 2104 10th St. in Sacramento, California, a stone's throw from Thomas' birthplace, Woodland.

The denouement of life in Sacramento was, apart from his youngest son, the dissemination of Mr. Batchelor's family. Kathryn was institutionalized: she was irreversibly committed to a sanitarium in the city of Auburn, located in the picturesque Sierra Nevada foothills northeast of Sacramento. It is truly tragic that such an imaginative, inventive mind/life was locked down. Next, Leon Edgar registered for the draft and was ultimately enrolled at age 20 on September 12, 1918. His military papers indicate he was born July 29, 1898, but the 1910 census indicates he was born in 1899. I suppose in those days a specific birth date was irrelevant. Leon Edgar (Lynn) Batchelor had inherited his father's passion for red wine and although he loved a good party, he was also a busy man, never without work. Prior to enlistment he was employed as a machinist's helper with the Southern Pacific Railroad.

Blanche, too, left home at a very young age. Wedded at 16 to her first husband of eventually three, she divulged to me that her first relationship was disastrous and short lived. However fleeting it was, she never again returned home. She effortlessly attracted men who cared for her and was never very long without boyfriend or husband. Exceptionally beautiful, flirtatious and sweet, she had inherited all the best of her mother, including a somewhat eccentric personality.

I don't know how long they were in Sacramento, but Jonathan said he first started kindergarten there. One would assume there existed any number of jobs for musicians in the state's capital. However be it may, at some point Thomas decided to move a full two hundred miles south, to another resort town, Visalia, located in the middle of the Southern San Joaquin Valley, somewhat between Fresno and Bakersfield.

For a man who relished the ocean, he was certainly far from it. Visalia did offer the beautiful Kaweah River. Typical of California waterways, it generously overfilled its channel from snowmelt spring and summer, downsizing to a trickle in autumn. At that time the river flowed free, eventually draining into Tulare Lake (and rarely the San Joaquin River). But because downtown Visalia was repeatedly inundated, (the deluges happened after Mr. Batchelor left) it was decided a dam was needed. Eventually Terminus Dam was built and thus was Lake Kaweah created. Preceding the dam, a dance hall and resort facility stood along the river's edge.

Because it is seemingly placed out in the middle of nowhere, Visalia may seem an odd place for a dance hall and resort. But during the 1920s, along with a diminishing train ridership, automobile travel proliferated. Henry Ford's affordable cars provided previous non-travelers the means to a vacation despite dusty, dirty, muddy, or rutted roads. The questionable early roads were a means to an end for local farmers. They stood to make a quick buck using horse teams to pull mired cars from sludge and sand. Despite poor road conditions, the Federal government encouraged tourists to visit our National Parks and local governments tried to improve dirt roads with oil and gravel.

Basil Clemons, Car Camping in the 1920s. Permission from University of Washington Libraries, Special Collections UW23113z: Early Photographers Collection. Ph Coll 334.

Car travel during the 1920s was iffy at best. Gas stations, service stations and their attendants and/or mechanics were few. But for those plucky enough to venture, there was much to see and do heading toward the towering Sierra Nevada. Not only is Visalia considered a gateway to Sequoia National Park, home of giant sequoia trees, but also to California Hot Springs Resort, a quick trip south and Yosemite National Park to the north. At that time, one could easily see snowcapped Sierras from the San Joaquin Valley (as opposed to today, where the view of the Sierras in summer is at best questionable, considering significant haze from smog and particulates festering on the San Joaquin Valley floor). Still popular, however, the clear-running Kaweah River is a haven for hikers, fishermen, and whitewater rafters.

Thomas Leon Batchelor was listed as 47 years in the 1920 census and his estimated birth year has moved up to 1873.

Although living without wife, he still listed her as his spouse on the government summary. His Italian neighbors, recollected with warmth and so clearly evoked by an eighty-year-old Jonathan, are also mentioned on the census. The Italian family, who made their own red wine, became close friends with the Batchelors. Although prohibition barred selling alcohol, there was an allowance for people who relished crafting liquor within their own homes. No surprise that Thomas was a frequent visitor. Jonathan remembered that first taste of red wine, the loud, raucous parties where his jostling-joking party-loving father shared anecdotes and roaring laughter with the noisy, affectionate Italians. In his latter years, the reserved artist loved to reminisce about those neighborly gatherings. He spoke of their daughter, the "little Italian girl down the street" (Jonathan's description) who, at the tender age of eight, insisted she marry Jonathan because she loved his red hair. His flaming locks, a prompt for schoolmates to call him carrot top (and oh how he hated that!) would be cradle to grave a magnet for the opposite sex.

Jonathan was, for all intents and purposes, a solitary child. Enfolded within immeasurable farmlands, Visalia offered pastures, orchards, and vineyards for exploring. The artist recollected bounteous unregulated roaming across fields and hills, following rills in the winter and dry washes in the summer. Hiking beneath California's limitless blue skies was an endless yearning, and would continue until old age held him from lingering walks. Even when elderly, to his dying day, his heart was outside: he loved going out at least once a day, to view and smell beloved Canyon ethos. The six-year-old redheaded scamp, unaccompanied and unobserved, found solace in the countryside. Trekking often left him famished. Too young to prepare his own meals, he learned to scavenge for scraps in local trash bins, the consequence of which was a bout of parasitic worms. It was the child's diagnosis that brought about a reunion between Thomas and his brother, John.

John Batchelor's existence was the absolute opposite of his younger brother's. Because he was good working with his hands, John was a handyman and had proven himself a skillful house painter to earn his way through life. After departing Santa Rosa, he established a permanent home base at 2929 Harper Street in Berkeley, California. Despite years apart, the brothers had kept in touch via mail and intermittent telephone calls. At some point, John heard about his nephew's bout with worms; the housepainter was alarmed that father and son were not thriving without Kathryn. He took time from work to drive from Berkeley to Visalia, no small feat considering no major highways and mostly dirt roads. His trip was fruitful; he persuaded Thomas to return and live with him, his wife Selma, and their children.

It is almost impossible to track a date of departure from Visalia to Harper Street in Berkeley. John and Selma Batchelor's children were, for the most part, adults. Lester and Clarence were married and on their own, but 19-year-old Frank, and 13-year-old Esther still lived at home. Jonathan remembered playing with Esther, but more importantly, the Nathansons lived down the street and their son, Ralph, was approximately Jonathan's age. The two boys developed a solid friendship that was to last the rest of their lives.

Berkeley was a flourishing 1920s city, with a population of about 56,000. Although horses were still used as drayage, the first Mack trucks had been manufactured and were gaining in popularity. The subject of paving for automobiles became a studied topic for city governments. But for the most part, people either walked, used bicycles or the trolley system. Stylish women wore either cloche hats or oversized hats with feathers and mink stoles; hemlines rose to mid-calf as more women joined the workforce and needed to step into cars. Men wore suits with vests and pocket watches beneath their jackets; boys still wore knickerbockers (Jonathan remembered wearing knickerbockers).

The Golden Gate and San Francisco-Oakland Bay Bridges did not yet exist, and several overlong docks were built for the purpose of ferrying passengers to San Francisco. Southern Pacific used a wide-ranging dock works (nicknamed the Mole Dock) built well into the bay connecting passengers with either the Key System or ferries. The Key System was a rail line and bus service connecting East Bay cities; it was busy and well served until the Bay Bridge was built. As usage declined, the Mole Dock was eventually demolished in the 1960s to make room for Oakland's modern shipping wharves.

Jonathan remembered the Mole Dock. The Mole Dock reduced the distance from East Bay to San Francisco to seven miles (the only other option was driving for hours completely around the bay). A favorite recollection was he and his father on weekend jaunts via The Key System and ferries to San Francisco's Ferry Building, where they ate roast beef sandwiches and the child was treated to his favorite candies, Applets and Cotlets. At that time, (1920s) one could still see the occasional tall-masted steam schooner, scow schooner, and paddle wheelers on the bay.

Topographically, Berkeley (and Oakland to its south) sit exactly opposite the Golden Gate; both are fixed between the San Francisco Bay to their west and the coastal ranges, a north-south set of hills to the east. Bordering the bay was an immense bay-shore marsh, expansive and extending from south to north, turning inland toward miles of delta estuaries. Much of Berkeley/Oakland was ripe for urban development but their western marshes, with their access to the bay, became convenient locations for profuse manufacturing plants as well as quays. Wetlands, considered wastelands in those days, were filled to create thick earthen berms for the Southern Pacific railroad, and the filling continued for decades. Consequently, West Berkeley/Oakland became an area that was a mixture of industry, marshland, and wharves.

Although Berkeley was a flourishing city, it still had dairy farms and immense tidal flats. The artist/child fell deeply in love with the still quite sizable marshes bisected by unforeseen and unpredictable sloughs. Jonathan cherished roaming miles through soaring cattails, sometimes following narrow pathways between plants taller than he. Once in a while he found a boardwalk made from cast-off planks, placed by fishermen or hermits who lived in desultory weathered huts, their corrugated metal roofs peeking above the reeds. A solitary roamer, he never felt alone, nor was he afraid. He loved all manner of flora and fauna, and deeply inhaled invigorating salty breezes blended with marsh pungencies. The Bay Area's residual marshes of today cannot match the acreage that was lost when both industry and the Eastshore Freeway, running the entire length of shoreline east bay, was built mid-20th century.

As a part of the Pacific Flyway, Bay Area marshes pull in diverse species of birds. Red winged blackbirds were, and still are, ubiquitous. The youth had a sharp eye and learned to recognize quail, identify snakes, reptiles; he caught and released amphibians and crayfish. Occasionally he spotted a clapper rail, now endangered, but considered fair game early twentieth century. Although Jonathan never hunted (did not have the heart to kill) it was fairly common for city folk to pick up their rifles and hunt not just clapper rail, but squirrel and rabbit as well. The lands surrounding Berkeley/Oakland were predominantly wild and huntsmen regularly made expeditions to the city's fringes for dinner.

In addition to wetlands, California's enchanting blue skies with wispy white nebulous clouds beckoned him easterly to the Berkeley/Oakland Hills. The youngster frequented long warm summer days with dusty deer trail, crackling dry, dead oak leaves and limp straw-colored grasses underfoot. Blonde savannah hills wondrously transformed to brilliant emerald landscape in winter. In those days, the ranges were predominantly savannahs, with scattered areas of lichen-laced live oak, Manzanita, chaparral, California laurel, and further inland, coast redwood. Summer dry washes of pebbles, twigs and leaves were transformed into rolling rivulets with winter's rainy deluge. All the current foliage one observes on the East Bay Hills followed housing developments as people planted and decorated their properties. It is easy to forget that at one time, the Berkeley Hills were mostly barren.

His self-fostering passion for wild lands was accompanied by a weighty love affair with books that led to an everlasting conviction that man cannot elevate himself without education. Pedantic and precocious, his vast reading interests included science fiction, mythology, literature, philosophy, poetry, and most of all anything about the sciences. Of Thomas Batchelor's children only one, Jonathan, displayed a propensity toward school and curiosity in the world around him.

Although the stability of Harper Street was a refreshing welcome for father and son, it was also short-lived. First Selma passed away in 1922 at the young age of 51, followed by John almost a year later at age 58. Because Jonathan's uncle was a house painter, he may have been affected by lead, which could be why he died at such a young age. At that time lead was freely used as an ingredient in house paint because it generated a superior color and long-lasting paint. According to Jonathan, his uncle displayed lead-exposure symptoms, such as high blood pressure, headaches, and joint pain.

After John's death, Thomas moved to a boarding house, 477 41st Street in Oakland. He continued his living as a musician but because vaudeville was waning (due to the nascent and popular movie industry) Thomas tried his hand at other trades, salesman and cabinet finisher among them. At this point he was through roving; all he wanted to do was stay in one place to make sure Jonathan received the education he absorbed like a sponge.

Sometime during the 1920s Thomas' other sons relocated to the Bay Area. Lynn, discharged from military service in 1922, set up shop in San Jose as an electrician but by 1924 was living in Berkeley on College Avenue. Alameda County voting records listed him as a cabinetmaker. Older brother Ralph soon followed. The following advertisement appeared in the 1924 Oakland Tribune, "Trombone lessons: Ralph Elliott's Trombone Studio, 5819 Dover Street, Piedmont, Oakland." Municipal concert bands were still in demand; not only did Ralph continue playing the trombone, but along with brother Lynn opened another dry-cleaning business in Oakland. One of Jonathan's favorite sentimental photographs presented Lynn and Ralph behind the front counter of their establishment, with prominent signage behind them, "No credit, no checks." Their thriving cash business and side-work carried them through the 1930s depression.

Both sides of the Batchelor families, Thomas' and John's sons, had a knack for working with their hands. Lynn and two of his cousins, Lester and Clarence, worked hard at their wood working business. At one time or another, all three were listed as cabinet finishers/producers in Oakland's (Alameda County's) voting records. From the 1926 Oakland Tribune there appeared the following advertisement: "Cabinet maker for fine furniture; none but A-1 men need apply. Batchelor Cabinet Shop. 2940 College Avenue, Berkeley." 2940 also happened to be Lynn's house address, shared with his cousin Lester.

Thomas' move to the 41st Street boarding house was serendipitous; straight down the hall lived a widow, another Irish lass, New York born and the daughter of immigrants, with the same name of Katherine. This Katherine soon became the second Mrs. Katherine Batchelor. Of her, I know very little. All photographs of her and her family taken by Thomas burned in the Canyon fire. I do know she had children that were older than Jonathan and he recalled pleasure being part of her family, as it gave to him stability and playmates. From the boarding house, the Batchelor's moved to 2621 Minna Avenue in southern Oakland where, at this point, Thomas tried his hand as a real estate agent. Although both Berkeley and Oakland were busy cities, there were still boundless undeveloped, rural grasslands and hills. Real estate was a booming business, as more and more automobile-infected suburbs were created. Jonathan's boyhood life revolved around his bicycle as he continued to explore both the western waterfront and hills to the east of town.

Below : Grinning from ear to ear. The artist, age unknown, possibly mid-1920s. Perhaps grinning because he no longer has to wear knickerbockers?

Mid-1920s, the artist would have been in Junior High. It was around this time he was introduced to backpacking. A friend of Lynn's invited the two brothers hiking in the picturesque Sierra Nevada. Awe-inspiring, nicknamed 'Range of Light', the lofty Sierra, running north/south along Eastern California, are laced with jagged, glacier laden, snowbound peaks (this all prior to global warming, which has reduced the ice fields). Jonathan exulted in the white granite boulders, glaciers, alpine meadow and forested canyon where rich, red timberland soils were a brash contrast alongside vivid mountain greenery. In those days, a train crossing the Sierra somewhat northeast of Sacramento dropped passengers off at the Cisco Grove junction (later changed to Cisco, elevation somewhat over 5,600 feet) and the trio walked north over unimproved fire roads to the Fordyce Creek/ Eagle Lakes area. In the early part of the twentieth century, the Sierra were unpopulated, pure, and pristine. A boisterous river, Fordyce Creek, had to be crossed, but there wasn't any bridge. To cross the deafening whitewater, one had to sit in a small one-person gondola and pull on a cable connected to pulleys on either side of the creek. Here, they could camp unfettered as long as they had supplies and food. The impact of this backpacking trip cannot be understated. The adult Jonathan, a man of rigid routine, would for the duration of his life, return to the Eagle Lakes area, which he renamed the 'Valley of the Gods'. Nowadays, Cisco is no longer a train stop, and Cisco Grove refers to a campground and RV resort located on the Interstate 80 frontage road in the Tahoe National Forest.

The developing artist idolized nature; living on Minna Street proved fortuitous as it was fairly close to Lake Merritt, a tidal estuary in the center of the city. In those days, Oakland was without gangs or young children with guns, and all manner of violence that prevails today could not have been imagined. The artist/child took off on his bicycle even late at night (sometimes he snuck out of the house without telling his parents); his destination was Lake Merritt's boathouse where the water-loving boy would sneak a rowboat or small sailboat and glide effortlessly across the brackish, dark water. In those days of low crime rates, boats were unlocked and available for the imaginative youth.

In 1925 a "necklace" of lights was strung around the lake

casting animated reflections into the water, which enhanced his enjoyment. Always observant, he kept his eye out for wildlife, which at night included geese, ducks, squirrels, opossums, skunk, an occasional deer, and once in a while, turkey. A dusky rosy sky was always littered with joyful sounding songbirds and was also heads up to return the boat, as he had to be careful to return it before daylight. Around 1920 a bandstand opened close to its shores; Jonathan recalled that his father and half-brother sometimes played there, his new family picnicking on the grass with the audience.

That California's acclaimed blue skies and ample grand roaming spaces impacted his life cannot be overstated. Surprisingly, the second Mrs. Katherine Batchelor indirectly altered his life's path when she insisted her new stepson attend the Catholic Church. Thomas was a secular Jew and hadn't any precise constraint concerning his son being taught any religion. However, he could not have imagined the effect Catholic mass and ritual would have on his son. The youngster loved ceremony and the Bible was fresh reading material that fit right in with his love of mythology; he absorbed the Bible and was able to recite lengthy passages. Although his years with the Catholic Church were overall few, for the doctrinaire, serious child, Catholicism was a beauty to behold. The adult Jonathan was complex regarding his Catholicism. On the one hand, he turned his back on Christian myth and disdained the idea of the virgin birth, even laughing about it at times. He found it astonishing that millions of human beings believed a virgin gave birth. On the other hand, he retained deep memories of his Catholic years, even telling me that in junior high school, he longed to be an altar boy. Of course, that never happened and he instead turned to the wilderness for inner restoration. A second consequence from the church was the effect of incense. Keenly receptive to aromas, he developed a love of incense; for the remainder of his life, he burned it wherever he lived.

Incense was not his only inebriating perfume. He fervidly cherished the scent of home-grown roses. Personally, I will never forget the fantastic potpourris placed all about Canyon house. Plentiful: crinkled petals were cradled amidst colorfully decorated ceramic containers. I was astounded as I lifted lids and swooned at the heady perfume of decades-old color-faded lifeless petals. That was new to me; I had no idea flowers could maintain their bouquet for decades.

> Below: Detail of a Batchelor painting. A young girl buries her face in roses and deep breathes their perfume. This was rendered in the 1960s or 1970s. Titled *Fragrance,* it is quite a large (size unknown) oil on canvas. One of his favorite subjects, he painted several with that label. He made sure to include scattered apples, a fruit he had great fondness for.

Jonathan, the redheaded, well-read youth, had by mid-1920s an emergent passion for chemistry. In those days, without rampant illicit drug use, and when a person labeled "terrorist" was foreign to most people's thoughts, chemical equipment and chemicals were readily available from The Berkeley Chemical Works. Thomas spared no expense and readily purchased the glassware, beakers, test tube stand and tubes, Bunsen burner, pipettes, and whatever chemicals the boy desired. Because Thomas did not drive or own a car, and he hadn't any use for his detached garage, it became Jonathan's laboratory. Why in the world the boy decided to make nitroglycerin is beyond me. Nitroglycerin, unstable, can explode for the smallest reasons, including a slight temperature change. According to Jonathan, he placed the compound on ice, and then left to go to the store. When he returned, his father greeted him with a "Well son, you've done it now." To the boy's dismay, the ice melted, and the garage was in pieces. What is most noteworthy is that Thomas never angered at his son. He took it all in stride and even made jokes about it.

It was while at Minna Street that Jonathan's artistic tendencies were noted, and he received a scholarship to attend summer classes at California College of Arts and Crafts, located in central Oakland. The father was proud of his precocious son. "Look to this one," Thomas periodically broadcast to anyone within earshot. "He is going to make a difference in this world."

He gifted the child a book of Edgar Allan Poe's "The Raven" with illustrations by Gustave Dore. That book became the child's treasured possession; a passion for Dore's illustrations followed with trips to the library all in the name of seeking Dore's work. The 16th century artist's surrealistic drawings with fabulously detailed line-work, intense darks and lights, phantoms, demons, monsters, and myriad eclectic people of all shapes and sizes immeasurably influenced the captivated youth. Dore became a muse as Jonathan developed his own skills and tried to create human beings of all stature and demeanor. Dore's drawings, to him, epitomized beautiful line-work. Artists are drawn to lines which can be a field of study: lines can be thick, thin, textured, cross hatched for shadows or for emphasizing or simply left out entirely and yet, we are still able to recognize a human with a few, well placed pencil marks.

Next page: *Tropic Drink*. Jonathan must have drawn this when he was in his latter twenties. In those days, he loved hob-nobbing in bars and making quick sketches. Here he has sketched an ample human being and defined her torso with just a few simple lines. It was drawn with sanguine conte crayon, one of his favorite tools. I dug it from the ashes of his burned house; the drawing is clean because it was sandwiched between two objects.

The impact of Dore and the influence of Edgar Allan Poe cannot be understated. The adult Jonathan, still an ardent Poe fan, had innumerable books of Poe's writings. In his Canyon home, I found not only the macabre stories assigned to me in high school, I also discovered to my amazement that Poe wrote hilarious, witty satire. Jonathan's burgeoning book fervor led to Junior High writing experiments. Around that time, he met Louis Smith, who had matching interests and the two became inseparable. According to Jonathan, they frequently sat on school steps writing science fiction or fantasy or adding to journals, daydreaming about their futures as authors. Jonathan was so advanced with his English usage that one of his teachers accused him of plagiarizing. The accusation deeply stung and to his dying day, he never forgot it and never forgave his teacher.

Prior to discovering Dore, the young artist fixated on drawing futuristic cities, full of astronauts in space suits with large helmets, floating through rocket-laden skies. He hadn't studied anatomy per se, but he was, as most artists are, very observant and even at that age his figures were well proportioned. The illustrations of Dore gave him new subject material bordering on fantasy. It should be noted that his burgeoning creativity was not limited to writing or artwork. Passionate about music, he picked up his father's violin (most professional musicians have any number of instruments lying about) and started playing.

The relative stability of life on Minna Street carried Jonathan through most of Roosevelt High School (named after Theodore, FDR had yet to become president). Unfortunately, the welcomed stability after years of chaos wouldn't last; Thomas' life took another tumble with the stock market crash of 1929. Real estate had been booming throughout the 1920s, but after 1929 home sales declined. His earnings as a real estate agent proved sparse; revenue was scarce and without steady wages his second marriage became uncomfortable. The final blow came when the second Mrs. Katherine Batchelor died April 20, 1930, at the very young age of 53.

I am not sure how father and son maintained an existence; the world was changing, and Thomas' compelling entrepreneurial spirit wasn't enough to earn a living. Although public transportation was good and efficient, sometimes one needs a car to look for work, and still he could not drive. The bandstand at Lake Merritt was their stronghold; as long as concerts continued, which they did through the 1930s, he had one source of income. However, the automobile allowed people to travel so they were not reliant on local entertainment. Across the nation, public bands were in a decline with the new technology available through radios and the developing recording studio. Slowly the radio and record player became a primary source of amusement and musicians who had once made a living with civic bands were thrown out of work. It is also worth noting that the cost of radios had come down to around ten dollars and although people may have dropped payments on such items as cars, sofas, tables or vacuums, many kept up their payments on radios. Not only did broadcasts provide inexpensive entertainment for some, radio was a social outlet for family, friends and neighbors gathering to listen. Thomas' declining musical career was altogether stopped short with a rude sailor on leave in downtown Oakland. The sailor who may have been a few sheets to the wind (although prohibition was yet to be repealed, if someone wanted alcohol badly enough, it could be found) accosted Thomas. Thomas was a very sweet and kind person, so I can't imagine what the sailor had against him. The two argued which resulted in Thomas receiving a knuckle sandwich. Because Thomas' mouth was damaged and teeth knocked loose, the musician was unable to play his euphonium or trombone. Thus ended his musical career.

Bay Area employees, as typical per depression era workers,

were jolted hard. Work was not to be found and countless middle-class families found themselves evicted. Households improvised, a community was made from huge concrete pipes, six feet in length, large enough to stand in, stored above ground in West Oakland. Each pipe section became home for a family; open pipe ends were covered with handy materials from corrugated metal to cardboard, to burlap or newspapers. The December 3, 1932 *Oakland Post-Inquirer* presented this description: "To qualify for citizenship in Pipe City you must be jobless, homeless, hungry, and preferably shoeless, coatless, and hatless. If one also is discouraged, lonely, filled with a terrible feeling of hopelessness and helplessness, one's qualifications are that much stronger. One belongs. Not all of Pipe City's inhabitants are that way. Some of them have learned that a philosophical attitude helps. One may tinge his philosophy with a drop of irony, even bitterness, and the concrete may seem less hard and the blankets less thin and the mulligan less watery. But it takes a lot of philosophy, you bet, to make concrete either soft or warm!"

Thomas' son Lynn offered financial help by hiring Thomas to finish furniture in his workshop. Despite depression privations, Lynn and Ralph continued to make a living through cabinet building, furniture finishing, and their dry-cleaning business. Ralph, as well, gave trombone lessons. Thomas' daughter, Blanche, a knockout with auburn hair and blue eyes had aspirations to be a model and actress and had a portfolio of headshots created for that purpose. She was by then with her second husband, Charles V. Lindo, and living in Los Angeles, one step closer to show business. She told me that many people made it known she was a dead ringer for Fay Wray and because of that, she felt she had a good chance of making it into movies.

Despite the depression, Charles Lindo, or 'C.V.' As Blanche dubbed him, was able to make a good living selling magazines and encyclopedias. At that time news was disseminated by newspaper, magazine, or radio. C.V. Lindo didn't seem to have any problem selling subscriptions to both magazines and encyclopedias: the demand for magazines went unabated, despite people out of work. Because her husband was handy at merchandising magazines, Blanche was convinced her smooth-talking father could do the same: she invited father and brother to live with them in Los Angeles. So it was decided Thomas would move south after Jonathan graduated from high school, which would have been in the early 1930s. Mr. Lindo had his own home and could accommodate them, even with his three boys and Blanche.

After high school graduation, father and son carefully packed their belongings including Jonathan's cherished books, art supplies, chemistry equipment, and chemicals. Bekins Moving and Storage was hired to haul their goods. Because Thomas couldn't drive, both father and son relied on public transportation via The California Transit Company, which was a precursor to Greyhound Bus Lines. In the latter 1920s, California's Highway 101 was completed, and there was bus service from the Bay Area to Los Angeles. Freshly finished, Highway 101 carefully followed 'El Camino Real', the road of California's Spanish missions. The only other alternative was Highway 1, a narrow, two-lane road that carefully followed the coastline, meandering inland to cross every riparian delta and estuary before returning to the coast, and terminating far north of Los Angeles. Prior to the opening of 101, traveling south meant weeks of driving.

Father and son arrived at Blanche's home before Bekins arrived. Blanche was living a decent, bourgeois existence and wanted for nothing. She was shocked at her father's and brother's appearances. In those days, men dressed nicely, compared with the casual dress of today. Men commonly wore suits with vests, slacks, hats, nice sweaters, jackets, ties and even bow ties; Thomas wouldn't be caught without a bow tie or fedora. Both father and son, not able to afford fashionable new clothing, had resorted to stitching and patching what they had. This was especially hard on Jonathan, who experienced typical teenage growth in high school, and showed up with charity driven hand-me-downs. Jonathan's shabby shoes, tattered from both day usage and hiking and biking, hadn't any soles. Jonathan had cut out cardboard inserts and glued them to the bottom of his shoes. Blanche took it upon herself to have the soles replaced with leather, a small factoid she never let him forget the rest of her years.

Their new beginning did not bode well when Bekins Moving and Storage lost all their belongings. Remarkably, Thomas spun the loss into self-deprecating humor. But Jonathan, barely eighteen, was disturbed. Gone were the only possessions he had ever owned and they had taken years to amass; his beloved books, prized chemistry equipment, costly chemicals, and a few of his mother's priceless art supplies. The loss was devastating for the studious young man, who at that time, desired to go to college to become a doctor, preferably a research physiologist. For the rest of his life, he never forgave Bekins Moving and Storage and in his later years, as Jonathan's mind wandered with reminiscence, multitudinous moments of annoyance were expressed as the loss of his books were once again brought forth from some cubbyhole in the back of his mind. For some reason, that memory, as irritating as it was, frequented his thoughts. Not that he hadn't made up for all that! By the time I moved in with him, he had the most wonderful glassware and chemistry equipment and so many books, there weren't enough shelves to cope with them all.

For all the trouble and effort moving south, Los Angeles was not a remedy. Thomas may as well have stayed in the Bay Area; chaotic and tumultuous were adjectives of the day. Mr. Lindo recruited Thomas to sell books and magazines door to door, Thomas Batchelor simply was not suitable as a salesman. Energetic and entertaining, he enjoyed meeting prospective clients but instead of selling, oft times he visited and chatted away his afternoons; many a time he left without selling any books or magazine subscriptions. Dialect comedy was fundamental to vaudeville and the peddler Thomas was eternally on stage. He was a natural comic; he would return home at the end of the day and regale Jonathan and Blanche with stories, miming not only people he met but also their foreign accents. Bent over with laughter, his children were in stitches and tears.

Blanche's stepsons were too young for Thomas' humor and to her the mischief-makers were exasperating. (Blanche eventually left the marriage because of the children. She often told me she would have stayed if he hadn't the boys). It was quite a full household and it soon became apparent father and son would have to relocate. Thomas found an apartment in the Boyle Heights section of Los Angeles which was chiefly Jewish and Thomas felt right at home in the lively community. Most residents spoke Yiddish, there were multiple synagogues, and countless mom and pop shops lined Brooklyn Avenue. Due to the early 20th century rise of communism, and its role in the labor movement, it was typical to find animated students or store customers debating politics. At that time, the entire community of Boyle Heights was influenced by left-leaning principles. Although Jonathan never actually joined the American Communist Party, he was unquestionably influenced by its vision and utopian philosophies.

The painter was a scholar without university; he unquestionably had an aptitude for philosophy. Quixotic and dreamy, Jonathan adopted from communism (or rather, his idea of what communism should be) a model worldview where there was no room for 'I'. It was always 'we' or 'us'. When I read through rough drafts of letters he had written from that period of time, more often than not they were addressed to comrade. He wrote letters of his idealistic notions about the future of humanity, as well as inquiring about meetings with like-minded people for deep-thinking conversation. When is the next get-together, he would ask. Thus began a lifetime love of gatherings and red wine that continued till the day he died. Thomas continued selling magazines and books, returning at night, articulating about whomever he happened to meet that day, and mimicking the many Jewish, Russian, Yugoslav, Chinese or Latino accents he heard. Jonathan recalled howling hysterically; sometimes he laughed so hard his sides ached.

Father and son had an awesome, exceedingly close relationship. However, because of his son's academic aspirations, Thomas felt badly. Of all his children, only Jonathan was educated, well read, loved to write and loved school. Thomas was in no position to put his son through college, and scholarships and grants were not as available at that time as are common today. Furthermore, although grades were never an issue for Jonathan, even if grants or loans were available, he would not have had the wherewithal or the patience to seek out personal information required or fill-out endless forms. With the question of college defeated, the artist did the only thing left to him. Ever frugal and scraping by financially, he continued to draw and paint, using a few tubes of his mother's surviving paints that he managed to hang onto, her old palette, wooden boards for canvasses, and an old chair for his easel. Tired of watching his son leaning canvasses against a chair backrest, he surprised Jonathan and bought an old cast-off easel.

Every artist has his/her own ardor to follow. As Jonathan

matured from boyhood to manhood, his drawings turned from focusing on science fiction to women in fantasy. Influenced by Art Deco, Jonathan repeatedly sketched women in various states of dress or undress, usually in long, flowing gowns, in his version of feminine powder-room goings-on. Drawn from his imagination, his figures would be doing feminine activity such as brushing hair or brushing someone else's hair, or admiring images in mirrors, or rolling stockings up legs. When he wasn't drawing from his imagination, his sister Blanche was a willing model and over the years he made numerous nude sketches of her. He had no qualms sketching his sister in the buff and she easily disrobed: posing nude was never an issue for her.

Early fantasy drawing of two nudes. He had not yet studied anatomy which presented a few awkward structural issues.

Although his mother was a painter, and he likewise enjoyed daubing with oils, art did not become an ambition until he attended an exhibit featuring the work of local Los Angeles artist Theodore Lukits. Theodore Lukits, famous for his portraits of Hollywood stars, excelled at drawing and painting human figures, landscapes, and still lifes. He had established his own art academy and named it the Lukits Academy of Fine Arts.

And in general, that is the way it is with artists. A student might serendipitously come across a style and fall in love with it, and then either copy the genre, or solicit the artist for instruction.

Jonathan, dazzled by Mr. Lukit's European-influenced artwork, immediately knew he wanted to study with the artist. Talking to Mr. Lukits was an entirely different matter. Unsophisticated and unrecognizing his own talent, the insecure young man wasn't sure how to approach the cultured, accomplished, and famed artisan. However, his thirst to paint well overpowered his inhibitions and he made an appointment to show his portfolio. Mr. Lukits was immeasurably impressed, so much so, that he agreed to take Jonathan as a student even though the young man could not afford tuition. A deal was made where Jonathan would attend classes tuition free provided he modeled for figure drawing students. Lithe and wiry, it was easy for students to discern musculature and bone structure beneath his skin. And although in those days male artists wore loincloths, Jonathan was never afraid to pose nude.

Mr. Lukits' impressionist-styled European-flavored artwork bewitched the emergent artist. At that time, the only option for artists seeking current art know-how from the opposite side of the globe was to travel overseas, or to buy books with art prints. When I moved into Canyon house, Jonathan had plentiful thin, oversized soft-covered tomes with almost poster-size reproductions. These early attempts by publishers to reproduce impressionist and/or modernist paintings never conveyed completely accurate hues, and some appeared dull compared to the real piece. Color reproductions at that time were poor and it was all but impossible to garnish any idea of what the actual hues were. Among Mr. Lukits' teachers were several who had studied at the art colony in Giverny, France, and had taught Mr. Lukits their knowledge of a style now known as Decorative Impressionism. Jonathan was awed not just by the classicism of Lukits' paintings, but also by the riot of color.

Above *The Cardinal*, oil on canvas, 33 ½ X 25 ½, 1918. Jonathan may or may not have seen this painting. I can only speculate that if he did, he must have been delighted. He loved much about the Catholic Church, if not their beliefs, then the rituals.

The odd size of *The Cardinal* was typical of that era. Stretcher bars (the braces of a mounted canvas) had not yet become standardized, and many painters made their own canvasses. Below that: *Introspection*, oil on canvas mounted on board, 38 X 28 inches, 1922. Again, I am not entirely clear if Jonathan saw this painting or not. *The Cardinal* and *Introspection* were painted prior to Jonathan's stay in Los Angeles. He may have seen them but if not, I can only imagine how inspired he was by any of Lukits' works with their brushwork, rendering, and shock of colors. Artists are inspired by fellow artists and of course, by musicians; Jonathan befriended and painted numbers of Oakland Symphony string players over the years.

Mr. Lukits painted exquisite portraits, and at times had his models dress in costume. The vibrant Los Angeles Hispanic scene occasionally influenced his multi-hued, dynamic renderings as in the case of *Viva Mexico*, above.

Inspired by Mr. Lukit's Hispanic renderings, Jonathan was motivated to illustrate a group of Latinos he observed assembled daily in the Los Angeles River basin. When water was absent they gathered loose windblown rags from the river basin, sorted, bundled, and tied them for resale. During the depression, everybody did what they could to bring in cash, selling rags among other things. Some of those stacks of bundled rags were ten feet high! The image above is a detail from that canvas. Titled *Mexican Rag Sorters*, it was by far the largest painting he had ever completed, and for years hung in a house in Northern California. Regrettably, as I was moving from that house, I hired nitwits to haul trash from the house. In my absence, they apparently also threw away the painting, for I never saw it again. Images of Lukits paintings are courtesy of the Jonathan Art Foundation (The foundation name 'Jonathan' has nothing to do with Mr. Batchelor.) To see more of Lukits spectacular work, please visit the Jonathan Art Foundation online.

Lukits' influence did not stop at art. Lukits was a craftsman who assembled his own paints from raw powdered pigment and due to the extravagant cost of frames, fashioned his own. Years into the future, when Jonathan had his own atelier, he followed Lukit's precedent of mixing his chosen medium with raw pigments and constructed frames instead of buying them. Furthermore, Theodore Lukits studied at the Barnes Medical College to garner deeper understanding of human anatomy. Jonathan never formally studied anatomy at a medical college, but the studious researcher did gain complete knowledge of anatomy on his own; he could name almost every single muscle and bone in the human body. Both Lukits and Batchelor drew anatomical studies of humans for their students. Jonathan was also good with comparative anatomy and enjoyed pointing out to me the different placement of bones in humans as compared to horses. (Why horses? Because they are my obsession and Jonathan was elucidating horse anatomy for me.)

Outside of Theodore Lukits, Los Angeles did not have much to offer. He investigated the Otis Art Institute, but there wasn't any teacher of interest to him from that direction. It was happenstance that brought the red-maned artist to one very breathtaking sculptural exhibit. In 1933 sculptor Donal Hord had his very first one-man show and his remarkable works lit a fire within Jonathan. The fledgling artist loved working with his hands and he also admired Auguste Rodin's majestic figures. Thus, he reasoned that the next logical step on his creative voyage was to meet Donal Hord. He packed, left his father in Boyle Heights, traveled to San Diego, and sought Mr. Hord, all in the name of acquiring sculpting expertise.

The move to San Diego was not easy. Although he could drive, he did not yet have a car. He resorted to the hitch hiking that was popular with transients; thumbing a ride had not yet become dangerous. Once in San Diego, not only did he have to find a room to let, but it was the 1930s and jobs were still hard to come by. The young artist always managed to find pick-and-shovel labor digging roads, ditches, and even graves. Although thin, he was naturally rugged, of unbelievable strength and made himself available for any type of manual toil. Working in a cemetery turned out to be a bonus: access to paupers' graves! Somewhere during the depression, at some graveyard, he obtained not one but two human skulls and the complete bones of a human body. Those were his cherished possessions; the skulls he eventually cleaned and varnished and put on display wherever he lived. When in Canyon, one skull embellished a piano, the other a shelf. Over the years, they were guaranteed to be the highlight of many a party. When our neighbor, Jeff Pratt, built Jonathan's coffin (at Jonathan's behest) the skulls were naturally centered on the lid, after the coffin, stored on the bottom floor, was brought up two flights to the studio for Halloween.

In San Diego Jonathan's affectionate relationship with his father continued through correspondence. His need to create prose was as central to him as his need to breathe. Composing journal entries and penning letters were uplifting; he believed the triumvirate of writing, painting, and composing music enriched and exalted humanity. His protracted, handwritten letters meandered about his philosophies, dreams, current politics, but seldom day-to-day activities. I found most of his early drafts in Canyon, in an antique wooden dispatch box his father had given him. "Comrade" opened letters to friends, but to his father, he addressed all letters as "O Genie", and he would follow with some such opening as, "time for a new missive", or "the latest epistle". When I asked him why he referred to his father as Genie, Jonathan softly replied, "Because I thought he was so wise, I thought he could move mountains, I thought he could do anything."

I am not sure how Jonathan introduced himself to Donal Hord. As a young man, Jonathan was unaware of how self-doubting, socially blind, and unworldly he truly was. Despite those obstacles, he was a great talker and tenacious about observing Mr. Hord sculpt. Mr. Hord did not offer classes, but Jonathan did meet him and from him learned how to create the underwiring and structure for sculpting. The influence of Donal Hord is strikingly noticeable, not just in Jonathan's sculptures, but also in the labeling. The poetic side of Mr. Hord manifested itself in such ethereal names as *The Spirit of the Hills*, *The Burden of Earth*, *Desert Summer*, *Dream of Night*, or *Wheel of Industry*. The dreamy young Jonathan would continue with many similar expressive titles over the years.

Next page: Donal Hord's *Morning,* is a wonderful capture. Don't we all stretch and yawn in like manner when we awaken? The lifting of the right arm is almost identical in both sculptures. I can only guess Jonathan must have seen *Morning* which was completed while Jonathan was in the Bay Area. I do remember photographs of him and his eventual third wife in Southern California, early 1950s. That would place him in the vicinity of Hord's work at the right time.

 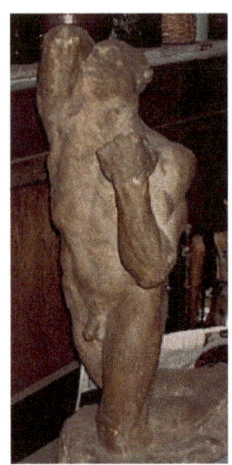

Donal Hord, *Morning* side by side with Jonathan
Batchelor's *Anguish. Morning* can be seen at the Port of
San Diego. This image is courtesy of Port of San Diego
art department.

Above: Donal Hord sketched potential works. Left: Study
for *Thunder.* Right: *Thunder*, carved from Jade, 1947. Above
pictures are property of Bridgeman Images.

Jonathan likewise enjoyed sketching possible works of art. Above left is his sketch for *Waterfall*. Right: The finished product.

It is hard to stamp an exact date for Jonathan's endeavors with Mr. Hord. Certainly, it must have been prior to 1935. I can only speculate that he may have heard of the Federal Art Project from Mr. Hord, who was accepted into the federal program and received a fixed salary ($75 per month, not bad for that era). Although Jonathan eventually would go to work for the WPA, when he left San Diego, it was for another reason entirely.

San Diego historically has had a constant military presence; it was from a military officer in San Diego that Jonathan discovered he could work as a civilian aide to military doctors in a facility located near the small-unincorporated town of Nacimiento, California. Even as a boy, Jonathan had admired people who were educated, scientific, and for his entire life he had a special affinity for doctors. Excited about the possibility of working side by side with his hero physicians, Jonathan left San Diego for Nacimiento. Because he was carless, he must have hitchhiked, taken a bus or train, and possibly detrained at a station located at the small town of Bradley, just north of his destination. However he decided to travel, he hauled with him skulls, skeletons, art supplies, books, but very little by way of clothing.

Below: Remnant of Jonathan's drawing of the Nacimiento boot camp where, as a civilian, he worked alongside military doctors. This is a fantastically detailed rendering, and how devastating that part of it was destroyed in the fire. Not only are the buildings highly described, but one can see the tiny figure of a drill sergeant saluting and a long line of tiny heads bordering the burn line. Jonathan often told me of his young 20/20 vision, which enabled him to see fine detail when outdoors.

Nacimiento was and still is a small-unincorporated community north of San Luis Obispo, California. Fixed within a narrow north-south river valley channeled by the confluence of the Salinas and Nacimiento Rivers, the delicate, tiny, riverine flatlands were surrounded by elevated hills both east and west, rich with rivulets, ponds, and lakes. I can only infer he was there in winter because California summers shrink vernal streams into parched washes. Jonathan's vivid remembrances brought forth visual pictures of typical expansive California grasslands dotted with chaparral and oak trees. Nacimiento is famous for its vernal pools, which enchanted the water-loving rambler.

Nacimiento landscape remnant, sketched in the 1930s. Typical of his sketches, it is rife with detail. Emphasizing the foreground, he left a huge, empty sky. Greatly influenced by J.M.W. Turner, he loved the openness of wide skies. Decades later, he painted a series of works he titled *"No Fences"*, all with spacious skies and usually one lone, solitary figure in the foreground.

Lake Nacimiento, formed when the Nacimiento River was dammed, was still years into the future. Ever fanatic about wild places, he relished the wild-running river and hunted for waterways by trekking alongside the river and over lush peaks. Roving wide-open spaces was nothing for the slender, healthy young man. Even in his seventies, I was witness to the fact that he walked thirteen miles from Oakland, California, over the East Bay Hills, to his home in Canyon. Vast distances were never an issue. Over the span of his lifetime, he found diverse forms of that precious liquid peaceful and soothing to his soul. That said, his love and curiosity almost killed him when in the Nacimiento bluffs, he found a brook that intriguingly entered a dark cavern in the hillside.

Curious and adventuresome, as young people are wont to be, he decided to dive into the stream to see where it discharged. Jonathan described it to me years later. "That was just a dumb thing to do!" he exclaimed, rolling his eyes. He said he took a deep breath and plunged. The stream seemed to cascade underground forever; at one point he truly believed he was going to drown. But right when he needed it, the stream burst forth from the hillside and Jonathan gratefully lay in the warm, refulgent sun, panting and catching his breath.

For all that he expressively conveyed about the remoteness and magnificence of the Nacimiento River basin, the same could not be said for his experiences working with ill soldiers. Assisting the doctors in a nursing capacity dimmed his imagined dreams of glorified doctorhood. When describing his experiences, he told me he simply grew impatient and tired tending to bedpans, wounds, STD prevention, and other ailments. For that reason alone, his experiences as an aide were worth their weight in gold. Although for the rest of his life he admired doctors, he also put away his dreams of curing and focused on the thing he was born to do: blossom as an artist. While at Nacimiento he heard about an artist's colony in a place called Carmel, California. After listening to descriptions of Carmel-by-the-Sea's splendor and its vivacious artist's colony, Jonathan knew he had to leave. With skeletons, skulls, art supplies and newly gained knowledge, he headed north.

Nestled in a small bay south of the Monterey Peninsula, Carmel is known for its bevy of twisted wind-blown cypress trees leading to warm, silky-white beaches. An artist's colony practically from inception in the early 1900s, Carmel was still in the 1930s affordable for a dynamic aggregation of artists; pricey upper-middle-class residential development was yet into the future. Arriving from Nacimiento, Jonathan briefly intermingled with local artisans. Fleetingly he met Armin Hansen at a show and was dazzled by Mr. Hansen's oceangoing scenes with elating, robust colors. Up to this point, outside of Theodore Lukits, the heaviest influence on Jonathan's color and brushwork was J.M.W. Turner. Turner's large canvasses show off moody rainbow-hued spacious skies with an emphasis on nature and less on the human presence. By comparison, Hansen's focus was more up close and personal with human beings and boats populating vibrant works. After observing Hansen's paintings, Jonathan knew it would require years of demanding study to develop into a fine artist.

Jonathan on a beach at Carmel-by-the-Sea,
taken during the 1930s. Carmel's luxurious
white velvety-smooth beaches front the town.
It is now known as a voluptuary destination.
The artist would return repeatedly over the
decades.

To stay in Carmel was highly appealing but when Jonathan
found out the Works Progress Administration (WPA) was looking to
hire artists at the University of California in Berkeley, he chose to
leave. He loved the beauty of Carmel, the artist's colony, the ocean,
and he would have stayed put, but he also had a strong need to
work. Jobs were scarce in bucolic Carmel and the idea of making a
living as an artist in a university was measureless; education was his
compelling inner push and working at a university was a potent force
he couldn't oppose. And although he could have stayed in Carmel
to develop artistically, his nascent adult tendencies of angst and
depression were fomenting and he was endlessly insecure about his
talent; he did not think he was good enough to make a go of being an
oil painter, especially after viewing Mr. Hansen's works. However,
he did have confidence in his drafting skills and whatever lay north at
U.C. Berkeley, he was sure he could do.

Franklin Delano Roosevelt's presidency provided a motivating crusade for artistic and creative people. There was concern by the government not only for the unemployed middle-class breadwinner, but also for people in the arts. Because of the many thousands of actors, actresses, vaudeville musicians, and artists out of work, the administration decided to include professional artists within the sphere of federal programs; it is estimated that five percent of the WPA's spending was earmarked for public art works, which has left us with beautiful murals, sculptures, and bas reliefs decorating public buildings.

Jonathan dashed off a note to his father explaining he was returning to the Bay Area. Thomas Batchelor, alone and not doing well selling magazines, also decided to return. Father and son converged on Lynn Batchelor's house on Emerson Street in Oakland. By that time Lynn was married but hadn't any children; he and his wife Laura (whom, according to Jonathan's spry, giggly, and elderly sister Blanche, was nicknamed Hippo by the family) openly welcomed father and son. But Blanche surprised everyone when she, too, left Los Angeles. She couldn't cope with the Lindo children, and despite being told she looked like Fay Wray, her calling as an actress was going nowhere. The charming Blanche, however, was never far from male assistance; due to a financial arrangement with Mr. Lindo, she was able to afford a hotel.

Latter half of the 1930s found the entire Batchelor clan back in the Bay Area. Prohibition had been repealed in 1933; the wine-loving Lynn was only too happy to share with his clan the occasional glass, usually of a red variety. The outdoor-loving group frequently picnicked at Lake Merritt, or they boarded the Sacramento Northern Railroad that had special "picnic" trains, that pulled coaches of people east through Oakland, through a tunnel below the Oakland Hills, and beyond Eastport, the first stop in the next county. Their destination was a lovely picnic spot set in a grove of redwood, madrone, and oak trees somewhat south of a place known as Redwood Canyon.

Picnic Specials were a distracting reprieve for many during the depression. Train fares were manageable and it was inexpensive entertainment. Despite hard times, Lynn and Laura Batchelor maintained through the depression without suffering too much. The do-it-yourselfer Lynn was still self-employed as a furniture builder, repairman, and finisher who worked from home. He also assisted Ralph Elliot with his dry-cleaning business. Additional family members in Lynn's home did not hurt him financially; Lynn and Laura were able to save by being careful with their money, planting their own garden, canning their own food, and buying day-old bread.

The grove in the photograph is in the heart of Canyon, California. One can see the bygone combination store/post office through trees. This is the picnic area where the Batchelor clan savored long afternoons. Photograph from *Old Times in Contra Costa: A Journey to the Past* by Robert D. Tatam.

Left: Lynn Batchelor in his work clothes. Right: Dapper, dressed to kill. Lynn worked hard to build a life for himself, yet he was a perpetual party boy who loved life, red wine and smokes, just as much as his dad. Photographs by Jonathan Batchelor.

Despite the Great Depression, San Francisco decided to celebrate the completion of two San Francisco Bay bridges (Bay Bridge in 1936 and Golden Gate in 1937). Never to do anything in a small way, San Francisco filled in part of the bay next to Yerba Buena Island, and christened it Treasure Island. The flat island, midpoint between San Francisco and Oakland, was originally contrived to be an airport. Instead, the Golden Gate International Exposition (GGIE) interrupted, followed by WWII, and the airport was never constructed. Using the island for a World's Fair seemed as good as any purpose. It was a big event, with President Franklin D. Roosevelt calling from Washington D.C. for the opening ceremonies.

Encouraged by people who regularly told her she resembled the actress Fay Wray, Blanche applied for a job with and was hired to perform as one of Ms. Rand's famous fan dancers. Sally Rand'svenue was featured on the Gayway, an entertainment zone christened as 'Forty Acres of Fun'. It was in the Gayway that stage-struck Blanche was able to show off her beaming face from behind one of Ms. Rand's gigantic fans. However, her fanciful stage calling came to a blunt standstill with the fan dance; she never participated in the Ranch, which exhibited women donning little more than fake six-shooters and cowboy hats doing ranch chores.

Sally Rand's Nude Ranch. Photograph courtesy of the California History Room, California State Library, Sacramento, California.

Nudity was never an issue with Blanche. Now and then, she had willingly disrobed and posed in the buff for her brother. She enjoyed her time at the fair and soon after closing chanced upon the man who would take care of her for the rest of her life, Mr. Hugh Smith. It didn't take long for Blanche Demeris Batchelor to assume Blanche Demeris Smith, a name she kept forever as she blithely settled as hausfrau. Mr. Smith, a veteran who worked for the Pullman Railroad Company, provided for her a good income for a full life and when he retired, two pensions. He made sure Blanche never lacked for anything.

Left: Hugh and Blanche Smith at Diamond Springs, Ca., 1956. Right: Blanche retained her regal beauty well into her later years.

On the first day of returning from Carmel, Jonathan straightaway applied for a position with the Works Progress Administration. A post was available in the entomology department at U.C. Berkeley for an artist who could depict detailed insect illustrations. What a perfect fit for Jonathan's 20/20 eyesight and masterfully detailed draftsmanship.

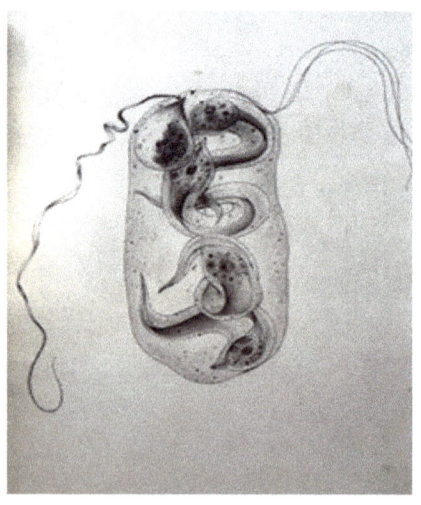

This drawing of a microscopic protoplasm was sketched at UC Berkeley.

The artist working at UC Berkeley. He worked in various departments depicting microscopic creatures, insects, and aided the diorama staff.

Charred remnant of insect drawn by Jonathan at UC Berkeley. This is a remarkably flimsy piece of paper, and I don't know how it survived the fire. I included charred drawings to show the world what has been lost. The detail on the insect is phenomenal; his early drawings were always very detailed.

Because he did not have an automobile, he used public transportation but more often than not, Lynn's gratifying bicycle. The young artist had always loved the sciences and he was both exultant and intellectually intoxicated by working at a notable university. He found the professors fascinating, mesmerizing; he prized conversing with them. Not only did he draw insects, but due to proficient detail-work he was also asked to paint the background for dioramas.

As a work rule, he normally sketched solo. Affable to everybody, he was popular with students and staff on and off campus. Among his circle of acquaintances were a few mischievous associates who, for merriment, made a surprise visit while he was on the job. Anticipating no one, he was putting considerable endeavor into a sizable sketch of a wee insect, and he scarcely glanced from his microscope. When he did, there stood a trio of WPA employees: Bart Frost from the university's diorama department standing next to Mildred Frey, who was Frost's girlfriend, and the petite pixie WPA acrobat, Mildred's roommate, Dorothy Mae Molica.

Fifty years later, in 1984, reminiscing to Dorothy Molica in a letter, Jonathan penned, "Remember Gene Towne? Then there was my friend Byron Guyer and his blonde wife. They both attended the university where I was a micrographer in the Zoology department. Remember Bart Frost and Mildred Frey? Mildred was your roommate in that petite apartment on Channing Way … when I first knew you."

And so it goes. Whenever Jonathan and I visited Dorothy (in her latter years, the 1980s-90s) he was fond of reminiscing and out tumbled names associated with their youthful ventures. I remember her asking, "How on Earth do you remember all those people?" Indeed, Jonathan's nimble recall is the reason I can write this book.

DOROTHY MAE DICKINSON

The man who idolized feminine contours hadn't much time or thought for serious female relationships. Not that he couldn't have had. Throughout his young life, in Junior High and High School, a smattering of young girls had been attracted to him primarily because of his colorful locks. The "Italian girl down the street" as the elderly artist referred to her, was his first childhood sweetheart. At the tender age of eight she had even proposed to him, way back in Visalia. As a youth in his twenties Jonathan was very serious about life and determined not to bring children into this world. Whether he realized he simply wasn't parent material, or whether he just wanted to focus on art and not parenting, for whichever explanation, children and romance were at the bottom of his bucket.

Conjointly, he had personal reasons for precluding children. Jonathan had inconsistent auditory complications that irregularly agitated him; it was challenging for him to be fenced in by any kind of sporadic noise, especially staccato type sounds. His focus on work from home precluded children who, if they are raised correctly, create pandemonium. He told me his hearing issues were from an infancy encounter with the whooping cough, which may very well have been true. But he was also the front-seat passenger in an automobile fender-bender that additionally may have played a role in his erratic deafness. The mishap, whereby a car ran off the road and hit a pole, must have happened mid-1930s. It took another decade before a doctor would diagnose a possible disturbed mastoid process. Reinforcing his anathema toward children was his observation of Louis Smith, his childhood buddy. Jonathan, the inveterate letter writer, had kept in touch with Mr. Smith. Bonded with his pal through their love of wilderness and dreams of publishing, the artist eagerly anticipated a visit after moving back to Oakland from Carmel. The youthful artist saw firsthand his comrade's descent into unanticipated reality: now a wage-earning employee, Louis, unsatisfied and discontented, had descended into alcoholism after marrying and fathering children. Jonathan was shocked.

Yet the artist worshiped, loved, sanctified women and everything the fair sex represented: adoration, comfort, shelter, nourishment, tenderness, all yearned for in his motherless upbringing. Therefore, it is surprising, yet not surprising, the first woman to passionately catch his eye was older, divorced, and already had two children. Because the artist was nowhere near ready for child rearing, her children were nowhere to be seen (with certain exceptions) when the two spent time together.

After an introduction to the elfin Dorothy (4' 10", if that) at UC Berkeley, what followed can only be described as 'Love at First Sight'. Dorothy admired the gangly supple redhead, who at times could paint better than he could speak or at other times couldn't control his ceaseless tumble of words. Despite the unprompted and unprepared introduction, the two were smitten; it did not take long for Dorothy and Jonathan to become a couple. Dorothy was Jonathan's first genuine ladylove. Her beauty prompted the artist to pen the following untitled half poem, half letter, referencing his scholarly love of mythology. "Epistle indited during the dolorously humdrum late afternoon of June 2, year 1938. To my darling Dorothy Mae, beloved little Anemone:

"When I sauntered alone this morning
Through the dark forest by the mer
I behold a seemly dryad disporting
By herself in a brief sequestered glade.

"Her antlered head was gaily adorned
By a diadem of palest flowers from the vale,
And her supple torse moved in quiet dance
Upon the nimble legs of a white roe-deer.

"The blowing winds played haunting strain
Of summons music high in the tall dark trees
And methought I heard the piping of a
Gilded syrinx somewhere near-about.

"And when I made to enter the fastness
Of that lonely hollow in the forest
The winsome solitaire gave vent a cry,
A melodious cry, - that haunts me still.

"Yet she did not flee, nor cower alarmed
There seemed some knowing amity, of
Whose truth, of course, I bore no father
And whose exotic beauty held me bewitched.

"She put forth a pearly, cloven hoof,
Tentatively, -a small, pointed hoof so gracing
A long slender limb, her waxen white
Arms held pliantly aloft, in frozen dances.

"A dryad, half woman, half gazelle,
Was my companion in the forest fastness,
With whom I held zealous consort
Where a garden of mauve hydrangeas bloomed

"And the piping of a gilded syrinx
Played rapturous strains of phantastic melody

Somewhere near-about that enchanted hollow
Where I loved and was loved by a lonely dryad."

The poem, expressed through waxing love, was followed by a second, much shorter poem titled, "Lethe".

"Where a garden of mauve hydrangeas blooms
I go wandering in the early morning,
Seeking some subtle analgesic wherein
A solitary voice intones oblivion.

"It is a time of trial, my darling, such as you and I, perhaps, have never known. But it is a time of growing jubilance and exultation such as we have never known! Its pathos is its felicity; and its digression, which is simultaneously its adversity, shall ultimately be its triumphant munificence…

"It is to be strong and zealous, and of firm courage; to dread naught, not be dismayed…Your Jonathan awaits."

1930s drawing *Pan Dancing with Dryad*, sanguine conte on paper, size unknown. Drawing courtesy of Cheryl Parent. Inspired by mythology, Jonathan's fanciful visualizations took flight.

Born in 1907, Dorothy's inauspicious beginning included a kidnapping. She was stolen as an infant and raised by a couple she truly believed were her parents. When Dorothy was four, there suddenly appeared a toddler brother. Obviously, he was carried off from another family.

When afflicted by childhood illness, Dorothy was fond of lying in bed with diverse dolls; oodles of them lived inside a trunk in her bedroom. Later in her seventies, remembering her life to neighbor Cheryl Parent, Dorothy (known as Dotty to everyone) explained how one afternoon her purloined brother peeped into her room and suddenly became obsessed with the succession of faces lined up across the leading edge of the open trunk. Impulsively, he jumped into her room and slammed the trunk's lid on the doll's heads, decapitating them. The little girl became bent on fixing them, and thus began a lifelong passion for repairing and mending dolls.

The young adult Dorothy managed to discover who her natural parents were. All parents, biological and those who raised her, astonishingly became good friends. At the tender age of sixteen, the lovely Dorothy ran off, dove into her first marriage, had two children, all by the tender age of twenty-one.

Two portraits of the lovely Dorothy Molica.

Left: Dorothy and her children. Right: Dorothy with her ex-husband and first child.

It is moot to note when Dorothy met Jonathan she was no spring chicken, and perhaps that accounted for her bold audacity in approaching the cautious artist. Ordinarily, she sought creative souls and unorthodox people: engrossed by him, she eagerly stepped to his side, endlessly gazing, giggling, and smiling. For all that Thomas Batchelor was a buoyant go-getter, his artist son was reserved, unassuming, and insecure; Jonathan used liquor to metamorphose into ebullience and sometimes downright silly behavior; under the influence, propriety disintegrated. Dorothy loved to hobnob at bars and Jonathan complied readily; together they dawdled, drank, and he sketched customers while she imbibed. The pair were occasional binge drinkers, which suited both. Inebriated or not, the artist was never far from conte crayon, pencil, and paper.

Untitled remnant, spontaneous sketch of a bar crowd.

Left, charred remnant of *Ol' Nick, San Francisco Bar Fellow*. The artist was fond of taking a black marker and sketching spontaneously: his superb draftsmanship was on display. I can sketch a face, but I need pencils and most importantly, erasers! I would never sketch spontaneously with ink. Right: *Young Woman at Bar*. I believe she was drawn at the Moraga Barn. More about the Moraga Barn further along in the book.

Years into the future, Jonathan painted *The Wine Tasters,* oil on canvas, 36" X 48", undated.

Besotted by Dorothy, it was only a matter of time before he again set pencil to paper producing this abstruse esoteric second letter. "Missive composed during the dismally dull late afternoon of June 7, in the year 1938. To my darling Dorothy Mae, adorable little sylph: A saturnine indecision of mind apprehends my sensibilities this evening. Some indiscernible factions of genes form a battery of tyrants, which pillage me of coherent imagery, burdening my soul like a cordon of cackling vultures voraciously dismantling a carcass. I gaze demurely upon a shriveled rosebud lying diagonally upon a sorely decrepit dun-coloured book resting cheerlessly on the table nearby, and very demurely at a cigarette-snipe disposed on the grey floor in a badly mashed and crumpled state. I peer absently into the tawny nape of some weary comrade-in-misfortune solitarily humped over a drab platitude of solitaire on his grey habiliment far across the shadowy barrack; and still more demurely upon the dim inauspicious page before me. I have dubbed myself a simpleton a score of times, and a plain bigoted curmudgeon even more often. In short, at times, I've totally had no use for myself.

"Now I can sit here and vaguely ruminate the variant character of the hundreds of thousands of hours that dance and whisper indecisively before you and me, a motley procession extending picturesquely into the dim magnitude of the future! What lies behind, at this moment, has little colour for retrospection. It was a lost and tempestuously chaotic pilgrimage, born of tumult and destined for tumult. This liberation which is nigh shall be a rebirth, a renascence wherein you and I, better equipped and accoutered with the grim tutelage of the old, are reincarnated, to embark upon a new pilgrimage, a new adventure into more notable realms.

"I feverishly await the arrival of this last hour of preparation. It is so vain of me to attempt a description of the great mirth which I shall know when I have you beside me again - if only for that delirious little hour. But I can wait with a dream to fondle me. I can sit here and just ruminate desultorily the amazing gamut of different hours that beckons beyond. Yet who shall verily proclaim or define for the human gaze what God shall ordain to do, and which celestial forces better elaborated have not yet chosen to divulge? Jonathan."

Two portraits of the couple. Both photos were taken by Jonathan. As soon as he had the means, the artist bought a camera and became a skilled photographer. He was fond of taking 'selfies' throughout his life.

Her husband's custodial retention of the children left Dorothy with time. She not only was employed within the WPA but was also easily hired by local theatrical groups, including a circus group. Jonathan and Dorothy, with their matching histories of fathers who had journeyed with vaudeville, made for the couple an abiding ethereal connection. Dorothy's father, a headliner in Chicago, staged himself as Rube Dickinson. Whatever the reason, genetics or just general interest, Dorothy found herself drawn to theater and the popular beauty had legions of theatrical friends.

Previous page: Dorothy had a creative urge and was attracted to artistic and original people. Hair in rollers, she spends the afternoon dabbling with watercolors.

Petite Dorothy has a competitive edge against her towering competition. Here she is a lead on stage with some of her theatrical friends.

Below Newspaper clipping from Oakland Tribune.
One-legged, the bicyclist Al Castle pedaled fiercely
while intrepid Dorothy performed acrobatics, 1935.

A THRILLER! Here's a sensational stunt by Al Castle and
Dorothy Dickinson as they performed before the throngs of
applauding boys and girls at the Christmas party.

A publicity shot; photographer unknown.

Two photographs of Dorothy on stage. Photographer unknown. All photographs were found with Dorothy's mementos. Images are courtesy of Cheryl Parent.

The couple found a house to let in Oakland and the artist applied for a new WPA position to be closer to home. Oakland had an early history of manufacture and the broad waterfront lent itself to mass transportation including ships, wharves, docks, railroads. I used to laugh when Jonathan tried to describe 'Pickle Billy' to me. Pickle Billy had a warehouse adjacent the waterfront, loaded with enormous barrels, some ready with pickles to sell, and yet others had cucumbers steeping on their pickling journeys. Hired by the city to draw waterfront scenes of ships and stevedores, the artist enjoyed his time along the waterfront, stopping in for pickles on the way home. Some of his Oakland sketches are below, courtesy Cheryl Parent. The first two in her possession are intact. Untitled, sanguine conte crayon on paper, sizes unknown. The charred ones all went through the Canyon fire.

Oakland's WPA hired Jonathan to draw waterfront activity.

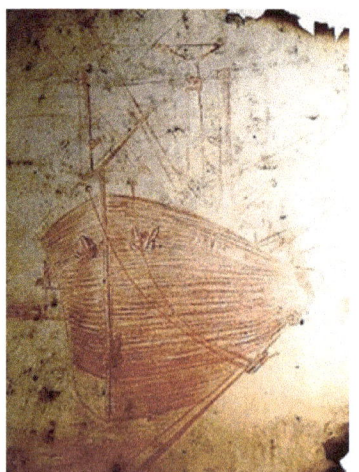 

Oakland's waterfront, late 1930s. The left is labeled *Shipworkers at Dock, Alabama* (the name Alabama is easier to see on the original fragment). The right is titled *Tractor Towing Boxcar*. Both charred remnants, sketched on flimsy newsprint, are sanguine conte crayon on paper.

This fragment is titled *Small Oil Tanker, Yerba Buena, Bay Bridge*. The hill in the background (to the left) is Yerba Buena Island, midway between Oakland and San Francisco. In the faint distance beyond the water tank is the faint outline of brand-new San Francisco-Oakland Bay bridge.

This last singed remnant is titled *Stevedores at Work*. These fragments were all tucked away in homespun cardboard portfolios within Canyon house. As many survivors of the depression were wont to do, Jonathan made do with recycling, reusing and reinventing possessions. He made many thick and sturdy portfolios for his artwork out of cardboard, tape and glue. He, and like-minded artists of his era, made unique wooden homemade frames for their oil paintings. It is almost miraculous the above drawing remnants, drawn on fragile paper, survived at all. As to whether the city of Oakland took possession or kept any of his drawings, I have no idea.

Although Jonathan eschewed the idea of rearing a family, he didn't mind intermittent outdoorsy jaunts with Dorothy's two. He was pleased with them: not only were they nice children, but their existence meant he would not have to contend with the maternal predisposition, something he was all too familiar with. Custody arrangements complemented their lifestyle: guardianship prevailed with Mr. Molica: the uninhibited sprite that was Dorothy was free to devote all attention to the artist.

Jonathan's WPA work gave him the means to purchase a car. Here, Dorothy is radiant while holding her daughter, Patricia, in the passenger seat while her son Jimmy mans the rumble seat.

Dorothy's two children. A small graphite sketch on paper, it measures no more than 5 X 8. It is in remarkable shape, considering it survived the house fire.

Next page: Although he did not want children, Jonathan did observe and appreciate Dorothy's attention to her own offspring. While he was dating her, he made this very emotional drawing of mother and child. *Untitled*, sanguine conte on paper, size unknown. Drawing in possession of Cheryl Parent.

Next page: Unfinished sculpture of mother and child, 1930s. Although he lacked motherly nurturing, he venerated motherhood and would do so for the rest of his life. Laboring on the mother's face, he gave her a 1930s hairdo. The baby, however, was never finished and lacks a face. To me, the woman slightly resembles Dorothy.

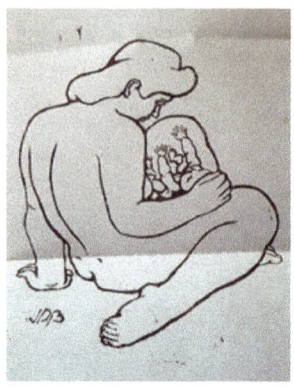

Top: Print of mom and baby, ca. 1930s. This may have been a study for the previous sculpture, considering the similar pose. Bottom: Trying to attract art students. He never lived on Durant Avenue, which is two blocks from UC Berkeley. Possibly it was a collaborative studio.

The couple wed in August of 1940. If they had a ceremony, I did not hear about it. Neither was zealously religious, although Dorothy wore a cross and conventional Catholic tenets at first played a serious role with Jonathan. Catholic doctrine was still fresh as he commenced nuptials; he thought the marriage would be everlasting and she his only wife. I am not sure how he reconciled those thoughts with their abounding socializing, carousing, and inebriation. How could any marriage survive all that bar hopping?

Two photographs taken sometime in Oakland during the 1930s. Left: Jonathan in his painting smock working en plein air. Exceedingly serious, he seldom smiled for photographs. Right: Domesticated Dorothy, wearing a cross, cracking eggs. I have no doubt when the artist saw her head and shoulders bathed in light with darkness encompassing, he must have felt compelled to capture the image. They were not church going but knowing Jonathan as I did, he would have weighed in on religious matters as a point of philosophical discussion.

Their marriage was conventional. He did not mind Dorothy working but he would have been just as content for her to stay home. His expectation was for Dorothy to have dinner prepared and the house orderly by the time he came home from work. Unfortunately, "old-school" did not always mesh with hedonism.

They loved wine, entertaining, parties. It was while living with Dorothy that Jonathan, who loved to dress in costume, began his favorite dress-up festivity. He became noted for his 'Edgar Allan Poe' parties; all guests had to deck out as their favorite Poe character. Dorothy's education was not as well rounded as her husband's and although she liked to read, she did not read literature voraciously; encouraging her, he regularly bought her books. Gleefully she anticipated his Poe gatherings and loved welcoming her theater friends. And although she loved to binge drink, with or without him, none of that mattered to him as long as she had the house tidied and dinner prepared: he could cook but hadn't time nor inclination for doing so.

The fastidious artist did not mind cluttered chaos after a bash, but insisted everything be shipshape as soon as possible after the merriment. He liked his house neat. He was fussy about hanging clothing properly; intermittent heaps of apparel on the floor a pet peeve; he insisted on unimpeded access. He wanted knickknacks oddments rags mishmash organized in kind to allow easy access for household or artistic needs. Not only is tidying a home energy consuming and time robbing, but also any artist will attest studios are a task. Artists tend to accumulate not just the raw materials to create their visions, but all kinds of bric-a-brac and curios for their own personal visual enjoyment. As years pass, a studio can become a hodgepodge of objects and is not always easy to keep orderly. His need for space created serious household clutter issues. In the latter 1930s, he began casting about for an art studio.

Dorothy asleep with bottle, books, drawing, and for the life of me I don't know how she managed to keep that glass of wine in her left hand from spilling.

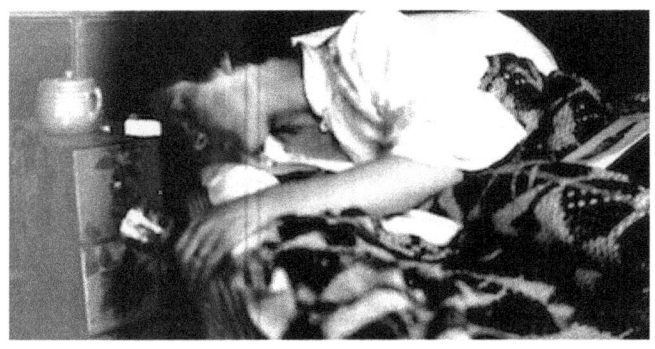

Dorothy asleep with tumbler still attached to hand. Why the wine glass is not on the floor stumps me. Jonathan must have gotten a kick out of her dozing with a glass in her hand, as he took many such photos.

In downtown Oakland, at the corner of 64th St. and Broadway, stood an old mansion well past its glory days. Jonathan recalled fields of acreage behind the mansion and offset slumbered a colossal old carriage house, crestfallen, desolate, depressed without horses, stables below and enormous loft above. With every drive by, the artist couldn't help but notice the abandoned building with multiple large windows on the second floor. Impulsively, he stopped at the estate and politely asked the owners, Mr. and Mrs. Mahl, about the forgotten building. Discovering the structure belonged to them, it didn't take but a moment for him to ask if he could rent it. The building had no electricity or running water, but the artist did not care. An older couple, the Mahls got a kick out of the artist. Pleased, they were generous; rent was set at $5 per month. Over time, the Mahls developed a fondness for both Jonathan and Dorothy. It is probably moot to say how ecstatic Jonathan was with his very own atelier (the wordsmith preferred 'atelier' over 'art-studio').

Decades into the future, the persistently incurable letter writer in 1984 wrote Dorothy a letter of reminiscence: "I recall the pleasure we shared walking together in the rain in the Berkeley hills. It was the way we were: years of sharing joys and pains. Remember the carriage house studio on Greenwood Terrace?" [authors note: that was a slip of memory. Carriage house was on Webster St., not Greenwood Terrace]. "When it was summer we slept on the little balcony, looking out into a wold of Lombardy poplars. A steep hillside arose in back of the house, extending into wooded countryside, interspersed with the ruins of sumptuous homes that were lost in the 1922 Berkeley conflagration. What wonderful parties we had there! I did a storm of drawings and writings in that place."

For a span of years, the carriage house art studio was Jonathan's identity, soul, purpose, spirit, psyche, sanity. The artist did not mind solo time and indeed, he thrived on solitude; he loved sitting in his loft writing journals, letters, poetry. "December 8, 1944, Friday: I have been sitting here for a long while, looking at the pale light shining on the mottled window panes. In the streets beyond, glittering vehicles careen with varying swiftness, casting flickering shadows on the murky pavement. But in the room I glance slowly from chair to table, to the floor. I look at piles of drawings and written paper, clusters of tools, bottles, looming sculptures ensconced on barrels and packing cases. My large easel stands to the left with the freshly begun portrait of Marjorie Paris. Nearby is the rude table cluttered with battered, half emptied tubes of paint, my palette, the Chinese sculptured bronze vase bristling with brushes, bottles of oils and turpentine."

Years into the future, he was commissioned to do portraits of the Paris sisters (Jeanette, Fayne and Marjorie). He was still painting in a very classical, realistic manner interspersed with hints of rugged brushwork. I received a very interesting email from Fayne Paris' adult daughter, Allison Knox Blankenship. Of her mother, Ms. Blankenship wrote: "She was one of his models while a student at UC Berkeley in 1946-1948. She always spoke of him with such loving adoration. My mother wrote a 30+ page memoir and here's what she wrote about Jonathan: "While I was in high school I visited the studio of Jonathan Batchelor, a teacher at the California School of Arts and Crafts. Jeanette had met him and had sat for an oil portrait. His studio was incredible. It was in a big barn, and you had to climb up a ladder and enter by way of a big trap door in the ceiling to his studio on the top floor. There were huge windows and lots of light, and there were many beautiful nude statues all around that Jonathan had sculpted, as well as his work in oils of nude figures. Some were couples entwined together. Jonathan was intrigued with me, and he asked me to sit for him. First he did sepia crayon sketches, and then he painted my portrait in oils. It was a very good portrait of me, but as a 16-year-old, I really hadn't seen what I looked like to others. My whole young life, I had always been referred to as "wholesome," and I guess I would have liked to have been considered somewhat more exotic.

"Jonathan was a very striking figure, a man in his 40s. He was tall and thin with a wild head of red hair and beard with very white skin and wore these big work boots. He was a real-life bohemian. He was a working artist and sculptor, and I was very flattered that he found me interesting. He said he wanted to do a sculpted head of me, and I sat for him. Now I saw myself in 3-D, and was disappointed as it was indeed me, and not some exotic creature. He said he loved my strong neck, and he even wrote poetry about me as a puma. He knew I was disappointed with the head, and he went through all the trouble of changing the head, making it more stylized and not an exact likeness, although you could tell it was of me. He entered the head in some art shows, and it won prizes. Now when I look at a newspaper clipping with a picture of *Concerto*, I realize it is a fine piece of work."

Graduation photo of Fayne Paris next to image of *Concerto*. He never revealed to me the bust was Fayne Paris, although he had mentioned Ms. Paris' name on countless recollections. She truly made a deep and lasting impression. For years the bust lived in the "Inner Sanctum", one of any number of bedrooms in his sprawling house in the woods. That room (all his varied rooms had their own nicknames) was located deep in the center back of the house, set against a hill. It was always chilly in the winter but on hot summer days, the Inner Sanctum felt like a swimming pool. I oft times went down there to escape summer heat and read numerous books.

Concrete bust of Fayne Paris; Young Ms. Paris full of life. The bust was titled *Concerto.*

My Carriage House Studio, 16 X 12, oil on panel, 1944. This old carriage house as studio, destination and respite was made for Jonathan. He was, for all intents and purposes, a child of the wilderness living in the city. Without electricity, evenings were spent penning next to a kerosene lamp. Old wine bottles served to bring water to his studio. Cold temperatures were not an issue; he was very hardy. Because he usually dressed nicely, one would not have known he lived so severely.

Titled *64th and Broadway*, 30" X 24", oil on panel, 1945, the oil painting is a portrait of the Mahl mansion. The mansion plays second fiddle to the ornate First Presbyterian Church, which looms over the left side of the painting. This intersection is now 27th and Broadway and the church still stands; the mansion was either demolished or rebuilt into a modern office building. Today, the same view hosts an expansive cityscape. Years into the future, this section of Broadway becomes 'Auto Row.' Billboards that advertise car prices flank the mansion; they foretell Oakland's industrial destiny.

Interestingly, I found this original drawing buried amidst a pile of sketches that survived the fire. It was rendered with sepia conte crayon. He loved conte sticks and relied heavily on sepia, sanguine and black.

Next page: Tres amigos! Thomas Leon Batchelor, slender and spare next to his taller sons, Leon (Lynn) Edgar Batchelor and Ralph Elliott. The entire Batchelor clan converged back to the Bay Area. Photographed by Jonathan Batchelor.

The latter 1930s not only saw Jonathan and Dorothy side by side, but also the migration of Thomas Batchelor and his offspring to the Bay Area. Thomas had his choice of households to couch-surf but preferred staying with 'Jonny and Dorothy' (the entire clan called him Jon or Johnny). Despite protracted hardships, animated Thomas remained a source of laughter. Well into his sixties, he still could not live without his beloved red wine and smoked like a fiend. The Social Security Act, signed in 1935, did not start until 1940. For people like Thomas who were of retirement age, the government allowed one-time lump-sum payments in 1937. Thomas took his lump sum and decided to purchase a house in the countryside. He remembered fondly the resorts that lined the Russian River from his vaudeville days and decided to settle there. Small cabins for reasonable prices were available at Camp Meeker, an old logged-out Redwood and Douglas fir area. The timber industry was long gone but those small cabins, built for loggers, were modified and sold as summer homes for people from Sausalito, San Francisco, and the Bay Area. Thomas' cabin was not roomy, but suited his purposes. He loved the countryside, never lost his passion for horses, and even as automobiles became the mainstay of urban life, he stubbornly refused to drive. For the rest of his life he and his adopted small black dog,

Rosie, split their time between Camp Meeker and Oakland; one child or another had to make the drive to pick up or return him. Dorothy enjoyed their outings and always insisted on picking up a growler of red wine prior to the drive.

Thomas Batchelor, above, was an avid reader who adored the western genre. When he passed away, he left an entire bookcase of Zane Gray novels.

Next page: Old colorized postcard depicting Russian River activity. Rio Nido had similar sunny beaches, swimmers, boaters, restaurants, a dance hall, skating rink, stage, arcade, and a bowling alley. Postcard is public domain.

Left: This 'Living Tower' of four redwood trees appears to be the last of the old growth redwoods in that section of Camp Meeker. There were seven landings to the top and it is said one can see seven counties from there. Right: Old Postcard of the Camp Meeker library. I'm somewhat assuming Mr. Batchelor spent much of his free time there. Both photos are public domain.

The Batchelor clan, but especially athletic-outdoorsy Lynn, valued the Russian River's enchanting sunlit beaches and beckoning entertainment. Camp Meeker became a family gathering place and was a convenient respite for both Lynn and half-brother Ralph, both of whom put long hours into their dry-cleaning business. Sadly, the 2004 fire of Canyon burned countless black and white Box Brownie photos of the family canoeing, swimming, and sunning along the river. Also in Canyon, Jonathan kept a bedside-framed photo of his father, standing in front of the cabin holding Rosie. Jonathan, like his father who always had a soft spot for animals, fell head-over-heels in love with Thomas' little black dog and he, too, decided to adopt a dog. After his marriage to Dorothy, in lieu of children, he and Dorothy adopted a German Shepherd mix they named Tanya.

Thomas Leon Batchelor enjoying himself at Camp Meeker. If you look carefully, a dog's leg and tail are peeping out from beneath his bent legs.

Dorothy was an early oil portrait. One can see this work originated with line drawing (as opposed to forming a face with shapes, or darks vs. lights). The master draftsman created an exact replica of his wife's features with precision. This image came to me as a photograph so I am uncertain as to dimensions or date.

Above: The couple loved their adopted pooch, Tanya. Left: The serious artist, who seldom smiled for photographs, beams with Tanya in his arms. Right: sweet Tanya places her paw over Dorothy's arm.

Of Dorothy, perhaps it can be said that she was a bit too wild. Customarily docile, she was also gregarious, full of laughter, and had many theatrical friends that she loved to party with. She loved her work and her husband did not mind that she worked with entertainers and neither did he mind that she had a great many friends. It can be said of the groom that he was non-possessive and hadn't covetous tendencies. However, he did have certain expectations regarding his wife's duties and there were times when he came home from work to find Dorothy gone, bed unmade, no dinner on the table and the house a mess. Sometimes Dorothy, who loved wine, get-togethers, and pubs, disappeared with her fellow performers for days on end. Bewildered, Jonathan did not know what to make of it. Although he dearly loved drinking too, Nutmeg's (his favorite nickname for her) irregular disappearances left the artist shouldering household chores. This was certainly not anticipated. Even tempered, the artist accepted her surprising absences and never lost his temper with her, even when she was occasionally jailed. "Missive Written during the dolorous, late evening of July 2, in the year 1939. To my poor little trampled flower..." He wrote. "My dear Dorothy..." Dorothy had apparently been incarcerated.

"Now, little cosset, though I feel you have erred, as you have so often, I must pause to tell you how utterly I grieve your absence from our world of mind and body, for not merely in dreaming, such as small humanity knows, can the warm pulse of life be felt most lustily, but to hamper what miserable lot of liberty we are rationed by this trite and gawdy little world we call civilized is to dull the edge that God has rendered to atone for humanity's vain stupidity! This stuffy structure of human device and drab stone and mortar and fast corroding metal shall one day fall asunder in a ruin of its own crass and fractious injustice wherein no men shall dwell except in their long-forgotten ashes and dust blown by wild winds and parched in a pitiless heat.... I await – Postcriptum: They kept me from seeing you yesterday, and since today is not a regular visiting day, I shall see you tomorrow. Please do not fret much, my dear. I forgive your little error because I love you profoundly...Your Jonathan, late evening, July 2, 1939."

Dorothy made up for her deficiencies in many ways. When she was not with her theater groups, she was a wonderful companion and steadfastly supportive of his art and poetry. And just as Jonathan put up with her sprees, so she put up with his imbibing. He loved red wine, sipped well into the night, and when he did, became chatty. Thin, wiry, energetic, he was somehow able to function on only three or four hours of sleep a night. After sipping wine in the evening, he would typically write prose or poetry and could talk philosophy or diddly-squat till dawn. Never an angry or abusive drunk, he would get his few hours of sleep and be on time for work the following day.

Above: Domestic tranquility. As the artist sculpts, his wife reads and smokes. I believe he was sculpting the piece pictured on the next page.

I call this piece *Pygmalion*, because it reminds me of the fantasy, "Pygmalion and Galatea". His left-hand grips chisel and his right arm wields a hammer.

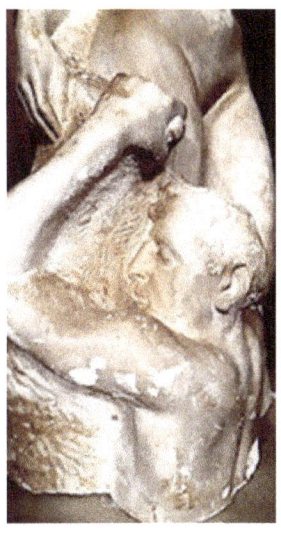

Another view of *Pygmalion*. I have often wondered if Jonathan intended this to be a self-portrait. The nose and body resemble his, not so much the eyebrow and forehead. Jonathan's hands were unusually large and rugged.

Impromptu sketch of Dorothy relaxing. She apparently liked to read and snack together, as there seems to be a plate on her lap. Sanguine conte on paper, size unknown. Drawing courtesy of Cheryl Parent.

Left: The finely dressed young couple, sometime during the 1930s. I can only conjecture they were relaxing and possibly returning from a symphony concert. His drawings adorn walls. Right: An early landscape, size and date unknown. As many artists do, he started his creative life as an illustrator, developing his impressionistic proclivity with time, knowledge, and practice.

"Nutmeg", when not on a bender, was very domestic; not only was she an excellent cook but she was great with knitting, darning and clothing repair, did all the laundry, and kept a sharp eye out for bargains at the supermarket. She filled their home with plants and enjoyed gardening in the backyard. She relished decorating their home, filling it with bric a brac and directing him to hang his artwork here or there. She provided dedicated emotional support encouraging his artwork and furthermore, she accompanied him on his many retreats into the Sierra Nevada; he still loved and needed the mountains and continued to camp in the backcountry of the Eagle Lakes area, his beloved 'Valley of the Gods' where he had spent many a long summer with Louis Smith when they were teenagers. Dorothy was game enough to try camping and she enjoyed it, especially with Tanya along.

Two photographs taken by Jonathan of his beloved 'Valley of the Gods'. Situated in the vicinity of Fordyce Creek, this area of the Sierra features multiple small lakes, marshes, meadows, lots of granite and diverse views.

Whilst driving home from one of his mountain jaunts he and Dorothy passed through lush Sierra foothills and discovered Diamond Springs, a small undeveloped area just outside Placer ville. He chanced upon property for sale in the middle of nowhere, one log cabin, no neighbors for miles. His thoughts went to the log cabin as art studio, not as a residence, even though it was livable. He also prized the undulating hillsides punctuated with oak and the cabin remained in his thoughts.

The Sierra was not his only haven. He remembered picturesque Carmel and its white and luscious, warm beaches. He was fond of spending weekends at the artist's colony.

Previous page: Top: Thomas Batchelor enjoying a nip in the white sands of Carmel. His son, wearing artist's beret, appears worried, even though visiting Carmel was a treat. Photographs of Dorothy next.

Perhaps the artist was concerned because Dorothy was not feeling well? Cigarette balanced between fingers, she has wrapped herself with draped jacket as though she were chilled. Eyes shut to the sun, she may have been hung over. I wouldn't be surprised if Thomas, Jonathan, and Dorothy all over-indulged the previous night. To be fair, I found another photo of Dorothy, perhaps from another day. Below: alluring in her swimsuit, she appears the personification of health and ready to swim.

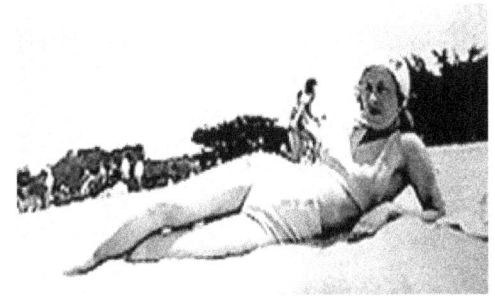

Very early painting of Jonathan's, reprinted from a negative, and not available in color. I gave it the arbitrary name *Landscape with Sylphs*, of which he depicted many, frolicking in the sun. I haven't any idea where this painting is, or even if it exists, but it does show his state of mind energized by myth, Gods and Goddesses.

Previous page: What an interesting double exposure, something that cannot be done with digital cameras! The artist was in his backyard (I recognize that bamboo plant from other photos of his Oakland yard). I get a kick out of that gigantic chicken in the background.

Life was good for the couple. Oakland was not a bad place to live what with a smaller pre-WWII population, less traffic and no rush hour. Public transportation was fabulous; the electric Key system connected all Bay Area cities to Sacramento and beyond, not to mention the new two-decked San Francisco-Oakland Bay Bridge, cars on the nearly empty upper level, the lower reserved for Key System Trains and trollies.

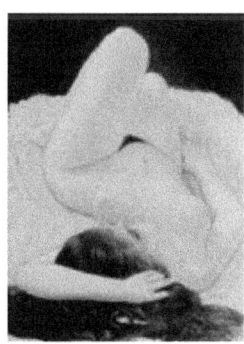

Jonathan and his 'Nutmeg' at home in Oakland, California. Note the sparse furnishings; the artist was not inclined to spend money on furniture. Two paintings including a reclining nude (above the couple) have been hung. The nude, printed here from a negative. This painting may or may not now exist. Visible against the window is a homespun turntable with an unfinished sculpture, later titled *The Lovers*. Undated, the photos are possibly early 1940s. He may have been browsing a large volume of reproduced artworks, pointing out different art styles throughout history, something he did with me frequently. Photographer unknown; it may have been Thomas Batchelor or Jerome Nowotny. More about Mr.

Nowotny later.

In the 1930s, left leaning politics and forward-thinking philosophies had created a Bay Area ethos of openness and free thought. This broadmindedness has always been a draw for people from all over the world, which contributed to the Bay Area's sophisticated multicultural outlook and continues to this day. The Bay Area has also been a stronghold for dissidents and protesters with serious union strikes by dockworkers and longshoremen. Some union members were also communists, which in those days before the cold war were not considered threats per se. The Bay Area became a draw for the creative crowd including novelists, poets, painters, actors, musicians, and journalists. Jazz became important to the local scene as Bay Area native Dave Brubeck flourished. Innovative people wrote, painted, and performed their way to express thoughts on racial and working-class injustices, which laid the foundation for the eventual Bay Area civil rights movements.

Missives were de rigueur. Jonathan had kept in touch with a small cadre of 'comrades' from Los Angeles. Imagine how pleased he was to receive a letter from a former acquaintance, Mr. Nowotny. To the artist's delight, his friend, a would-be thespian, sought to relocate in the Bay Area and requested to temporarily reside with Jonathan and Dorothy while the actor looked for work. Describing himself as a performer, he wanted to pursue his passion within the creative juices of politically left-leaning Bay Area. Jonathan looked forward to his comrade's visitation, as he referred to it in his reply. The Nowotnys arrived by Greyhound and were greeted with gusto by the Batchelors.

However altruistic the Batchelors were, their relationship with the Nowotnys at length crumbled: Mr. Nowotny, chronically out of work, and his wife, candidly made use of the household, including food. Jonathan was away at work during the day, unmindful of everything, and probably would have let the couple continue their mode of sustenance if it weren't for distressed Dorothy. Concerned, she pointed out their dwindling finances, the disappearing food, and explained to her husband in no uncertain terms, that even though they were his friends, the couple just had to go. Dorothy, docile by nature, left it to Jonathan, socially oblivious, awkward with communicating, to take care of it. Their peaceful house became unpleasant; one could cut the tension with a disconcerted knife. Pressures arose, arguments escalated, and one afternoon while Mr. Nowotny was away, Jonathan had one final argument with Mrs. Nowotny and simply asked her to leave. He escorted her to the door and shut it behind her.

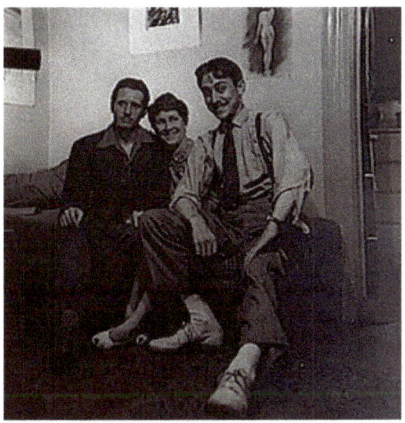

Jonathan, Dorothy, and Jerome Nowotny in the couple's home. Face beaming, Dorothy appears to be making eyes at the would-be actor.

Mr. Nowotny, a very handsome man, easily could have been a leading man. On his photograph he penned: "Jonathan Comrade, may you get what you desire FAME Jerome." He could not have known Jonathan very well, if he thought the artist was after fame; Jonathan was always utilitarian in his outlook. Although he never expected to be wealthy, he also never anticipated chronically modest earnings. Photographer unknown, Cheryl Parent owns the photo.

Vindictively, the Nowotnys filed charges against Mr. Batchelor. Unbeknownst to him, Mrs. Nowotny, although not showing, was pregnant, and throughout that era it was illegal to discharge a pregnant woman from a house. Jonathan was charged and sentenced to six months in jail. Thus began a tornado of missives between husband and wife. At that time, the postal service, in top form, picked up and sent mail twice a day. Writing from jail, the artist remonstrated with page after page about the injustice of it all. Dorothy, not one to wax philosophic, simply tried to be as encouraging as she could, softening the edge of his impatience to be home. She wrote of the more mundane matters such as where she had been shopping, what family members she may have been visiting, a plant she bought for the living room, where she placed it, and how nice it looked, or simply who happened to stop by for a visit. The deluge of posts continued, and just as suddenly, from Dorothy's end, they stopped. Presently, she was able to write again. "Guess where I am?" she scribbled. "I am in jail!" On another binge, she had been arrested while driving under the influence. Her jottings continued, with husband and wife writing from their respective jails.

She was presently released and about the same time Jonathan was transferred to a minimally supervised custodial work farm outside of the small town of Clayton, California. Although still officially in jail, at least the work farm was not in the city; surrounded by lush green hills dotted with California live oak, it was marginally tolerable for the nature-loving artist. The letters continued unrelenting until Jonathan was discharged some three months later.

After his release, Jonathan, solo, drove north to retrieve Thomas from Camp Meeker and when they returned, Dorothy had vanished on another spree. Troubled, resolute, Jonathan set about putting the house in order and preparing meals for his father. After several days, and no Dorothy, Thomas quietly asked his son, "How often does she do this?" Thomas was shocked when he found out how frequently she stepped out. "Well," he replied, "What is good for the goose is good for the gander".

It is generally noted that some young people are confused about life and Jonathan was no exception. Excluding a few minor years with his stepmother, the lion's share of his growth was spent with his father, and indeed, he and his father were very close. Any spousal concept emanated from the Catholic Church and not from home life. When his marriage started disintegrating, he didn't know how to cope. He had entered into matrimony believing Dorothy was his for eternity. Life with his father had not prepared him to communicate with an oft-absent wife nor did he know anything about repairing a broken relationship.

Those words, "What is good for the goose, is good for the gander", set Jonathan on a course far different from anything he had ever imagined. Following his father's advice, or using his advice as an excuse, he began consorting with other women. He was, of course, not available for a partnership but at least he was honest. He made sure his dates understood him to be married, and he also continued to seek older divorced or separated women, preferably those who already had children. Without question he did not want romantic love: no young lady who might pine for his baby! The upshot is that Jonathan discovered for the first time in his life he could charm and entice the gentler sex. At 5' 10" and never weighing more than 120 pounds, he had always considered himself a skinny, plain, average looking guy, somewhat unworthy and unremarkable.

His love of parties continued unabated and when his wife disappeared, he attended social gatherings without her and was astonished at the number of women who edged up to him for conversation. In his younger years, Jonathan thought himself a serious scholar and nobody's romantic dream. Not realizing that human behavior is backed by motivation, he was truly clueless. He did not recognize that women can't resist a man who *listens*, and Jonathan, as self-absorbed and non-empathetic as he was a charmer who also gave heed. But how to stay versant, when one possesses capricious hearing loss? I am an artist with decades of mishearings. Let me just say I have spent a great deal of my life reading lips of which intense scrutiny is required. When I am talking with someone, and that person turns their head away from my line of sight, sounds become mishmash. If the audience is oblivious to the narrator's hearing issues, I can see how the listener can misconstrue concentrated lip scanning as personal interest.

While I was with Jonathan, I attended social events, his social events, as I had none. I was always cheerful to be his chauffeur and I found his meetings and CCAC alumni dinners animatedly enlightening. I cannot speculate how many women he met at these events who doubtlessly became captivated by him. As I was relegated into the role of secondary guest, he and his brand-new acquaintance dropped into an exchange of their own. They had intense eye contact with each other, neither looked at me, and I was left out of their sphere. I think I should mention, despite his actions, my feelings were never hurt; I simply dropped into my character as witness. I could see his obliviousness to me, and it helped me to recognize how Dorothy or any of his later wives may have felt snubbed.

I can only speculate that his very intense lip surveillance may have flattered some women, as certainly in their eyes he must have seemed fervidly absorbed. Not to mention, going beyond lip scrutiny, artists who are fond of drawing the human face are all prone to stare. We are taught it is not polite to stare, but we cannot help it. We try to disguise our staring, but the fact remains, we do on occasion stare at an interesting face. How can we not? How could any woman resist this flamboyant, red-haired illustrator who gazed attentively and held onto her every word? Furthermore, plied with a little red wine he was magical and flirtatious all without realizing it. He was simply being himself and women prized him.

Red wine was gold bullion; he prized it as much, if not more, than his father. With alcohol, Jonathan lost his propriety and became overly dramatic, at times the life of the party as he hammed it up or jumped on a chair to dance. Thomas Batchelor had been a born performer and never needed liquor for stage appearances; his son became an entertainer only after consumption of red wine. And indeed, in his latter years, when I accompanied him to many a party, all it took was a glass or two and Jonathan could embroider any story or mimic an awesome Cockney accent. He was exceptionally comical. The ironic thing is that in the morning, he hadn't a clue!

And thus was inaugurated Jonathan's penchant for dating, sometimes hiding it from an extremely jealous Dorothy, sometimes not. For all that he was bereft of womanhood when he was a child, he made up for it as an adult. The man who worshipped women was now able to meet, get to know, and enjoy the company of many adoring women. He did not necessarily bed them all; sometimes he was simply enamored of womanly conversation. The few he became intimate with evolved into friendships that in some cases lasted well into years. For his part, he was keenly interested in each and every individual and relished discovering her persona; his preferences were for intellectuals who could talk philosophy, God, or the universe.

Below: *Those Who Worship Women*, sepia conte crayon on paper, 20 X 16, 1940s.

As per the hedonist Dorothy, the artist never tired of satirizing her. Following are some of his lampoons:

Of all the drawings that survived the fire, I was surprised to see this *Parody of Dorothy*, 1938. Jonathan used to howl with laughter at it. Of course, it looks nothing like the petite, svelte woman that Dorothy was. Her drinking habits were spoofed; she holds a martini in her right hand.

Also mocking Dorothy, this is clearly exaggerated, and her theatrical friends surround her. I have no idea if she appreciated his lampoons, but she did keep some of them mixed in with mementos of her life. All these sketches are courtesy of Cheryl Parent.

These are both deliberate satiric exaggerations of Dorothy. Why he chose an elephant, I'll never know. Black conte on paper.

Left: On the reverse of the bowing elephant the artist noted: *Baroque Dance Terpsichore or Burlesque.* Right: Jonathan had printed Dorothy's initials in the bottom right-hand corner. If she at all felt ridiculed, she may have smiled when jotting "Jon" beneath his sketch of a pig.

Early 1940: Thomas needed a lift from Camp Meeker; he was in agony. A doctor examined him at Oakland's Highland Hospital. After a brief exploratory surgery, he was quickly diagnosed with cancer and sewn up; the Batchelors were told there was nothing doctors could do and gave him six months to live. Thomas quickly put his affairs in order, participated in his last and final US census (where he listed himself as widowed although his first wife, Kathryn, was still alive), listed his highest educational grade as the 4th grade, and listed his age as 68 although if he was born in 1870 he must have been 70. He then stayed with Jonathan and Dorothy until he seriously needed hospitalization. Although dying, Thomas never lost his lightning-fast wit or sense of comedy. His wisecracks affected hospital staff; the nurses laughed so hard they were in "stitches" (Jonathan's pun). Thomas also repeatedly asked his son for red wine but the artist could not get himself to sneak even one bottle into the hospital. For the rest of his life, Jonathan was ever remiss that he never delivered the wine, but at that time he thought it would be the wrong thing to do. Time and again Jonathan remonstrated if he had to do it over, he would unquestionably take that wine into the hospital, rules or no rules.

Thomas, the man who loved horses and never learned to drive those hated automobiles, finally passed on June 20th, just shy of Jonathan's birthday, which was June 29th. He was laid to rest in Mountain View Cemetery, in Oakland.

> Next page: After his father's death, Jonathan, aching but unable to cry openly, expressed sorrow with this self-portrait. The slender youth, lying on bedrock, reaches toward a fractured tombstone, his head turned away from the viewer as if trying to grieve with some privacy. This drawing burned in 2004 and I am markedly grateful to Jonathan's daughter, Pamela Lorence, for her vast inquisitiveness. She took many photos of items that piqued her curiosity, including this one.

Thomas Batchelor had very little to leave his children. The two eldest boys, Ralph and Lynn, were busy running their dry-cleaning business and did not concern themselves with his personal effects. The red-haired son was left with some clothing including a top hat and tails that he dearly loved and would use as costumes for both Halloween and Edgar Allan Poe parties. He also inherited some of his mother's paintings, and a few assets in the form of stock. The issue with the Camp Meeker cabin was entirely different. It was left to all his children to be used as a retreat. However, he made no written provision and before Ralph, Lynn or Jonathan realized what was going on, Blanche took it upon herself to sell the property, using the profit to purchase acreage and to build a home in Pleasant Hill, California. I know nothing of her husband's finances, but I do know he was a WWI veteran who also worked for the Pullman Railroad Company, and eventually retired with two good pensions. However be it may, parsimonious Blanche paid no heed to her brothers, expressed no empathy, and chose to further her own interests.

Ralph and Lynn were far more upset than brother Jonathan who took the sale in stride and was too soft-hearted to take his sister to task. Both older brothers, businessmen, were far more imbued with finances than Jonathan. Not bourgeois, his attention was forever with his work. Finances, retirement, property values, were non-existent in his mindset. For the moment he let go of Camp Meeker (years later as a senior, the whole sordid episode would haunt him). He told me he tried to console Lynn, who deeply mourned the loss of the Russian River weekends. But comforting any human being was a foreign language for the artist. Because he was never mothered, he was not one to coddle any person and he told me he simply did not know what to do with a crying individual. "What's done is done," he told Lynn and besides, what could he do? His reaction to Lynn was very typical of the introverted artist: calm and constrained. Although his life, to that point, had been anything but secure, he maintained a strong need for very measured discipline, including emotions. He was, however, an occasional binge drinker and as is well known, binge drinking devours control.

On the other hand, moderate tavern drinking brought Jonathan together with an Oakland police sergeant and they became pub buddies. The sergeant owned the yawl *Pango,* and the artist found himself pulled into the ancient craft of sailing; skimming across San Francisco Bay dovetailed with the artist's love of everything wild and water related; whenever he wasn't at home or working, he could be found at the Berkeley Marina with his newfound friend. Characteristic of the scholar, he began to read every book on sailing he could find. He and the officer became great sailing mates and what better pastime than hot tea infused with whiskey after a long, cold sail? Jonathan became such a proficient sailor that on one afternoon, when the police sergeant (I apologize, I do not remember his name) fell asleep on the boat, Jonathan alone took complete helm control and at day's end, after returning the yawl into its berth, the sergeant finally awakened and was startled to find himself back at the marina.

Study of Oakland Police Sergeant, oil on canvas, 18 X 15, 1930s. He sold his boat to Jonathan, and the artist continued to sail until the very end of his existence.

It did not take much to convince the young captain/artist to cash in his few inherited stocks to purchase *Pango*. Sailing was deep-seated and as much a part of his psyche as art. In those days, sails were still made from cotton canvas; each and every time he sailed he had to lug them home to unfurl and dry. He was a natural, taught by a timeworn sea dog and he became an old-school sailor. Those years that I sailed with him (different boat) he seldom used the outboard motor. I learned to sail into and out of the Berkeley Marina on sail, something I noticed that very few people did.

Next page: Captain Jonathan Batchelor with his first mate Dorothy, in captain's hat, sitting at the helm of *Pango*. A natural at sailing, perhaps the DNA of Captain John Batchelor, some half century earlier, played a role in the artist's love of seafaring. Note the very loose, shabby, and crumpled pants. He seldom, if ever, purchased new clothing, favoring secondhand wear. He preferred spending his money on living necessities.

Previous page: Flaming locks wildly awry, Jonathan Batchelor aboard *Pango* late 1930s. With few exceptions he favored beards. Oft times, post-sail, a stiff drink is warranted; the San Francisco Bay and biting winds are chilling, even amidst summer. There is nothing like hot tea with a dash of rum to warm a frigid body.

Early 1940s. The United States' economy was strong enough to abolish WPA programs; Social Security remained as the only benefit. Husband and wife lost their relief jobs and although Jonathan continued to oil paint, money was at best intermittent. He tried to sell his art (mostly by word of mouth) to gain portrait commissions. But the painter was not confident; his low self-esteem, lack of bravado and timorousness (but only without drink!) kept him from hawking his skills successfully; as many artists are, he was poor at handling the business end of things. Although grateful for the WPA programs, it was difficult for him to create his own artistic path; selling oneself is difficult enough, but navigating our world when one is without social decorum or the moxie required to negotiate one's expertise can be rocky. Although in his 30s, he was still very immature in both knowledge of people and expectations of them. He had tunnel vision of a humanity that bordered on utopia; he thought most people were grand and it never occurred to him any living person would not be interested in art. Indeed, he wandered through a great deal of life without recognizing that human behavior is backed by motivation, which at times can be contrary to one's own belief system. Without such insight, transition from any walk of life is nigh to impossible. In my opinion, mind blindness, or the inability to 'read' people, is responsible for holding back many a career.

No longer with the theater, Dorothy was a content hausfrau; but his art did not give them security or stability. He continued to seek employment any way he could, usually as a general laborer, and spent all his spare time at the art studio or on the boat. Intensely thin, he was extremely strong with mountainous rugged hands; he could hold his own with men twice his weight and taller. Digging graves and building roads was always available.

I am not clear as to what prompted the following letter to Dorothy. Perhaps Jonathan's extensive reverence to his father sparked some of Thomas' entrepreneurial spirit into his son? In August, 1939, he apparently traveled to San Francisco, attempting some kind of business enterprise: "To my darling Dorothy Mae, most precious little cosset, Having just now arrived at Onofria's ménage, the desire to make you happy waxed so great that I must pause to draft a few lines to you, before any more ado." [Author's note: Onofria Cataldo was an artist's model and an oil painter. Ms. Cataldo's studio was in a large boarding house on Russian Hill in San Francisco. The house had a ballet studio on the bottom floor and often the artists would sketch dancers, who gladly performed. Ms. Cataldo regarded Jonathan highly. She set store by him and posed regularly around the bay area for many artists, with or without clothing. Jonathan made sketches of her but did not commit any pose to canvas until the early 1980s.] He resumed: "This is to say, of course, that our darling friend has been so gracious as to furnish me with the essential stationery and the time to rest enough to get these things written.

"So far yours truly has not had much success in commercial matters none to be had. Can you imagine that? The whole damned business makes me sick. I think that I shall go back to painting and writing just as I please as you please!"

[Author's note: Jonathan has crossed out the next line which reads: "However, I hope to spend the night here" and then beside that, he wrote, "This" {spending the night} "is out. Onofria has gone sour! I suppose you are responsible for it!" [I do believe that last sentence was intended to be a joke.] "Granting that dear Onofria's hospitality remains extant. And I pray earnestly that you, my sweet, are not too lonely praying that you have had company and some good things to do. I may be home sometime Saturday evening. Don't count on it, though. If I am not there, my dear, please do not be unhappy. It is so very painful to me to think you are unhappy. Remember, you must take good care of your little body. Much is lost when you have broken your health."

His prose spun into poesy. "Remember: I pause to freshen my pain-dulled senses, to take anew a thought of those hours not yet unwound from the skein of time, wondering dimly what God may do yet mysteriously undone.

"It seems there are no petals from
Those sullen flowers burgeoning densely
Along the dismal shores of the wild Orcus
Which have not fallen in our cup of wine!

"My pen formulates painfully those
Pale, almost forgotten mysteries only
Your own sad soul has come to understand,
For my wayfaring has not led me away from you.
With Love, Jonathan"

Wary, prudent, Ms. Cataldo kept him from staying the night. They were good friends, and although he was flirtatious, she was a fortress of fortitude and Jonathan, of course, paid heed. What with all the wolfish men in the news today, I would like to make it clear that preying on women was out of his vocabulary.

> Next page: Jonathan made many sketches of Onofria Cataldo, but this is the only pose he rendered into a painting. The eponymous canvas is titled *Onofria Cataldo*, oil on canvas, 24 X 36, 1981.

As much as he loved his lady friends, without a two-way come-hither, intimacy did not prevail. On the other hand, when a human being experiences 'mind blindness', mistakes are made. Among Dorothy's mementos was this note, written by an unknown woman who wouldn't even write down her name, (calling herself 'M') who was determined to get Jonathan off her back. I can only speculate 'M' had received a love note or poem from the artist. Composed one week prior to the Batchelors' wedding in August of 1940, she penned, "Dear Dorothy: Jon always contends that he means no deliberate harm to anyone, so last night I gave him two alternatives: to let me alone, or to continue to interfere in my life and do me nothing but harm. This is very clearcut, and gives him the opportunity to be either decent or completely and maliciously selfish, with everyone understanding his motives beforehand. However, I do not intend to be the goat. I can leave my home if he makes it necessary, and he will certainly not be able to find me.

"Since you have what you apparently want, I think you owe me a little consideration. In Jon's copy of the epistle I received this morning, will you see that all direct reference to me is destroyed? It would be a very dangerous document to fall into the wrong hands. Sincerely, M. This is not written in anger. It is a cool and considered statement of the way I feel."

Unfortunately, I did not know of this note until years after Jonathan's passing. I would have asked him about it had I known, but all I can do is speculate. Whoever 'M' was, she certainly did not play any role in the couple's future. I can't even begin to imagine how this note made Dorothy feel but her reaction must have been negligible; a week later she was happily Mrs. Dorothy Batchelor. After the message from 'M' was the following undated missive from Jonathan to his wife: "Most cherished little flower that God gave me: I have drunk some of your good wine. I am so pleasantly ensconced in a chair, having drunk your good wine, that I would fain write thee a few words of the fever that smoulders in my soul.

"I tell thee that I yearn for thy sweet lips, that I yearn to press thee in my arms, so that I may tell thee how immeasurably I love you. I need tell thee little of the fevers in my heart. You must know so much of them. And I would write more, but the moments escape my eager grasp.

"Again I tell thee that I love thee wholesomely, and that I shall be with thee tonight. Keep me, Dorothy. Your friend David...." David was Jonathan's middle name, and this is the first and only time I ever saw it used. Pleased with his name, he rarely but proudly reiterated that Biblical Jonathan and David were best of friends.

Their dubious marriage began on shaky ground. Both were adulterers and Dorothy, a classic binge drinker, may not have realized how often she disrupted his life. Jonathan binged as well, his affairs had less to do with drinking and more to do with his wakened sensibility to womanhood. Wedded bliss evolved into a wearisome fugue; dawn to dark might be amicable only to be sporadically disrupted by mixed contentious moments. Months passed with irregular bickering initiated by Dorothy. Her tiffs were disruptive; he could not work after a quarrel. Yet even as Dorothy brought on the spats, she maintained friendships with her many theatrical and hedonistic colleagues and on occasion disappeared with them. The artist bore no enmity. Nevertheless, he would have preferred dinner on the table and a clean house, no matter where or whom she had been with. And although they pursued social events together, he also persisted in consorting with older women, either in his carriage house studio, on his boat, or stepping out to local pubs when Dorothy was away. But one unique older woman, Anna Gertrude McNamee, became a bane to Dorothy.

I do not know when or how Jonathan Batchelor met Anna Gertrude McNamee. I can speculate they may have been introduced by mutual acquaintances Cliff Melrose or Onofria Cataldo. Cliff Melrose was a Bay Area commercial artist and fine-artist wanna-be, who admired Jonathan's work interminably. Onofria Cataldo was a friend to both the Batchelors and Anna. I can only guess Anna may have heard of Jonathan somewhere, if not through Cliff or Onofria then through Anna's own busy-bee flitting; she invariably sought avant-garde circles, poetry readings, and art shows. Berkeley was the perfect city for cerebral Anna McNamee: In the early twentieth century, Berkeley, as it does now, nurtured the unconventional and was a magnet for wide-ranging cultures, a city of eccentrics and expression.

In her younger days, when she was a library science major at UC Berkeley, Anna McNamee frequented the Archetype Press, where all the non-conformists dallied. Run by Wilder Bentley the Elder, an artist and writer who welcomed all freethinkers, it was a convenient gathering place for enthusiastic young individuals. I did write to Wilder Bentley the Younger, and although he was a child when Ona stepped inside his father's print shop, he did remember her! He wrote: "During the first decade of my life (my father) was involved in the printing trade (and craft). I am fairly sure that Ms. McNamee must have dropped by his print shop, which was outside of one of the gates of the University of California, as he (my father) was a literary type and the place became a magnet for intellectuals in those days. That is doubtless how she became acquainted with myself, and she encouraged me to stop by her apartment and visit. It was not far away. I was between ten and twelve years old and she seems to have been finishing up her studies."

Mr. Bentley continued with this anecdote, "However, years later, when I was in my mid-forties, I had an exhibit at the library of Mills College, a young ladies' school in Oakland. I soon received a call from Ms. McNamee and she tried to get me to fire up my car and drive all the way to wherever she was and give an address to a poetry club that she was a member of, an offer which I had to decline, since I was more or less broke at the time, and since I could barely remember her in any event!" That was certainly the dynamic and vibrant Anna McNamee!

Anna Gertrude McNamee, or 'Ona' as Jonathan eventually nicknamed her, quickly became a good friend for Jonathan, and she remained so the rest of her life. And although he did not become intimately involved with Ona for a very long time, Dorothy clearly did not trust her. Ona and Jonathan were intellectual twins with kindred thoughts taking imaginary flight. Thirsting for knowledge, the two had a robust background of intellect and Catholicism; certainly Dorothy must have witnessed many a vigorous conversation between the two. Nutmeg had good reason to be jealous of the broadminded, literate and cultured Ona. Whereas Dorothy hadn't any college, Ona had attended UC Berkeley, and undoubtedly Dorothy was aware of the artist's esteem for the well-educated. Furthermore, Ona's upbringing reinforced achievement; she and her siblings were able to assertively hold their own when it came to discussing authors, books and philosophy. Jonathan began presenting his prose and poetry for Ona to evaluate and she eagerly assisted him with her interpretations.

Surely their profound exchanges must have annoyed Dorothy. Eventually, long before the artist and Ona became lovers, letters were traded. Impassioned altercations were unavoidable when Dorothy was acrimoniously liquored. Every so often Jonathan would evade his wife's real or imagined narrative by spending time on his boat or at the carriage house art studio.

Their world shifted dramatically with the attack on Pearl Harbor. Thrown into the war, the San Francisco Bay Area became one of several national urban settings where war manufacture became vital. It was only natural for Jonathan to seek employment in the shipyards. Although very healthy and physically fit, the artist, around thirty, was unfit for the military because of sustained chronic hearing difficulties. He blamed his auditory complications on a childhood case of the whooping cough, of which there was an epidemic in Bandon, Oregon, in 1913. Not only did he have difficulty hearing the higher registers, but he was also acutely sensitive to staccato-type sounds that hurt his ears and caused agitation. To cope with shipyard noise, he resorted to earplugs.

Dorothy was content to be a stay-at-home wife and take care of the house while Jonathan went to work for Moran Engineering in San Francisco: because of his skills as a draftsman, he was valued for his talent to make precise blueprints. Even though the newly built San Francisco-Oakland Bay Bridge had very little traffic at that time, he tired of the commute and eventually found work in Oakland at Moore's Dry Dock at the foot of Union Street, first as a draftsman, and later as shipfitter. As the ships returned from battle, it was his job not only to draft diagrams of damaged hull sections, he was also part of a contingent of men that had the unpleasant task of removing the occasional dead body from below decks. No matter what job he did for the war industry, he worked very hard and was highly esteemed. As shipfitter, he was respected for his ability to determine precise cuts around dents or holes in metal that required patchwork. To place himself closer to work, Jonathan found a house to rent at 1770 Goss Street in Berkeley, a stone's throw from the shipyard, and close enough to bicycle to work.

Shipyard work gave opportunity to live well. For the first time in his life Jonathan was able to save a substantial amount of cash and because he did not trust banks, he buried all of his extra greenbacks and coins in coffee cans in his backyard. His 'savings account' wasn't without purpose. For many years he had longed for his own art studio and well he remembered the property chanced upon when returning from a backpacking vacation. On that property, in Diamond Springs, was the only structure visible for miles; a small, spacious, but well-maintained log cabin in a stunning area amidst rolling hills and streams. The artist vowed that if he were able, he would purchase the property and make the log cabin his art studio.

And indeed, he made his wishes come true. Before his yearly backpacking trip, in the autumn of 1942, he stopped in at the realty office in Placerville and gleefully plunked on the realtor's desk several bags of coins, some $2,500 worth, for the property. The Mountain Democrat, Placerville's local newspaper, placed the following in their September 3, 1942 issue: "Twenty acres near Pleasant Valley sold to Jon Batchelor of Oakland." The artist was elated. Not only did he love the beauty of the California foothills, he was one step closer to realizing his dream of his own atelier. He visualized himself, Dorothy and their German Shepherd Tanya, living in the lush, tranquil countryside. Because he and Anna McNamee were busy writing letters to each other, I can't imagine how he envisioned her in the game plan.

Original log cabin at Diamond Springs. Photos by Jonathan Batchelor.

Juggling became his forte. Somehow he managed painting, sculpting, writing, working, sailing, red wine, epistles to Ona (who became his lover, with the carriage house their hangout.) August 1942 he penned: "Remember when you said something about never losing your gloves because you would wear them? Well, you didn't wear them this morning when you left. I have them in my deep drawer, now. I found them this morning, later, just before I left. It made me very joyous, somehow. I picked them up, knowing instantly they were yours, and I kissed them as the dreamer kisses a lavender lotus. They were something close to you and I loved them because you had worn them.

"Ona, I was, somehow, like Leander who touched again the pale, lovely feet of Hero. I think that you must understand how I felt to have in my hands a palpable token of the music of your voice and the precious tread of your feet in my dooryard. It was not hard for me to recall kissing your hand in the early morning. It was not hard for me to recollect the last, lingering sounds of your voice; nor was it difficult to remember how I enjoyed the delicate colors in your soft flesh as I watched you sitting in the lamplight in the brief hours you were here. I hold the gloves in my hand, pressing them lightly, wanting only to press again the quiet, human hand they covered.

"This late afternoon I returned from my weird somewhat varied occupation" (shipfitter). "I found it amazingly engrossing. The giant ships in which men go down to sea assume a surprising magnificence of shape and color in the broad cadence of abundant sunlight. I climbed down into the deep hulls to envision an immense new realm made of colossal, squatting hulks of myriapodic, crepuscular grandeur. New men were there and new things they made. And the days are great with sunlight and the poignant smell of the sea and the anticipation of longer hours with you.

"This is the last hour of the scant day which began with your laughter. I terminate this last hour with these words. I end it with a glance at the face of the electric clock on the table before me and a look into the wide, mysterious eyes of the black kitten (named Eurydice) ensconced nearby upon a pile of books. The little things which we do are really beautiful things. If only there were more time to do the little things which make the world lovely. This is the end, then, of this last remarkable hour of a remarkable day. This is also the end of an attempt to tell you how profoundly I love you and how strongly I want you to be an eternal part of this life of mine...."

The artist is clearly besotted with Ona. He wants her to be a permanent part of his life, yet Dorothy was his wife. I have no idea how he fudged the two in his mind or how he fancied the situation would conclude. And Ona too, unquestionably knew he was married. He hid nothing from Ona. He even invited Ona to Dorothy's birthday party in August. Because of the edgy west coast atmosphere (residents constantly afraid of a surprise Japanese attack) he thought another Edgar Allan Poe party was due. I was lucky enough to find this rough draft to the invitation in one of his surviving journals. "Tuesday evening, August 18, 1942. You are requested to be a visitant at the residence of M. & Mme. in the evening and late hours of Sunday, August upon which Walpurgis-like night the tarns shall be fathomed, their host of the gristly and gruesome summoned forth and, before you, rendered a weird, remarkable life; and, when all is seemingly voiceless, the numerous people of Mendes shall issue forth and entertain you abundantly in a kind of voluptuous manner which you will find vain to forget.

"And you are requested on this eve to appear in some subtle guise best fitting the story-character of some poem or prosewritten by the amazing Edgar A. Poe. Let your fancies rise unshackled by precedent or convention, please, and take heed to that precious detail and sentiment in your chosen mummery most likely to arouse remark and wonder.

"We await, then, beloved friend, your coming on this prearranged evening of carnival. You will, it is urgently desired, find the time comfortable, and the occasion one of immeasurable delight. For, as I have neglected to intimate, it is the birthday celebration of my dear spouse, D.M." (Dorothy Mae). "And the night, it is assured, will be prolonged and redundant with unusual and diversified viands and libations." Not only did the artist enjoy 'dressing up' his verbiage, he also loved to dress in costume and had any number of them, including an old waistcoat with tails and a stovepipe top hat inherited from his father's vaudeville days. He cherished that outfit and wore it on many occasions, including Halloween parties, where he loved to dress as an undertaker.

The above photo of the artist was taken at a Halloween party in Canyon, California. Behind him with unfinished painting was a massive oak standing easel; one can see his palette down at the bottom right. Oxymoron: he was the tidiest oil painter! My palettes are forever disorganized and paints accidentally mix. Not him! He was very controlled about himself and his habits. His colors occupied their spots, no uncalculated mixing of hues, and when he was finished with a painting, the palette was cleansed. There can be seen in this photo, behind him, part of a French door. That was the left double door that opened from his studio into the 'Dream Room' that housed a substantial dining table, leaving very little space to circumnavigate the room's margin. I loved the Dream Room. It had huge picture windows with sixty-year-old undulant glass panes that distorted outdoor greenery. Multiple plants hung from the ceiling beside the row of windows. Shelves accommodated hot-pink Christmas cacti vibrant in the midst of winter. All manner of glassware including wine and punch glasses turned into walls of sparkling diamonds that was very fun to look at in the late afternoon when sunbeams smote that part of the room. Old ceramic vessels and exotic urns contained dense thickets of paintbrushes, many of them unused for years. His favorites were kept on the easel.

The sophisticated Edgar Allan Poe summons is prime representation of Jonathan's writing style: bookish and wordy. Encouraged by Ona's support and helpfulness, the serious artist began writing short stories in earnest. It can be said the early to mid-1940s was an enormously productive time for Jonathan: although he had composed journals from a very young age (latter 1920s when he was a teenager), after his association with Ona those entries mushroomed with prose and verse; handwritten stories became sheaves of pages after he purchased a Royal typewriter. Although some short stories survived, sorrowfully, much was lost in the 2004 house fire, with a scant few located elsewhere. Same with his journals; commonly observations or 'mind-wanderings' his jottings are not structured and have no set beginning, middle, or end. They remain copious expeditions of his intellect.

To attend Dorothy's birthday party, Ms. McNamee must have had supreme derring-do as well as an over-ladling of chutzpah. Always a snappy dresser, she arrived at the Edgar Allan Poe party displaying tremendous poise and self-confidence. Endlessly bursting with joie de vivre, she loved laughter, and although somewhat fifteen years older than the artist, she never suffered any sort of age disparity. Undeniably, it was a relief for the sculptor to know he was with a lover who would not pine for a baby. Age meant nothing to him; he was in love with her mind and truly, if there was any one person who could be said to have been his soul mate, Ona was it.

Nothing, not even the existence of Dorothy, could block Ona's gravitation to Mr. Jonathan Batchelor. At the University and as a librarian, Ona had collected bohemian colleagues and associates; she was eager to include the colorful redhead. Not only did Jonathan find Ona's unconventional colleagues fascinating, but also Ms. McNamee was a great patron for the artist, both by introducing him to creative contemporaries and also by becoming a commentator to his writings. As per the moniker Ona, she enthusiastically adopted it and never restored Anna, except for legal paperwork.

Mr. Melrose was a commercial artist who longed to be a fine artist, and although he doubted his abilities, he created some very nice artwork. Above: Cliff Melrose's *Old Bandon Light House,* block print on paper, 6 X 10, 1982. He traveled widely and sent letters to Jonathan from different parts of the world. Years later, he settled in Port Orford, Oregon and continued his correspondence from there.

Ona McNamee taken by Cliff Melrose while she was modeling in his San Francisco art studio. I don't know who met Melrose first, be it Ona or Jonathan, but Cliff became a good friend to both.

Prior to Jonathan's death, I had photocopied some of his journals and sent them to Ona's niece, Rosemary McNamee Waller. Because the fire had destroyed most of his writings, she mailed her copies back to me. It is those mind-journeys I draw from for most of this book. Normally he never dedicated his logs, but he did for Ona. "To those who live on love I offer the things in this volume, in the beginning of the month of August, in the year 1942. To A.G.M."

(Anna Gertrude McNamee). The first entry, a whimsical fantasy, is dated July 24 [Author's note: Dorothy's birthday party, the "Edgar Allan Poe" evening previously mentioned above, is yet to come on August 18]. "The night is outside like a gigantic bird crouching in the mountains, extending prodigious dark wings over the houses of men. Far in the distance weird players are intoning slow strains of a music I have heard while sauntering in the deep town. I read again and again the quiet, lovely words inscribed in a quiet writing upon a bit of parchment.

This parchment I hold is of an angel's making. It really matters little, what the time may be or how shadowy the skies have grown. Nor does it matter how faint I have become in the late hours. I shall pause again to wander raptly over the soft texture of this piece of parchment.

"Countless diminutive hands are reaching about my face. I do not brush them away, because I love them. The books lying about and the papers with words on them, alone make me aware of solemn reality, the reality of time and the deep town. Flowers are on the table in a bowl. The bowl is pale green like the green of rose leaves. And I can hear the murmur of night-winds in the hydrangeas.

"It is hard for me to think of what the time may be or how dark the skies have grown. The hour is late and I must leave my books and the papers with words on them...."

Next page: The ruin of a drawing titled *Remembrance*. Notice the detailed mystical and fantastic humanoid shapes surrounding the figure. He loved fantasy immeasurably, and in his artwork, he also loved to distort the human figure.

I found the original drawing on one of Dorothy's negatives. Unfortunately, the face, which resembles Dorothy somewhat, is marginally blurred.

Remembrance, details.

Remembrance, details.

What the two drawings on the next page represent, I have no idea. Above: Elderly stick-thin men, all mirroring Jonathan's self-image, i.e., he thought himself ultra-thin and plain. Below that: I call it *Fantasy Drawing with Faces*. If there is a story to this drawing, I do not know what it is. The woman appears to be in the throes of orgasm, possibly because of something the young gentleman to her left is doing. He has the face of an ancient Greek with curly hair, full lips and straight nose. Fascinated by Greek lore, the artist typically pulled from mythology as he created many of his early works. He was, as many artists are, obsessed with faces. The three skeletal faces in the upper right corner I call the voyeurs.

Different shapes with faces on them. The
background discoloration appears to be a part of
the piece; it is not. Stains are due to fire damage.
Who puts faces on globular cluster doodles?

Next page: Another irreparably damaged fantasy
drawing. For most of his life he had excellent vision
and drew Lilliputian details, even in the smallest
of sketches. This one he called *The Dance*.

I tried to enlarge a portion so you can see all that amazing detail on *The Dance*.

Some of his journal entries were philosophical, weighty, and serious, as is the following reflection on life dated July 25. "They have said that "hard" work never hurt anyone. But too much work will starve a man's soul to death. It occurs to me that those who speak so loudly in favor of much "hard" work are those whose lives are sheltered by the laboring humanity of the world…

"Hard work, is that work which men are compelled to do in excess of natural processes and limitations which one small, dominating minority exact in order that it may gain more power to oppress and control. It has always been like that and it shall remain like that so long as the multitudes are kept in an impoverished and mentally inferior state.

"I have been asked why I maintain a "hopeless" stand in defense of the people of the world why I seek a new and "ideal" world order wherein men and women shall dwell in magnificent cities uncontaminated by published lies. I shall answer that I am one of the people. I have suffered with the people. I have known the hideousness of poverty and the humiliation of that kind of public charity, which is given only as a balm or a sedative to temporarily stupefy the senses until a war may be mustered to sap and consume the vitality of a nearly rebellious proletariat.

"All this I have written is mere doggerel. I don't think anyone will ever read it, because people do not like the truth about unpleasant things. In fact, unpleasant things and unpleasant people are really out of my category of thought and emotion."

Quixotic at times, the catalyst to create his own world was wrapped about unfavorable aspects of reality. To make life delightful, he tried to depart from the dismal and dispiriting World War II and its deluge of war bulletins. In 1943 he composed this darker poem, certainly a world away from his prose to Ona: It was dated March 20, and untitled:

> Black, hideous hours, these. There is a gray skull
> Rolling along the road The lonely, old, old road,
> Much traveled road. Many have gone that way!
> It is the roar and the rage. It is the chill of iron
> And blood in the mud.
> Monsters are crawling on the breast of the earth,

Eating the lovely fruit. The little men are under.
Their arms are torn off. The water rises and falls
Forever in their ears. They have had gravel to eat.
They, too, have known the sudden chill of iron
And blood in the mud.

Jonathan did have a darker side that he seldom shared. Because of his need to be completely in control emotionally, no one could have guessed how depressed he could be. Sometimes he released his stresses and/or anxieties through drinking and/or drawing. He often told me when he was young he tried to draw emotions.

For a man who said he could not comfort very well the artist certainly grasped the concept of sympathy. The title of this drawing is, obviously, *Consolation*. Even if he could not offer solace himself, he may have understood analytically how to comfort.

The Burden. Faceless figures sluggishly climb, bent under loaded packs toward a graveyard populated with vultures.

Although the war was far across the world, it is easy to see how the dark side of war influenced Jonathan's writings, thoughts, and artwork from that period. His paintings included expressionist pieces depicting people and soldiers, most completed with beige/grey/black tones and a bit of red here and there. Unluckily, many of those paintings were devoured in the fire. *Tread Softly* was one of his World War II paintings.

Next page: *Tread Softly,* oil on canvas, 36 X 24, 1940s, is typical of his wartime work. The artist leaves himself in many of his works, the ultra-thin subject with a sad angular face and muscular neck hints of Jonathan. Subdued hues are a far cry from his color-filled wonders. The door in the painting is so obviously askew, it makes me wonder if the door is a new opening, or if the subject is shutting out the past. The ambiguity is evocative of Jonathan's mind.

This drawing is titled *And the Dead Claim Their Due*, black conte on paper, 14 X 10, 1945.

This is one of the saddest paintings I've ever seen. Titled *Holocaust Victims*. It is quite large, 44 X 26, oil on canvas, painted in the 1960s. The holocaust was a sore point with the artist. Although he still carried Catholic ritual in his heart, and never totally let it go, he had fully embraced his father's Judaism and indeed, the scholar fell full force into studying Jewish history. Thoughts of the holocaust deeply saddened him the rest of his life, but as if to offset that horror, the self-educated insatiable reader enormously valued the fact that education was a mainstay of Jewish religion; he carried that tenet with pride.

Within concealment of his carriage house universe, succumbing to his predilection, the pencil pusher ofttimes withdrew from the world. In November 1943, the shipfitter's mind-wandered: "There is noise in the world today. Sometimes noise is trouble. Men are making engines with huge, grey metal, huge and full of noise. I stand by and watch, feeling dull pain and misgiving. Men are not wise today. Men are making engines in the rain, engines full of noise and trouble." [Here he drifts off into a more typical prose]: "I have been sitting here listening to some music, watching the rain outside through the tall north window. I have been watching the wild wind blowing the graceful stems of bamboo in the garden." [And now philosophy]: "At the other side of Hell men are mourning. The endlessness of change and the whimsical nature of things come upon me like hordes of small, angry monkeys. What may they do next? Is it the world that changes things, or is it simply the property of human beings to be forever twisting the fibers of their lives?"

[Now, the draftsman fires-up his fervor for life, nature]. "There is something marvelously prodigious about the state of the night outside. Night-winds, mostly, drive the rain noisily against the panes of the tall windows. The bamboo lashes fiercely about the earth and the walls of the old house, the long, pale leaves glistering with the wetness of rain. These things I love as a drunkard loves his drink. It is a passion in me. The black cat crouches on a cushion nearby and watches the fantastic contortions of the long bamboo-stems. I wonder what it is thinking about."

[And now he juxtaposes music with the war machine.] "People are playing violins in the distance. Monstrous iron machines are moving with dull deliberation about the agonized world. I have not asked for much. Most of what I have I took with great struggle. Some I must have always had." [And now waxing philosophic]. "The world is unhappy only because men do not know what they want of it. Men are making metal monsters much more of metal than of intrinsic value. Men are mad because they mold metal monsters in Hell's crucibles. The matrix of Hell. I have watched them pounding metal into the shape and hue of monsters more of an idiot's device. Men are mad with the madness which the clangor of metal brings."

This is the type of drawing that Jonathan sketched in the stable loft during WWII. A soldier lies prone on the ground, head on the left, one leg with shoe on the right. His guts are scattered everywhere. The artist never saw the battlefield; such depictions are invented. With his vivid imagination, it is no wonder he detested war. Paper is discolored due to fire damage.

Somber notions occupied his visions. Above are two decapitated heads. I cannot begin to imagine trying to sketch something like that. Intensely sensitive to life, he rarely killed any living creature, including ants and spiders.

This drawing is a metaphor, with war represented by a hulking, cudgel wielding figure, ready to smash humanity. He drew this in 1926, when he was in high school; he had always detested war.

Jonathan jotted this quote, written by Ernest Henry Schelling, American pianist, composer, and conductor. It reads, "God, how the dead men stand aloof and moan in vain above the roar and horror of the cannons and the victory toll!" He penned it inside one of his books. I do not know which book; the book is gone; all that is left is that one single page.

Employees at the Moore Drydock singing the National Anthem, 1942. Jonathan worked at Moore Drydock as a shipfitter. For all I know, he may have been in this photograph. Paul Robeson stands left of center front, in a nice suit. Photo courtesy of San Francisco Maritime National Historical Park B19.40264n.

From fledgling childhood, Jonathan had been a keen observer and deep thinker. Reasoning, philosophies, ideas, logic, thoughts, concepts, all were essential to the budding artist. One can almost say he was profound and serious from birth. In high school he was no different. (Theodore) Roosevelt High in Oakland presented not only capitalistic thought, but to round out education, history instructors also taught Karl Marx's concept of utopian classless society. The cultural ideal where every human being is equal is a compelling argument, especially to a young dreamer. Speculative thoughts burgeoned as he mingled with youthful eccentrics during his stay in Southern California's Boyle Heights and it is easy to see why, working for the WPA and observing the depressed economy, he believed some of those quixotic Marxist tenets; he was in love with the notion of a world where everybody was egalitarian. His steady WPA paycheck garnished stability and certainly helped further his perspective. Steadfastly, he adopted left-leaning doctrine as his outlook. To clarify: pure communism was never part of his mindset and Jonathan was not alone: communism per se was not even in the psyche of American members of the communist party.

Prior to World War II, earlier in the twentieth century, the Communist Party in the United States (CPUSA) was never about Russia or revolution; it was never about Marxism and only minimally philosophic. It was an umbrella of loosely packed socially-minded reformists with a progressive bent. Members wanted to end discrimination and racism, others wanted workplace improvements, better working conditions, better pay and benefits. CPUSA can be characterized as diversified causes under the umbrella of communism. Their meetings, misunderstood by the mainstream after World War II, did not consist of plans to overthrow our government. Although CPUSA of the old order felt unanimity with Russia, when Stalin came to power, many members were aghast and dropped their memberships. Most members only wanted social justice, a tolerant society, peace, and fairness. Although Jonathan knew members of CPUSA, and although as a young man he wrote letters that opened with comrade, there was no question as to Jonathan's patriotism or love for America. Logically, not emotionally, he embraced the communistic ideology of egalitarianism for all. But that was the end of it. He never yearned for revolution, never attended meetings, never hated America, and embraced heartily the freedoms and beauty offered in American society and wilderness.

The garrulous artist was apt to express his ideals of a visionary society not just at home, not just in front of Dorothy or Ona or in his journals, but in front of anybody who might intentionally or by happenstance be listening, including co-workers. His principles were not in support of Russia as much as they were for his support of the underdog, for civil rights, and for the idea that all individuals are created equally; he was a devotee of the common laborer and believer in the concept of sharing wealth. But he was gregarious to a point; he did not seek out social groups because he was too busy developing his art. Although there was a membership surge of the Bay Area Communist Party during the 1930s, Jonathan never joined. Political conservatives may have been aghast when Franklin Roosevelt instituted policies that paid for artistic endeavors with government funds but in the shipfitter's opinion, the Roosevelt presidency correctly supported a wide spectrum of public programs that included painters and illustrators and for the rest of his life, Jonathan remained a loyal Roosevelt Democrat. Scads of his politically oriented drawings (usually done with pencil or conte crayon) from that era, portrayed corporations as gigantic, greedy, demon-like monsters gobbling mountains of miniature, frail human beings. Regretfully, most of his political drawings burned in the 2004 fire.

During the war Jonathan drew myriad political cartoons. Many of them showed some type of creature (the above may be a rat, I am not sure) devouring small, frail human beings. This one he titled *Corporate Greed*. Hanging from its mouth are people.

Long-winded as he was, he easily spoke of his philosophic visions and values, even at work. It never occurred to him his views and general anti-war rhetoric (not against World War II, but against war in general) was triggering alarms within his fellow shipyard workers. Self-absorbed and mind-blind, he was unable to discern social cues and most probably did not realize when he caused his coworkers discomfort. In due course, several employees were anxious enough to contact our government. His co-workers could not differentiate between his rants against war in general and the current ongoing war that he felt was horrific but justifiable. His co-workers also could not understand why a seemingly able and fit man was not in battle. I am not clear as to who contacted our government, but federal agents were sent to investigate. The upshot was a decision to send Jonathan to a conscientious objector camp. It was not so much that he was considered dangerous to our country; it was more that our government did not want the artist to have an adverse impact on the morale of wartime workers. Many healthy, fit-for-battle people were sent to "Civilian Public Service" (CPS) camps for the same reason. Although healthy enough to fight, conscientious objectors simply could not participate in an activity that involved destruction of human life.

Jonathan was stunned when notified he would be sent to CPS camp. Equating it to prison, he was aggravated. The harsh stridency of shipyard cacophony agonized his deafening ears, yet he would have preferred his dockyard calling, despite the occasional dead body. The worst, however, was yet to come. One afternoon, as he was preparing for his involuntary transfer, he, upstairs, overheard his wife, downstairs on the telephone irately spouting, "Send him far away. As far away as possible." She was speaking with the government agency responsible for his relocation. For the rest of his life, Jonathan remembered that phrase, and during his golden years when reminiscing, he would occasionally recap those two sentences. Dorothy's words left him dismayed, befuddled, upset, and he did not know how to address it. It wasn't until decades later he finally discovered Dorothy was merely jealous and wanted to send him as far away from *Ona* as possible. But at that moment of misunderstanding, Jonathan felt betrayed. Furthermore, for some reason he never understood, his wife was tending to openly denigrate him to their friends. I can only speculate she did so due to his philandering, whether it be real or imagined.

Amid his emotional fog he could not examine his feelings, nor communicate clearly to his Nutmeg. He simply did not know what to do or say. Those last few days at home must have been awkward for both, with Jonathan confounded and Dorothy not realizing how hurt he was. Anxious, apprehensive, not only did he pack for Waldport, but he also delivered books, records, and artwork to Ona's apartment for storage. He had already internalized that he did not want to live with Dorothy any longer, but he probably did not say such to his wife. I don't know if Dorothy realized he was casting doubts about the marriage; perhaps the overheard phone call was just an assisted push out the door. He bid her an uncomfortable goodbye as he left and was helped to the bus station, not by Dorothy, but by Ona.

June 18, 1943. CPS Worker 000429 - Batchelor, Jon. D., landed at Waldport, CPS (Civilian Public Service) Camp #56. Located on the coast of Oregon, the environment was a feast for his soul. Conifer forests, oceans, beaches, marshes, lakes, ponds, and lagoons beckoned. The camp, founded by poet William Everson (formerly Brother Antoninus, an erudite educator, poet, counterculture figure, and printer), was located in a facility built for the Civilian Conservation Corp, but run by the Church of the Brethren. Once there, the men built roads, planted trees, watched for forest fires in a nearby fire lookout, worked in a vegetable garden, or assisted in running the camp by cooking or serving food, working in the laundry, doctoring, or directing recreational programs. Numerous artistic, creative types were sent to Waldport: known as "The Fine Arts Camp", it brought together poets, writers, painters, musicians, photographers, and actors. Jonathan recalled poetry readings, chamber musical soirees, putting on plays, printing their own newspaper (called The Tide) and magazines (called *The Illiterati*) as well as books of poetry (published by Untide Press). It was at Waldport that Jonathan met the author Henry Miller; a friendship was forged that lasted well into the future. Interestingly, another writer who was to become an esteemed friend of Jonathan's, Alan Watts, was interned at the CPS camp #37 at Coleville, California.

Miraculously, I found one copy of *The Tide* in Canyon's burned rubble. Left: The front cover. Right: the back cover with an explanation of the silk-screened plant gracing the magazine. The artist (not Jonathan) featured the rhododendron, the "most striking of the Western shrubs. It grows from 5 to 10 feet tall, is the Washington State flower, and grows in abundance in the Oregon forests surrounding our camp."

 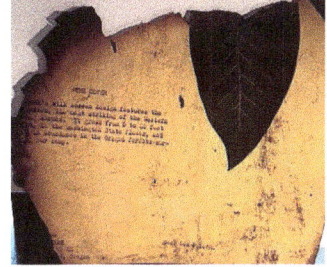

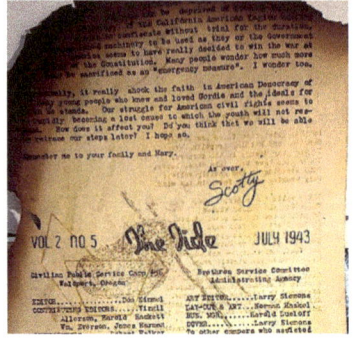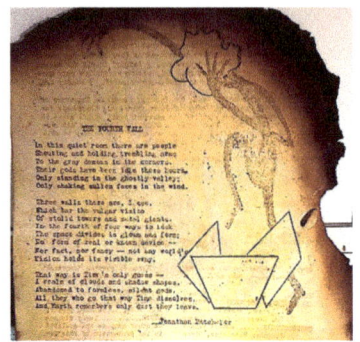

Left: Inside cover of The Tide, July 1943, with list of contributors, including Jonathan Batchelor.

Below: His contribution, a poem, "The Fourth Wall".

The Fourth Wall

In this quiet room there are people
Shouting and holding trembling arms
To the gray demons in the corners.
Their gods have been idle these hours,
Only standing in the ghostly valley;
Only shaking sullen faces in the wind.

Three walls there are, I see,
Which bar the vulgar vision
Of stolid towers and metal giants.
In the fourth of four ways to look

The space divides in gloom and form;
No form of real or known device
Nor fact, nor fancy not any world's
Minion holds its visible sway.

That way is Time's only guess
A realm of clouds and shadow shapes.
Abandoned to formless, silent gods.
All they who go that way Time dissolves,
And Earth remembers only dust they leave.

Before unpacking, before investigating the barracks, the latest Waldport newcomer was captured by his compulsion to write. Spellbound by unfamiliar vegetation while simultaneously deep breathing redolent greenery, the first inescapable prose poured forth. The previous day's awkwardness with his wife was far-flung as he wrote: "Wednesday evening, June 18, 1943. To little Dorothy. You are waiting as I am waiting. It is the night, and I have been sitting on the earth watching the sea dancing in the sun. The sky laughs and I laugh back. And the winds laugh in the tall, lovely trees. This is a magnificent land. It is the land of gods and the spirits which grow out of deep, sweet earth. I am joyous because the earth is sweet.

"When I go out the door, even in the night, I can remember the sound of growing things – the symphony of waters and sod. The men talk only of ripe philosophy and the writings of sages, and the comings and goings of great musicians. They talk of god only at meals, of music the rest of the time, of sweet women some of the time. They are essentially strong, young intellectuals who know better things about life, and who are growing like the young rhododendrons growing everywhere in the forest. This is just that a paradise of growth and verdure and laughing waters. This is a land such as you have never suspected to exist on this earth a land of giants and voluptuous pleasure and flowering youth. God! How magnificent it is! Even the high mountain vistas do not rival it. Today I have seen God! Jonathan."

Clearly, he had no idea how wonderful Oregon is. Camp 56 gave him space and opportunity, something scarcely obtained in the Bay Area. New and old worlds passed through mind explorations. He was both ensnared by Oregon's beauty and missing Dorothy, even as he realized he could not return to her. "June 20, 1943," he expressed with imaginative poesy. "Dear little widgeon, I have been watching the sun dancing in the deep waters all day. Deep water played a great symphony, orchestrated by seven people on a sailing craft. Immense, brown sails, hemlock-dyed, swung full to the wind; and I caught the halyards flying in the gale and drew them taut, and the neat little craft slipped eagerly over a coruscating gulf.

"This was today, the joyous. Six young men and a woman. She is Everson, his wife: Everson, the poet. He lives here, too. So does Mrs. Everson. She is a teacher in grade school. Lovely people, I think. And William Everson is a poet, one who loves fine music and art and life.

"This was today, the magnificent. The boat was constructed here in our camp. A young man, a good carpenter, one of the six young men who sailed the bright little bark today, designed and built it in our "shipyard". Some of the men keep working there, building boats. Later we will go to sea in them. And lie on our backs on the smooth decks and laugh at the wheeling gulls which follow us. Yes.

"Everson, his wife, came here a week ago. She lives here in camp. Lovely person, Mrs. Everson. School teacher. But she doesn't exactly like to teach. She is a sculptress. She prefers farming and sculpture. They, the Eversons, have a small grape farm at Selma, near Fresno. Lovely young people. Of course, Edwa Everson, his wife, is on her vacation. And this is a splendid land where a man may be alone with his soul and his ecstasies. Alone. None but the lonely heart. At times the loneliness is insufferable. But I can't go back. I cannot revert back to the freedom of yesterday not yet. This is the temple wherein I worship. It is the castle. I am captive here.

"Many of the men have full beards. Fine looking specimens, tense with character. I find no vulgar moron-knave here, no fanatical humbugs, nor fools, nor hateful hoodlums. Jonathan...

"You must take care not to tell people too much of the good things about this camp. I have just been telling you some of the beautiful conditions, close to the ideal. There are the harder things, too. The isolation. The separation from one's beloved; and there are the urgent biologic problems. There is the hard work without pay. But we must not let people think that we may be happy at all. We are supposed to be suffering here because there is a war. We do suffer. But we cannot deny the loveliness of the land. We cannot deny our own profound reservoirs of reason and capacity for understanding the splendor of God..."

Freed from work, he yielded to an abundance of forced downtime with scorched reflection. Thoughts of war, along with his wife's betrayal (the Oakland phone call to send him far away) reeled chaotically amidst mind flights of the unfairness of his confinement. Yet mixing with all that was the beauty that is Oregon. He juxtaposed

Oregonian paeans with startling journal passages: "Though spleen has never been greater for me, I shall have to go on waiting for the idiot-mind of civilized man to cast its momentous decision, whether for life or for death. It is bitter stuff to swallow knowing your life rests in the hand of the most hateful creatures that ever crawled out of Acheron, moronic humanity! How may I evade their insidious clutches so that I may perform, unmolested, the tasks of my soul? Few may ever know or understand how extremely I have suffered in these last few months."

Postcard to Dorothy written June, 1943. "Dear little bird – Getting on and on into a fantastically beautiful world of mists and shadowy, gigantic forms. The sun emerges from mottled abysses of azure and pearly green, and I am able only to watch futilely, with majestic grandeur within reach. Have lost complete contact with my baggage... Oh well, don't fret... Jonathan". (The lost baggage contained his art supplies.)

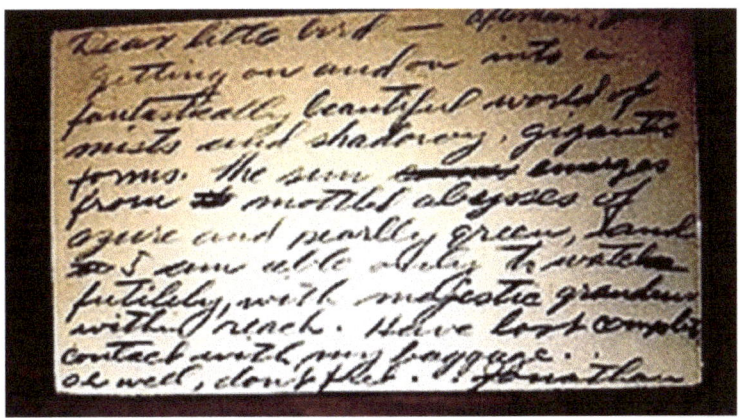

Jonathan the zealous absolutely could not be without a means to paint. He never did find out where or how the mysteriously disappearing baggage decamped. He bemoaned lost luggage to both of his special lady friends, and they separately sent him art supplies. Dorothy sent a paint box (and a special birthday gift! More on that later) but Ona sent sketchpad, pencils, charcoal, and best of all, a fresh, blank journal. The incurable letter writer continued his passionate prose chiefly to Ona who, along with Oregon's rainforest, became an endless source of inspiration.

Although Camp 56 detainees were assigned quotidian chores, Jonathan never spoke to me of his camp responsibilities. As per appointed duties, I know he would not have made a good team player. His solitary hankerings or his partial deafness may have precluded some social interacting. Although chores and regimented duties were assigned, on off hours, the men were not closely guarded. They could wander off to visit Waldport, the town, and the folk. The artist found it easy to meander through isolated and wild and his own secret places and this he often did. He told me he was approached only once by an alarmed military staff when he was painting a beach scene. Confiscated, the painting vanished and he was thus advised not to paint at that spot, as if one painting could generate any secrets to the enemy! Solitary by nature, there were occasions when he would join his fellow camp-mates, especially when drinking was involved. Yes indeed, put a cluster of hedonistic creative folk together and the occasional raucous party is unavoidable; there were moments when the folk of Camp 56 had libations, usually beer but occasionally wine.

For those who are interested, there is a wonderful online pdf. file available titled, *"Camp 56: An Oral History Project: World War II Conscientious Objectors and the Waldport, Oregon Civilian Public Service Camp."* Published by the Siuslaw National Forest and also the History Department of the Portland State University, it is a lengthy read of some 254 pages of dialogues by men who spent time at Camp 56. I came across one interview of Myron Miller (questioned in 2003) and how could I but chuckle when I came across the following paragraph? When asked if there were any incidents between any of the soldiers patrolling the area and men of the camp, Mr. Miller had the following to say, "There were no incidents that I recall about the soldiers. There was an incident with the Coast Guard that picked up one of the fellows one time who was deaf. He was down there painting a scene of the ocean. They confiscated his painting. He didn't understand what was going on. You weren't supposed to take photographs, but I don't know what a painting would do. He was deaf and he didn't know what they were talking about." (Page 175).

Knowing the artist as I did, I can only imagine his huffiness and belligerence as they commandeered his painting. It wouldn't surprise me if the situation devolved into shouting and/or a grabbing match and Jonathan, not hearing them, trying to talk his way into repossessing his painting. He told me they asked him to leave the area, but they never took him into custody.

Jonathan's obvious deafness precluded not only military service, but it should have kept him from the conscientious objector camp. It would be an understatement to say in Jonathan's case, mistakes were made. The upshot was a decision by authorities to send the artist to a specialist in Salem. The following June 28 missive, sent to Dorothy, outlines a few of his hearing difficulties. "Dear little minx, I now have two" (from Dorothy) "letters: the one telling of Morning's illness and the one containing Joyce's". [author's note, that would be Joyce Lobner. More about her further in the book].

"I cannot tell exactly how serious Morning's disorder is." (Morning was a cat). "I would have to see her in order to make a diagnosis. However, if you find that the scaling or slumping away of the parametrical matter" (skin) "includes much of the interior, that is, if it goes very deep into the material, there isn't much you can do. If, on the other hand, you find it to be a mere superficial scaling, you can try brushing her off with a dry cloth. If this has no promising effect, try wetting the cloth with a little alcohol. I do not advise using water, but you might try a little on some insignificant area. If it seems effective, you might give her a light sponging, taking precaution not to mar the significant areas, of course.

"I guess I need not tell you how delighted I was to get your letters. It is very easy to get despondent up here, especially this one. A psychiatrist might diagnose my malady as dementia melancholia or just plain paranoia. I seem to be more susceptible than most people I know.

"I hope you are not suffering much. There is a kind of loneliness which is experienced in the midst of the throng. It is really a kind of hunger a hunger for tenderness and the caress of the beloved, which, lacking afflicts some of us in strange ways. Some of us it merely annoys; others, it makes drunk; some people it makes restless, so that they desire to wander through alien lands and places of unusual character. Still others, it drives to almost suicidal madness.

"But I have word of something which may bring me back to my sculpture and my life, even in the near future, although I have been informed that it may require several months.

"When they sent me into Waldport for my final physical examination, and prior to that occurrence, my hearing had been getting worse. The M.D. told me (he had to write out much of it) that I had chronic Mastoiditis, a condition that calls for a surgical operation performed by a specialist. I was told about this many years ago by the eye, ear, nose specialist who extracted my tonsils and adenoids. I let it go. In fact, I forgot all about it. I think that auto accident had much to do with hastening the effects of an infected mastoid. The violent blow I received on the mouth and chin forced my jaw far back, bruising the sensitive tissues about the auditory canal, thus weakening these tissues and leaving them open to inflammatory processes. If you remember, the blow was more to the right side of my chin, thus accounting for the right ear's advanced condition. I recall now, though I thought it inconsequential at the time, that I suffered considerable pain and irritation, accompanied by noticeable distention (swelling) about the right ear where the jaw fits into its socket in the cranium. The left ear was a little sore, too.

"So it is. And so am I ... of course, the M.D. recommended an immediate discharge for me. This, however, may take some time. As usual, in governmental procedure there is necessity for much wagging of old men's heads, the writing of documents, and the signing of such by the numerous higher-ups. I will be sent to Salem, ultimately to receive an examination by the state board of medical examiners. It is they, of course, who will render the final decision. Until then I am like a squirrel in a nut house! And, as it stands, I go around here in a daze, unable to hear much of anything that goes on (my right ear is completely deaf! And my left ear rattles like a box of diamondbacks!)

"I know, now, what Carusi meant when she talked of hearing symphonies being played over and over." [Author's note: Madame Carusi was an opera singer and friends with the Batchelors and Ona]. "Remember that night when I complained about hearing thousands of birds singing? At three a.m.! I can hear all kinds of birds singing now. It is not very unpleasant, but their constant chatter drowns out everything else ... in fact they make so much ado that they keep me awake nights!

"Well, it isn't really that bad, but I am nearly stone deaf!

Occasionally there is a shifting of the barrier and I suddenly become aware of a new kind of noise the roaring of the wind and the clatter of horses' hooves upon paved thoroughfares. People all begin to talk at once then they, quite as suddenly, calm down, the horses vanish, and the wind fades away to the breath of a little child. All is silent again. I can see people's mouths moving, see them moving about but it is as though they were denizens of another land, and as though I were viewing them through some magic window, which failed to register sound. I can hear sound but that sound is not of this world.

"Anyway, I am eager to get back to my work to a new studio and a new beginning...

"I am pleased to know you are taking care of yourself. Keep it up. You will never regret it I know. Goodnight, little one. Jonathan.

"No package yet. I hope you haven't spent any of your precious money!!! You would like it up here. It ranks with the most beautiful land I have ever seen! I have used the paint box. One self portrait painted in the forest yesterday afternoon."

The above was dispatched on Monday. On Tuesday, his birthday, Jonathan received a special gift from Dorothy. He was only too pleased. "For little Dorothy" he wrote, "I have the cross and the silver chain on now. But it was your cross. I lost your other blue one. I am very happy to have it. It must last forever, never to be lost or broken. And I was certainly surprised on my birthday. I have the artist's box, too. And it will always remind me of you. That, too, was a gracious gesture. We never forget these precious, intimate things. They become part of our souls, eternally. But I appreciate the cross and chain. It is something I can wear close to the heart. But, to me, it shall always be yours, because I made it for you.

"I painted another picture today .... *Sisters of Earth*. Two young girls, brown like ripened fruits they might be Maoris or they might be Tahitians. It does not matter. They are young women, close to the earth, filled with its warmth, its vitality, its passion, its fecundity. They are like the huge bowl of fruit on the table before them ripe and edible. Tomorrow I think I shall paint another one.

"I will be glad to get back to normal life. One sometimes can become very morbid when the natural functions are hampered. This especially applies to this one. It is ironical to be so much in touch with natural forms without oneself being natural. This is, indeed, an unnatural life. I really am very foolish up here. Everyone is very foolish. There is a great deal wrong with a world wherein things such as this happen. The wrong kind of humanity is in power. Perhaps soon I shall be free. I am so terrifically impatient about things like this. Jonathan.

"Remember you are just a little bird and you should must be very careful with yourself." After thanking Dorothy and mailing the letter, he must have sent a post card that same afternoon. The postal service, in fine fettle, delivered and sent mail twice a day in that gentler and less populated era: "June 29, Dear Widgeon this is a postscript to my last letter...I neglected to tell you that you must have Roykin go out to the car and get out the jack and some wooden blocks from the rear compartment. That tire will be ruined if the car isn't jacked up. Roy probably knows how to do this. Have been down with an earache the last few days be happy Jonathan." [Author's note: Dorothy had an occasional need for masculine assistance. Jonathan's absence left that gap in Dorothy's life. I am not clear if Roy was a local neighbor, but because Roy offered to help her, Jonathan was pleased. He was clearly hoping that Dorothy and Roy might strike up a friendship, or possibly something more].

In the meantime, Jonathan's birthday package arrived. "July 1, Dear little Bugg this is to convey my profound feelings upon receiving the box of your cookin's. A few tears were in it but I brushed them away. It makes one feel good inside, to let fall some tears occasionally...All things are well with me except the ears, of course and a pain in my groin now and then. Be a good little Bugg. Jonathan."

Oregon Coastal Rainforest, oil on masonite, 12 X 16 1943. Painted near Camp 56 in Waldport, Oregon. The Brethren watching over the Fine Arts Camp allowed various artists to hang their paintings in their barracks.

Left: *Created Head*, pastel on paper, 15 X 11, 1940s. Right: *Created Head*, sepia conte crayon on paper, 15 X 11, 1945. The two Asian sisters alluded to in Jonathan's June 28 letter would not have been difficult for him to paint despite lack of models. Once the study of anatomy is down pat, artists have the solid foundation from which to create any type of face they want. He drew and painted diverse heads from his imagination.

We next hear from Jonathan on July 5. "Dear Little Minx, the sweet fragrance of pine mingles with sand verbena's perfume, and the wind carries the brine-dank tang of a restless sea. Wild birds stir in their forest lairs, contemplating nocturnal slumber. I stand out here thoughtfully looking down the long, silver path which leads to the homeland. Two months, it is; two months, ringing truculently until it becomes a hoarse shout two months! Every hour will count even the hour of sleep. It may be longer. God forbid! But it is written thus. They make out the meticulous epistles and write their intricate signatures while I go on suffering.

"The elders in Washington: they planned it all. But soon they shall be dust, forgotten, nameless, blown by fevered winds. When the day comes we shall not be waiting. We shall have forgotten, too...

"The food is alright. And the peppers are holding out comfortably.

"I do not mingle with the groups anymore. It is no use. As for the rest that, too, must be disregarded. I find it painful not being able to carry on a pleasant conversation. They have concerts and intellectual gatherings this, too, must go. I do not even hear the announcements. Life here, for me, is not joyous it is confounded and agonizing, bearing but one soul-preserving element, being the element of almost ecstatic anticipation. I am not one to endure prolonged bondage. There must be a break soon.

"Of course, between now and that moment of liberation I will, I must, compose my tormented senses. Poems are to be written, sketches made. Perhaps I shall even remain in the environs for a while when I am free. Only when I am completely free may I find real joy in the land. But that cannot be for long, because my hearing demands immediate attention. Prolonged neglect may ultimately bring complete deafness with all its accompanying unhappiness.

"Tears? Rachmaninoff never played that for me. It must be some recent publication. It has not been much played or I should have heard it in the past.

"I received a small, insured package over a week ago, but I believe I told you about it the red cross and chain. A second package I also told you about. But that is all, to this date. Is there a third?

Tomorrow I shall look. All this is a great source of relief and mitigation of hard-felt want for contact with the homeland. And it must be considerably troublesome for you, too, what with all your economical and domestic problems. My heart goes out to you and Roy and the rest of the ménage. No harm must come to you. I certainly hope you are not having too great a struggle... Rest well, little one and do not fret. Keep yourself well. It pays. Jonathan..."

"Dear little Dorothy," arrived July 12. As if an afterthought, he tacked on "and Roy", underlining and he knew he could not live with Dorothy any longer, and I'm sure he was hoping Dorothy and Roy might become a couple. He at least wanted to maintain a friendship with his wife: despite severing the relationship, he loved Dorothy, always would, and continued to correspond with her till her passing. "It was a mysterious package," he wrote, "I opened this afternoon. It seemed light, but there was a rather ponderous aroma about it which seemed a little "fishy" to be sure, before I had unwrapped it I was quite sure there was something fishy about it that package! When it was completely unwrapped and lying suspiciously in the middle of my lap I began to think you were feeling very sorry for me perhaps I wasn't getting enough to eat, or I needed some real nourishment something 'strong.'

"I peered sheepishly about the dormitory from beneath heavy brows, wondering whether anyone had been observing me. Assured that no one was looking, I mustered enough stamina to push back the lid of my 'sea-faring' box...

"In an hour I was savoring the warming character of a chili pepper mingling spontaneously with roast lamb, gravy, potatoes, salad, etc. Yes. We have a fairly equable board here. Of course I do not enjoy it the way I would if I were free.

"But, so far, they have been very kind to me here. Mr. Mills, camp director, has been particularly prompt in starting the legal machinery which should release me in about two months.

The final examination at Salem will materialize in about three-or-four weeks. Then it will be a month before the board will deliver my release if granted. If they do not grant it I shall be a gibbering maniac within the following month.

"Being nearly deaf is a miserable state to experience. But being in this cruel position is quite intolerable. It is amazing how much agony I am going through. It is difficult to give credence to this wild, senseless oppression which seizes me.

"I haven't entirely disconnected myself with the people here. Everson writes messages for me, not wanting to shout. And I have delivered one-or-two readings. My work is accepted with suitable enthusiasm. They want to publish some of my poems. I may let them have one-or-two. Aside from that, I am definitely and tremendously miserable. Long hours, long days interminable weeks. Regardless of what I do, or think, the hours gnaw into my blood like ravenous ghouls; and I am consumed by a misery more insane than anything I have ever known.

"It is not merely the sense of being imprisoned which agonizes. There is something else, more hideous, - immeasurably more evil. It is the world which horrifies me. It seems, since there are so few things to occupy me here, especially since I do not hear, the true ugliness of the world we live in takes full possession of my faculties. Those damned men at Washington; the crazy contraption of war. It has become a grim, overpowering obsession – now that I dwell in a realm of silence; now that the normal course of my life is being forced far out-of-bounds.

"I know, now, that most of my happiness before was due to sundering myself from the world and its idiotic warfare. I was engrossed in my work and the essential good things which were happening to me. Now that I am severed from most of this, especially the happier principals, the wicked principals break down undefended barriers and occupy most of my emotions. Getting back into the progressive channels of my life will probably remedy the condition nothing else will. Hopefully –Jonathan. For the peppers - thanks and hello for Roy..." As if to emphasize his rant, the artist attached "C.P.S. is the abbreviation for Civilian Public Service. No God-damned government officials here praise the Lord!"

July 15. "Dear, little Dorothy ... and Roy." (He extended his heading with "not dear, but little, though". I am not sure why he wanted to diminish his greeting of 'dear', except that he knew he wanted to break with his wife. He adamantly added Roy's name.) "The box of cake, including the manicure set, was a pleasant surprise for me this afternoon. Applesauce cake! No good wine to soak it in though. Sad very sad. But I munched a large cut of it for dessert tonight. You know how I enjoy it.

"A strange, somewhat disquieting silence has fallen over everything. Often I do not notice it. My mind is, fortunately, quite active. I hear music and voices 'inside.' It is a kind of inner world I dwell in. All is peaceful there so long as I can force out the monstrous visions of the war and the distracted people who are conducting it. Later, if I am doomed to become a wanderer in the meadows of silence, I may find it all very beautiful...no sound to disturb or alter the constructive trend of my spirit, no raucous noises to shatter time-worn senses. I think I shall always be able to hear music if it is loud enough. And I believe I shall always be able to hear a voice if it is uttered closely enough. But silence does not frighten me. Blindness would, but not silence. And I have so much work to do. God! How I yearn to get under way: What little I can do here is cramped and stilted. I simply cannot relax. It is a paradise in hell...Goodnight, little friend... Jonathan. Please look into my papers and find Blanche's address. Send it in your next letter along with Cliff's. If you can do it, send me my green address book although it really isn't necessary. You can write out the addresses as I call for them."

"July 21. Ten or twelve more days to go before word from Salem for finishing examination. Dear little Dorothy, - God speed these last few weeks. It is a tantalizing wait.

"I am wondering what you told the Mahons. I guess it is satisfactory to let them use the painting you mentioned. They must understand, of course, that I may want it in the near future." [Authors note: All throughout his younger years, the naive artist was quite willing to 'lend' out a painting or two. He did so for years, until he began to realize no one wanted to return them. They were obviously not true friends and 'ethically sloppy' to boot.]"Four new black members of the feline tribe. That means I shall have at least one.
"Incidentally, could you throw any light on the case of Lyman to whom we were so attentive for awhile before I left? I do not enjoy suggesting it, but I have begun to be a bit curious about it; especially, since you have been so silent.

"Well, anyway, granting that, inasmuch as you and I are concerned, all things are well with you, and that they return me to my own resources, the future is held intact in our own hands not someone else's. That seems to be the essential question with me. I want to be free. What do you want? It must coincide with what I want. Freedom must always be within grasp. Without it life is really devoid sense and joy. If there is love it can only live on if you do not try to clip its wings so it cannot fly away. You can never put love in irons and you can never find it written on legal bond tucked securely away in marital archives. The moment you place love in irons it deceives you and changes into water which quickly evaporates and is wafted out the window by a slight gust of wind; or it becomes a flame which swiftly flickers out and escapes in a faint cloud of vapor. I mean to say simply that one can never imprison love in any way. You can only nourish and keep it alive as a mother cares for her baby – tenderly and with no end of fond affection. But you know all this. I am merely reciting, Dorothy. Sometimes it is good to mull over well-known words. Truth is never monotonous when it is taken with faith. Because new words come always to fill the worn places of the old, there is brief tedium involved in the taking of new steps in a land of freedom...Jonathan"

His statement, "If there is love it can only live on if you do not try to clip its wings" was his very ambiguous way of telling her he wanted his freedom. In his letter greetings, he emphasized 'and Roy' as if encouraging a relationship. I suppose ambiguity might add a softer landing. Dorothy was massively hurt and even before Jonathan left Oakland, she was inclining to spill vitriol.

"July 29. Dear little bird, I have carried your little gift far into the wilderness to my bower of refuge where I have just now finished opening it, reading the brief message, and staring pleasantly at the precious contents. All your sweet boxes and your little manifestations of care and affection do things to me. In them I view all your goodness, your generosity, the better principles of your dear self. They are gestures peculiar to the kind little Dorothy I have always tried so hard to know and love. They call to mind essential notes which make for your happiness and mine namely that, though we be utterly free, we are never alone. Remember that, little one, though you are free you are not alone. You have friends who love you. That is important.

"Somehow, I know you are too wise to sell your dream" (at first the log cabin in Diamond Springs was Jonathan's dream, but the soft-hearted artist, beset with guilt, encouraged Dorothy to live there) "even at a double profit. Money really means so little. It is soon carried away by strange, restive waters through unrecognizable channels. But your home" (meaning the log cabin) "is always there an eternal refuge in a tempest-wracked world. And you need have no fear. There will always be someone who will love the good little Dorothy to help and cherish." [Authors note: I do believe he was referring to himself helping her. But how he expected to be there for Dorothy while she was in Diamond Springs and he in the Bay Area is a bit of a stretch]. "And you will be amazed at the ease with which you can live in that wilderness abode. Those things always come easily to the right spirit.

"The pressed amaryllis did much for me. I caught its essential essence, too. And well I remember how beautiful they looked in the early mornings as I trudged through the front gate, pushing a weary bicycle. (God spare me the hideous sin of another shipyard. You certainly know how it agonized me).

"Indeed, this war casts a grim shadow upon the land. May humanity learn in this instance the woeful destitution of real progress in this sort of business. Let this be remembered by all; the world is my country, and humanity my countrymen. Goodnight, Dorothy. It surprised me that Lyman has not completed the proceedings. I thought it was to occur within a couple of weeks. What happened?"

Dorothy may have had her faults, but she was definitively a vibrant cook. "That honey bread," crooned the post script. "is excellent. I like it as well as the 'Persian wine cake'. Trot out the vittles! Do not give away all those eats! Be sure to save me at least one good meal."

Without Dorothy's letters I cannot determine when she understood her husband was leaving her. But I do know that Jonathan was the primary breadwinner and without her husband's income, Dorothy was not thriving financially and rent had to be met. Years into the future, Dorothy, who eventually did move to Diamond Springs, was interviewed and featured in a small local newspaper, *The Mountain Democrat*. Responding to the reporter's query, she states she knew she needed to find a job when she realized her husband was leaving her. Because she was hired in August, my best guess is that she knew they were separating prior to his return to the Bay Area. She spotted an ad in the Oakland Tribune calling for women to train as welders, the training period merely one week, and she figured to have a job shortly. She was spot-on and soon working at her husband's old workplace, Moore Drydock. Because of her height and weight, the plucky petite was hoisted and lowered mid-ships for spot welding. One day an industrial hook eighty feet in the air came loose; using her acrobatic acumen, the intrepid woman climbed the hoisted crane and was able to fix the loosened clip. Afterwards she received no end of shipyard respect. But her fearlessness was no match for the frigid San Francisco Bay west winds that hurtled through the ship's hangar bay; she caught pneumonia three times while working there. Presently, by a stroke of luck she met another woman with boldness to match hers: Elsie Vivian Teaney. Teaney (as she preferred everyone call her) worked one of the toughest shipyard jobs: inspecting the bottom of ships where the ribs came together, a job considered one of the worst because of the cramped quarters and stagnant air. I am confident she was assigned her task because of her height, some 4' 8", two inches shorter than Dorothy. Sometimes in life, two people meet and are equivalent to interconnecting pieces of a jigsaw puzzle. The consequence is a sincerely profound friendship of two individuals meeting each other's needs. With Teaney, Dorothy found an advocate. It did not take long for the women to become close confidants.

In her letters to Jonathan, Dorothy at first makes no mention of her evolving shipyard friendship with E. V. Teaney; I am not sure why she omits her acquaintance but makes mention of Roy. And Jonathan, who had already separated from Dorothy at least in his mind, very purposefully added Roy onto letter headings. Although Roy was there for manly assistance, emotionally he could never take the place of Teaney.

On her single income, Dorothy was not flourishing. One or the other of the two women (I'd place my bets on Teaney) cooked up a scheme to rent spare bedrooms in the sizeable Goss Street house. In one of her letters to Waldport, Dorothy mentioned the game plan of renting to which Jonathan added a postscript to his reply: "When people are once established you cannot evict them, you know. Are you sure you must take in roomers? Or am I mistaken about this? I hope so, if you really have to rent those rooms."

Converting the Goss Street house into a boarding house for shipyard employees meant Dorothy no longer struggled financially. Dorothy and Teaney worked conjointly as landlords; together they pooled everyone's ration tickets, and on their day off went grocery shopping and did laundry for everyone. Although they at first had men and women tenants, Teaney decided the men were too sloppy in the bathrooms, (shoddy aim!) and thereupon rented to women only.

Teaney more than made up for a missing husband in Dorothy's life. Because Goss Street was so close to the shipyards, both women rode on Jonathan's bicycle to work, Dorothy in front with her legs over the handlebars, Teaney fiercely peddling; eventually, they graduated to a tandem bike. They earned a good living with $1.37 an hour wage on top of tenant's contributions. According to Dorothy's neighbor, Cheryl Parent, who over the years spent considerable time conversing with the two women, Teaney could be a bit cynical about shipyard work. Teaney mentioned walking a good quarter mile for the woman's room. "And if you had to go to the bathroom and you had your leathers on, it was not fun, shipyards are not designed for women," was Teaney's conclusion.

I am not sure when the two left Moore Drydock. Perhaps Dorothy's bouts with pneumonia were the push to leave. When they left, they came across an opportunity to run a hamburger stand located within Oakland's emerging black community. There, a tall, stout, neighboring occupant befriended the tiny women, became their unofficial bodyguard, and made sure no harm came to them.

Of the two women, Teaney had a rougher start in life. Born in Kansas, the youngest of ten, her sharecropper parents survived the dust bowl by moving from place to place. All the children had to work as they were growing and when they independently left home, Teaney was the only one left to take care of her aging parents.

Eventually Teaney left home to try her hand at earning a living; her first job was with a textile factory in upstate New York where she had to dress like a man, or she wouldn't be allowed to work. In the course of time she landed in Ithaca where she did a stint at an ammo factory.

Above: Teaney amidst coworkers at the ammo factory in New York. She is front and center, and obviously the shortest. Despite her size, she was driven and willing to wield tools. Below that: Teaney on motorcycle in Miami.

Proudly, Dorothy wrote to her husband about her work. His reply shows concern, "August 8, Dear Dorothy, If you have begun your rather novel occupation, you have undoubtedly discovered a number of barbs in the net. Have you found it difficult to control the welding arc? Usually the rod has a deucedly ornery habit of clinging to the steel. I suppose they admonished you to watch out for burns, flashes, and the like? Arc welding can be very dangerous. But, barring its hazards, and once you have mastered its numerous peculiarities, you may find it quite the thing. It really isn't always a very "hard" job. Stay clear of hemmed-in jobs, "double-bottoms", tank-interiors, etc.

The fumes from the arc, burning metal, flux, are sometimes extremely harmful. And, of course, you will have to be very cautious about walking about the yards. Will you go into Moore's yards? East yard, or west yard? The west yard is really better, cleaner, more modern, less hazardous, etc. Of course, they have means of ventilation, blowers, fans, and the like, but you still suffer, especially cardiacally.

"It is encouraging to know that you are using precaution about yourself. Also it is pleasing to know that you are getting your life into an orderly state. I am quite confident you will succeed in your new enterprise. If you do not, however, there are countless other things. Are you communicating with Margaret? She should be quite able to assist you in overcoming welding problems.

"I have been doing some painting. My state of mind, the equivocality, restlessness, suppressions, etc., are not conducive to much creative activity. It is all so tremendously and agonizingly frustrating. Somehow, I do not feel at all well. I have lost much weight. My teeth are bothering me. My head rumbles. I have gastric disturbances, weaknesses. I am enervated and fidgety. I have hallucinatory tendencies violent, terrifying dreams which awaken me, following which I hear voices of all sorts, high and low, and cannot go back to sleep. I lie awake, night after night. Often I look around, suddenly, wondering where I am, visualizing numerous nondescript formations in the darkness. Strange sounds are audible; musicians tuning their instruments; hounds baying; the clatter of horses' hooves upon pavement; the ringing of innumerable bells; the whirring of wings, hissings and coughings; the sounds of falling water; vague voices. It is frightening. I think when I get back into normal biological and mental channels all this will disappear. Much of it is a kind of product of anxieties and frustrated creative demands, which must be suppressed. Wistfully Jonathan. How about that goddam "Lyman business"? Nothing definite from Salem yet. I have let my beard run completely wild. It is all right, I guess." [Author's note: Jonathan was doubtlessly with a group of bohemians where he should have had a very good experience. To be surrounded by brother artists, actors, musicians, poets, writers, sculptors, what more can a creative human want? But he was miserable. He wanted to avoid hurting Dorothy, almost impossible to do, he couldn't hear conversations, had manifold earaches, how could he possibly value his experiences at CPS Camp 56?]

August 18. In this pedantic missive, the artist virtuously placed their marriage discord upon himself. Again, without Dorothy's letters, I cannot entirely know how she was taking their marriage strain, or if she even understood he wanted to break it off. As per Dorothy, I can only presume she finally mentioned Teaney to Jonathan. "Dear little Dorothy," he started. "Perhaps you can vaguely imagine how pleased I am to know you are progressing satisfactorily. That you have someone, some friendly, congenial soul who shares your new world, who looks into the same problems and singularities, who is also a person contributing to the general needs and maintenance, I aver, gives me great confidence in your ultimate happiness. It is chiefly because I understand fully what you are going through that I have been a bit anxious. But, as you have doubtlessly already found, this new experience will be, I feel, instrumental in arousing much of your neglected sense of responsibility. I think I have done you an immense favor by retiring from the picture." [Author's note: He was right. Although he did not cause her to binge drink, without his presence and love of red wine, she ceased abusing alcohol and gave up cigarettes. Or perhaps that was Teaney's influence.] "It was a forced alternative, but, I trust, you will see how damaging my influence has been. To be sure, I have wanted it otherwise, but my efforts were successful only in cultivating certain intellectual features in your personality, which evidently had been lying latent within you". [Author's note: Jonathan bought her books, mostly classical literature, and was endlessly encouraging Dorothy to read]. "But, in the total effect, I think my capacity for benefiting you has become exhausted. Perhaps you have observed this. Certainly it has been very obvious. In this, of course, I am referring to my influence as a husband.

"There are numerous reasons for concluding that any attempt to prolong the actualities, especially as they have existed would be an act of sheer refusal to comprehend the true significance of past misfortunes. I can only go on cherishing the remembrances of the precious, beautiful things. Ugly details evade me. I do not seek them. They dwindle into complete oblivion, leaving only the scar-tissue a knowledge of fatal possibilities arising from wounds which, fortunately were not fatal in any direction.

"There are, of course, associations with people inseparable to you which I find unbearable essentially because they have made themselves poisonous to me, even in the face of my attempts to be friendly even in spite of the tender feelings which you know I tried to keep alive." [Author's note: Although Dorothy was a very sweet person, she could be spiteful. I was left speechless when, nearly forty years later, Jonathan and I visited her and as we chatted about her kitchen table, she snappishly became scornful with Teaney rudely jumping right in and disparaging Jonathan! I could not believe what I was hearing! How can any human being hang onto anger for decades?] "And, as things are," he continued. "I believe you are aware that there can be no reconciliation in that direction. The sinfulness lies not in my heart. I bear no grudge. I forget the causes - only the scars remain to remind me of past wounds which might have proven fatal - and the grim realization that a repetition of similar associations, bringing me in contact again with the inflictors of those wounds, can only mean a furtherance of similar conflicts.

"In all this, as you may have noticed, I do not stress, or demand any choice of an alternative. That must lie in your own hands. With me, it is always this way. I do not know what has been done. There is nothing specific. But whatever you have done, or intend to do, remember always that my inner feelings remain irrevocably the same. You have accounted for the power of words. In doing this, do you recall the endless stream of hopes and yearnings and thoughts which I conveyed to you in nocturnal hours in prolonged discourses on matters of tremendous import to our happiness - our life as a combined unit? It seemed they, alas, were only of importance to me. To you they seemed to mean nothing. Words had no power then. Perhaps I was all wrong. Perhaps I said the wrong things, or utilized the wrong words to convey my meanings. Whatever it was I failed. The words, no matter how I uttered them, had no affect - no power. I even sensed that a kind of contempt had grown within you a contempt for oft' repeated phrases, anxious entreaties which always seemed to you to be a form of reprimand - even cruelty, as remote as I tried to make them, and as remote as they actually were from any such verisimilitudes. Words had no power. It was beyond me to make them seem right to you. But I am resorting to words even now. Perhaps they still have no power.

"But I have pleasant tidings. The journey to Salem has been completed. I was examined by a specialist - to the affect that I am to be released in about three or four weeks. He diagnosed my hearing troubles to lie in the sinuses rather than, as had been previously suggested, in the mastoid processes. That my hearing will always be faulty he intimated might be the case, but he lauded the possibility of arresting further development of the malady... Looking forward, as ever, Jonathan. No films, no pictures. However, I have a surprise in store."

I don't know how much of his surprise was meaningful to a fuming Dorothy. Resentful, she was unable to keep that side of herself from mutual friends. "There are, of course," he wrote, "associations with people inseparable to you which I find unbearable essentially because they have made themselves poisonous to me, even in the face of my attempts to be friendly." Regarding Dorothy's flare-ups: At that time and with that more gracious generation, outbursts rarely included vulgar language. Dorothy's tantrums were a list of accusatory actions accompanied by finger pointing at Jonathan. Although she tried to raise her voice, it was soft, never strident. And of all things, her complaints zeroed in on Ona, even though Ona, at the time of our visit in the 1990s, had passed away!

Jonathan's promised surprise for her, dated August 24, was a poem. "To little Dorothy on her birthday - "Portraits".

In the swift, fearsome flight of years,
Unnumbered and bearing each its bundle.
Of strange sorrows and inexplicable joys,
Some precious jewels are carved out
Of the living stuff - which we hoard away
In concealing caskets, never to be lost
Or stolen or spirited away by chance
Or even death: -
From these, through some subtle alchemy,
We paint these portraits of our saddened souls,
Which live on - defiant, strong, and lovely

To cast immortal eyes upon a wondering world.
Jonathan D.B."

I can only conjecture that Jonathan's August 18 missive distressed Dorothy to no end. Jonathan did try to assuage her hurt feelings with this August 27 reply. "Dear Dorothy," tumbled from his fingers. "I have never wanted it to appear to you that you have actually lost what you have loved. It is not possible. If you have loved, or found, anything of value in me you certainly have not forfeited it. That every feeling of warmth I ever held for you still exists, I can well assure you. An analysis of my own reactions to different words, inferences, recollections has made it quite clear to me that nothing connected with you has been altered, reversed, or discarded. My whole life has been patterned after a tenacious retention of all connections, namely, that no portion of anything experienced or anyone loved has been expunged from my psychic apparatus. I have not ever found it possible to say - 'I no longer love you.' I cannot deny that 'love stays.' The poet spoke with amazing precision about an inner process which, once set into motion, can never be obliterated.

"But there are numerous reasons to conclude that neither of us can ever accept the faulty structure of the past without considerable risk. As I pointed out to you in my last letter, there are forces with which you cannot be disconnected which contend against permanent happiness - and, of course, there are those countless peculiarities in the wielding of psychic forces of a marital nature between you and me which have never been clearly understood by either of us. This does not signify that connections are impossible; it merely enhances the statement I made to you some time ago to the affect that further kindredship such, and only such, as we have known can only mean a return or a reversion to those faulty structures which have contributed so much to our mutual unhappiness.

"However, Time is an endless stream upon which many barks disport -

"The sun which shone yesterday shall impart again the same light and warmth tomorrow….

"I have already said something for your birthday. What is left shall be retained forever. Jonathan. Were those your own words on the back of the envelope?"

By September 9, whatever rattled Dorothy must have abated. "Dear Dorothy, your missive of September fifth is with me. It has been a rare joy to read it again and again. In this vicissitude which has engulfed me, joy comes only in those brief occasions when contacts with the things that I love are made somewhat tangible - as in these letters I receive.

"But I am afraid I shall have to remain here three or four weeks yet. Many obstacles have fallen into the narrow gorge I travel, making the journey painful and wearisome. Many things I shall tell you later, which will facilitate a more vivid understanding of my woe. There have arisen great hordes of problems - numerous of which are almost incredible. I shall never forget these ugly days as an incident, not as a detail. I grant that there is etiology which must surely explain the underlying causes of all these peculiar problems.

"It is pleasant to me to learn that you are enjoying your new world at least you may not be lacking the few good things which freedom brings. Perhaps it is freedom, more than all else, which the prisoner wants. But you may be surprised, after all, to find that it has been the paucity of your own individual initiative which has made you unhappy in the past. I think that I have really contributed something to you as sufficient atonement, perhaps, for the enrichments you have bestowed upon my life. Nothing can mar the flawless surface of those carven gems with which we have adorned each other's souls! We shall cast out the waste matter as it is cast into the lake of fire.

"You will allow me this unconditional prerogative: to remain ultimately someone in whose life you have found shelter and goodness, someone for whom you bear the fondest friendship - and the love which is therein; and that you must always know that you have recourse to a mediator in whom you may unfalteringly find hope and condolence...Until Jonathan. These entertaining aphorisms you are jotting on the backs of your envelopes are steadily growing in number. It occurs to me that you must be doing an unusual amount of good reading to harvest so many pithy abstracts."

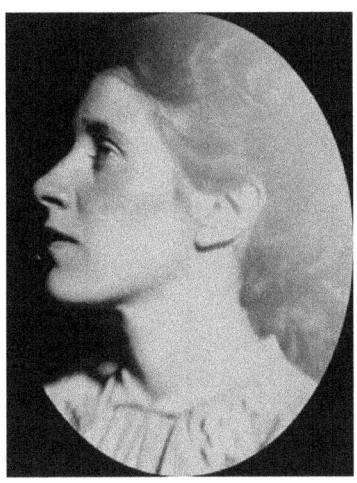

Dorothy in profile. All artists have their notions of beauty, and all have their favorite parts of the human body to observe, from the arms to the torso to legs or faces. Jonathan prized a woman's long, slender neck. He was only too pleased when a model wore her hair swept back in a bun. Photo by Jonathan Batchelor.

Anna Gertrude McNamee in front of U.C. Berkeley.
Photograph by Jonathan Batchelor

Dorothy kept her husband's correspondence with her keepsakes. Regrettably, we don't have her letters (house-fire incinerated) and can merely guess her exchange. With Ona, it was oddly opposite. Her archives did not present any of his Waldport communications, but I did find a passel of letters by her to the artist in Oregon. I can only conjecture that Jonathan returned them and they were saved amidst scads of missives to and from her own family members.

Jonathan's lady friends continuously intersected: one coming in with another on the way out. It was no different with Dorothy and Ona. Ona, the refined and polished bibliophile, wrote beautifully and had sent to Jonathan a most remarkable letter, scripted at least nine months before he left for Waldport, postmarked in September of 1942. Curiously enough, Ona mentioned Dorothy but only briefly, as an aside. The librarian had the temerity to send the letter to 1770 Goss St. in Oakland, the residence of both Jonathan and Dorothy, and yet the letter and postal address were to Jonathan, as if he were single. Opening the paean to him, she penned: "Words during a radio concert Sept. 1 by an audience among the cushions" shadowed by the greeting: "For you, Jonathan," with no mention of Dorothy. "There's a wind in the willows, beyond sing the woods. Don Quioxte is roaming somewhere in the garden far below - or else on the roof. I hear the gentle clank of his armor and the champing of his Rosinante beast. I caught something in the music that made me change my purpose tonight - For I can now see the faces of the two who were here last night. Now and in the future I shall not forget just how those faces are drawn. Even if there should come a time when, perhaps, I would not be able to see you the painting will still hang on my magical gallery wall.

"Pamela, not Peter, arrived on earth on Sunday at the hour when we were Poe and Israfel. I have candles burning and flowers blooming here for the Peter who stayed in Paradise. Pamela will be sure to pick out those errors in our knitting." [Proclaiming Jonathan another 'Poe' to her 'Israfel' testifies to the similarities of Jonathan and Ona. Jonathan commonly adopted literary figures as metaphors for himself and his lady friends. The literary figures changed with friend and circumstance.]

"The Affair Beanshooter," she continued, "went this way today. He came in with thunder over his beautiful little face. He took everything out of the typewriter desk, examined all carefully, replacing contents with disgust at its general lack of possibility. Then he looked at me sadly and said, 'I guess I let you down last night. I meant to take you out to dinner.' He makes honorable proposals, in the gallant idiom of the ten-year-old, that we live together for the remainder of our blissful lives. He says the reason is that he is "fed up" with his parents, who withhold the funds necessary for our dining out.

"Poetry should be read to one or two only, I think - Perhaps your Poe guests were exceptional exceptions". (Here I can only surmise she had previously met the artist, had attended an Edgar Allan Poe party, and in his house would have seen his artwork tacked to the walls, had access to various and sundry journals, and the artist would have had paper and chalk ready for sketching his guests.)

"Is a letter being written in your journal of tonight, Jonathan? Last Saturday I found an odd letter in my box. Very bulky it seemed and was. There were eight thick, large pages. But I think ironically, it began with a salutation followed by a blank sheet. Turning over, all the other sheets were blank, carefully numbered at the top of each (the next time I will answer my letters all!) Toward the end of page 8 were the words: "This is an exact duplicate of my last one to you." I had not kept the last one because it was like others by the same writer, very like. Yours are most unalike but one does not need duplicates since they will be, sooner or later, a part of your journals. However, Jonathan, it is beautiful to read your letters. What I miss most in my other letters are the cathedrals and especially the lotus grown lakes in which one can disappear when the middle of the worldly week is too long.

"The idea of the Poe play (called - Trial by Fury, or Poe Unposed) was that Poe had brought a case against you before Jove the Judge, on Parnassus, claiming that you might out-rival him if allowed to go on writing. The Angel for the absent Defense (Anna) wins your case and converts Poe to a special friendship for the new poet. During the trial the Angel calls long, long distance Earth - Te2829 where the said Jonathan is at the very moment writing that which will insure his seat beside Poe. And that will be all tonight.

"To you a star to wear - and my love to you both - Anna."

Not only was Anna McNamee's missive curious, but most

women would not compose to a married man. Coming from a family of fervid note droppers, perhaps to the presumptuous librarian letters, in her day commonplace as thistles on weeds, could be jotted to anybody at all. I can only speculate that Jonathan permitted Ona to read some of his journals, and she must have discovered scrawled rough drafts to all kinds of people. Indeed, his journals encompassed a wide range: letter drafts, myriad thoughts, witticisms, life observations, prose, poetry, and fantasy. August of 1942, he penned a fantastical metaphor, but whichever woman was going through his mind? "Sleep?" he wrote. "Was it sleep? Was it sleep which came to me and seemed like a sea of irises into which I fell like the autumn-leaf falls into the lotus pool in the garden? Was it a lust for that unraveled skein of time, which makes eyes stare, mystified, into the deep grasses, deep, watery grasses which cover long slopes in late tides of the year? Or was it just my sad fancy which held you in eager arms and kissed you as one kisses petals of flowers growing near a deep tarn where Naiads lie resting? But it was only my own wan mortality which dared not peer too intently into the deep land.

"I was engulfed by the long look coming from your sudden nearness. The summer night swallowed me and I was swept along like Autumn leaves which fall in bottomless waters and are borne away by a secret torrent.

"I remember, late at night it was. The streets with their dark trees - the ultramarine sky - extended into the quiescence of a slumbering realm. The dooryards. The endless rows of silent houses went out into the shadows. The night was late, dark as the tarn waters where the lotus blooms. Could it have been sleep, then, which made me enchanted or did I fancy you were there, and I a lonely farm who chanced upon you in the deep forest?"

Subsequent Ona's original missive, Jonathan felt a sincere urge to correspond with the obviously scholarly and well-read librarian. He was infatuated. A good nine months prior to parting for Waldport, he wrote (Sept. 18, 1942): "My Anna, I have been thinking all day about the little tree that has just thrust its small, pale leaves out of the dark, rich earth to feel the warmth of the sunlight, the cooling caress of unknown winds, the majestic tranquility of the nights dusk. It burgeons from the fruit of some mighty goddess. It shall spring from the gorgeous earth. It shall become the Titan in the wilderness. All the world shall bow before its grandeur.

"I have been walking slowly along the long corridors in the house tonight. I pushed open a door to another room. I have never been there before. It wasn't a very large room. But as I ventured deeper into its fantastic luminosity I saw how far away the walls were. There was a night such as I shall never forget in the middle of the long shadows near the end of the room. There was a piece of paper there with something inscribed upon it. It read in a strange, forgotten diction. The old vines were still clinging to the long latticework about the tall windows and betwixt their slight tracery issued the joy of another land. I had watched the long shadows that fell across the tables and chairs and the people sitting against the walls slowly breathing the leaden fumes that blew in through the narrow doorways. It was enough to tread that benighted sod where all slept and dreamed of the leaden light coming out of the clouded day.

"Yes. It is not hard to recall the way I felt when I lay in the evening hours at the far end of your garden watching the tiny white moths fluttering over the deep water under the muttering willow-leaves. You must remember, beloved, they were not all mine, those flowers you let me kiss. Were they? Were the roses mine? What does the hummingbird think when he steals the fragrance from your eglantine blossoms? What does the clumsily deft caterpillar think when he creeps into his chosen hollow and swiftly becomes a chrysalis? What does he think when in the bland comfort of morning sunlight he crawls out of a dead husk a thing of singular beauty, possessing unused capacity for pleasure, and knowledge of splendor, and unshackled desire? Yes, you must remember, beloved." Still wedded to his 'Nutmeg', he was already calling Ona beloved. Truly, any relationship direction once offered by the Catholic Church had long perished. He had not yet learned how to love and did not know how to acclaim one woman, his wife, above all others. As self-absorbed and oblivious to humans as he was, he never felt shame. His first letter to Ona was followed by a second, dated Sept. 21.

"Dearly beloved Anna," he purred, "Very near to my table is a black dish upon some books with a few dead leaves of the vine and some twigs from an old repast. The dim, equivocal light from a day growing to dusk makes me aware of last, lingering hours, the tarrying fond glances into unimaginably profound abysses which yawn within the amorous gaze. It seems that somewhere, perhaps often, in aeons gone by I have sought the same, nearly intangible images lurking far within those flower-shrouded abysses - as the bewitched faun who peers raptly into the serene endlessness of some recondite rural lake to retrieve the glimpse of a naiad who had stolen out of her watery lair and kissed him while he slumbered nearby in the early afternoon. The black dish upon some books in the corner of the room filled with dead leaves gives me pause to recall how the flowers nodded their lovely heads in the vineyard in the balmy afternoons of days long sunken in the dark mud at the bottom of the pool of Time.

"It is hard for me to tell you just how I feel about everything. But I shall try always to render you as voracious an account as possible to human diction. Sometimes the look in the eye and the turn of the face are far more efficacious than the word. But when I am writing to you it is so much like writing to something or someone inside of myself. You will never forget this, will you? And you will think about it when you are lying snugly on your couch to slumber in the late evening when the gray dusk changes almost imperceptibly to the dark night. And you will dream of the chalice on the wall, and the huge kalpis being emptied of its purple wine.

"It is not always just like that, Anna. You are my "tender and generous" Anna. I can only be to you what God has made me. If I can only extend some profound kind of joy, some of them voiceless things which come out of a lovely land then I shall not have striven vainly to be worthy of God's beauty. Few shall ever entirely know what sublimity this is. I have some pale colored flowers for you, my goddess. It is my humble but sincere and gratuitous offering at your shrine in the secret naos of our temple.

You will be waiting there, my sweet, my gentle and benevolent Anna."

Those two, Jonathan and Ona, were profusely alike and entirely besotted with each other. How the illustrator managed to fit Ona into his mind while married to Dorothy is to most people, baffling. But it does seem to fit with his abstruse persona. When it comes to artistic and creative people, our society lends an air of flexibility. Sometimes it is OK to be a little offbeat, a little odd, somehow different, when one has that creative streak. Cartoons and stereotypes abound of the brilliant prodigy that just cannot live typically. Possibly the artist's life would have been ordinary had he not dated while married to Dorothy. After all, his brothers all lived normal lives, and Catholicism rang deeply in his young, cerebral soul and although not faithful to Catholic tenants, he did cherish Catholic ritual and routine. Unquestionably, he told me when he had married Dorothy, he sincerely believed he would be with her the rest of his days.

"You are a jewel to me in the ocean of mud which I am compelled to traverse," he penned to the librarian. "It is an old book which I am reading over and over. You have opened the new volume for me. I have read and reread the same antiquated sentences. The book of my life has been furnished a new zeal. I have been observing the drab coloring in the faces of things of late. It is a change of green to gold and loftier hues. You have lengthened my book. You have refreshed the worn grooves…

"I cannot ever end my book. It is a long book about the lives of lovers. And the music is the marvelous lake in which one swims of autumnal afternoons when the smell of a woman's hair" (Jonathan had an extraordinary sense of smell) "has driven all belief of ugliness into an empty paper bag to be enclosed and never torn open…" With Ona in his life, painting, sculpting, prose and poetry exploded.

A beautiful rendering of Anna McNamee, or "Ona" as he nicknamed her. *Untitled*, oil on masonite, 24 X 36, ca. 1940s. Painted in the carriage house atelier. Painting owned by Deborah Waller.

Ona, the social butterfly, busy with librarian work, took time to write, both to Jonathan and her immediate family. On June 22, 1943, she dashed off a letter to Jonathan in Waldport. Cherishing countryside retreats, she had taken respite in Saratoga, California at The Lundblad's, represented on the letterhead as a 'Real Home in the Country'. She hand-scripted: "For you, In the garden. Friday - Last night I could listen, and an enormous clarity and silence surrounded the voice insistent and entreating. But this morning the garden is infected with placid, fat, wealthy well-meaners. I must take the horse to the hilltop where, unfortunately it is difficult to put down words - When Blue Boy is left for a moment he races homeward, leaving the rider to her own locomotion. I thought to find no friends at the Lodge this time, but people who come here, it appears, are all friends. One listens when it is necessary.

"However, I am taking a voyage Northward and I dwell on the fog-laden coasts where the world is green.

"Your picture (Cliff's) is on my table." [Anna's reference to Cliff was their mutual friend, Cliff Melrose, who apparently took a photo of Jonathan. Anna set the snapshot on her motel room table]. "The house cleaner, a college student, said, 'Is that R.L. Stevenson?'

And I had thought of R.L.S. When I saw you hurrying into the S.F. Station, with coat and books and easel, etc. Somehow going along loyally with their voyager - 'Aes Triplex.' Do you remember that essay by the R.L.S. Who so often had to step off into the unknown?"

After completing her stay at the Lundblad's, solitary and strong-willed Ona boarded a bus north to Crescent City, California; it was as if she longed to be near the artist as much as she could be and to think of him by the foggy, brisk, Pacific Ocean.

"Saturday. It is raining, softly, quietly as summer rains came in the morning to those white rose trees over the vast lawns among the old buildings along the Oregon Campus. I have relinquished the log fire and the chatter for a corner in a well canvassed lawn swing . No one else out except one small bronzed bird who is balancing in the bird-bath, having a tub and a shower together. He calls to me to note his gay ablutions.

"Fuchsias bend delicate necks submissively. Beyond, in great colonies, hosts of pink to purple blooms try still to hold up their massed faces, bringing remembrance of yesterday's sunlight. The red plum trees, laden like the jeweled branches in Aladdin's underworld, has been all studded with crystal sparks - Only one great, patrician dahlia has quietly abdicated from her sway over us all yesterday. She dreams no more - Peace to her slumbers - Her offspring, several inquiring, innocent buds, rub sleepy eyes as the raindrops tap their green bonnets.

"Soon I will go to the great roar of the sea - Your Crescent City word has come I wait for more…. This is the great forest. Alone, I remember the advice to the newly lost: Select one direction and adhere to it, lest by walking aimlessly you make a circle of hopelessness -

"The Filipino boy is ringing a bell to assemble those who sleep and those who wander among the great trees. I am looking in vain for the tallest, the tree who left his fellows below, mumbling as they have been told to mumble, whispering the litany of the crowd."

Perhaps the blustery, frigid, dramatic weather overwhelmed her. Three days later, the letter continued from balmy Carmel. To get there, she had to take a bus south along the coast, no mean feat in those days. The road south, Highway 1, is narrow, meandering, time-consuming; but she was strong-willed, loved the coast, and relished her many Carmel friends. Impassioned, she wrote from her usual resort. "Tuesday morning. Jonathan. The arrival late last night, and the cool (cold!) plunge into the Pacific this morning brought me to realize that so far I have been talking with you only, not sending any records by mail. It is the great white stretch" [the white sands of Carmel] "and the ocean which I so needed. So I have found in the sketch book a few words I meant for you before this and within the next day or so more will be sent.

"Two little books I bought on the early walk to the sea. I will look over them once more and then send them to you - ambassadors of Carmel. You are absent from that particular section of the California coast which must remember and ask for your swift return.

"To us mortals, dear Jonathan, absent things are those important to our existence. Now when gifts (talents) have been limited upon a man, he will not only lay them at the feet of the gods intended, as angels do too often, but he will carry them through fire, pain, and cold, making this substance part of his own, until the end of time reclaims them

"Now I have both letters. 17th and 18th - The words came shining through before I had the envelopes opened. They will be reread down by the sea and there I hope to hold them so that all the various lights and colors will again be of comfort. This (letter) must go now. I shall answer your words in the next.

"Eurydice (black cat) also sends a duplicate of that which I send you by sea and air. She is in charge at home. Anna. And aside from pain, upheld by fortitude, there must be found hope"

Despite Ona's hopeful and lovely correspondence, the Camp 56 jailbird continued to suffer depressions. Letter writing not only lifted her spirits but certainly receiving them must have made his soar. "Wednesday, June 24. The cove below Robinson Jeffers' tower," she wrote. "For the wanderer -

"The distant, white-breasted gull
Glides from the sea-lions rock
Effortlessly and with joyful cry,
Feeling the magical lift and pull
Bearing him swiftly upward - sideways
Into the burning light.

His shadow neatly crosses my heart,
Darkening my breast an instant
As I lie still in my cove,
A small bit of flotsam tossed by the waves
Awaiting the next high tide

"Your name is whispered into the jeweled sand
It is sounded in the caves below the winds,
Caves darkly sculptured in the other years
Before I found my cove of sleep and dream.
A current flowing southward chants a name.
Scarce audible beneath this endless roar:
It is my own - as I once heard it spoken
It stirs my heart.

"Yet, but a moment since, I thought myself
A bit of seaweed colored by the sun -
Forgotten, nameless, stranded
In this cove - A-

"The books I will mail tomorrow. The poems by M. Welch please keep for later. They are out of print. With Chekov do as you wish.

"Now comes your birthday. Let us have a little party at both ends of the line. I have not yet found which jewel should be sent, but hope to find one worthy.

"Tomorrow night, perhaps, I go to Oakland. This morning the people at the breakfast table prophesied that I would live here permanently in future years. That seems true. It is beautiful. At Sea View Inn I sleep in a wood-paneled high room. A little shelf holds a picture I brought, my books, papers and a bowl of blossoms in various pastels. From huge casements, swinging open one sees only trees, many, and the garden of roses, larkspur, etc. far below.

"There is a garden and studio for a sculptor nearby but no sculptor. Later perhaps the sculptor will be there. I feel certain about it. No perhapsing. A few salt drops have just hit my face. Something bright is coming landward in the oncoming tide - It looks much like a head I have seen shining in sunny hills. (So much I need not say - you know already -) Anna. (Did you ever try to write while lying on your back?) I wait for all words you will send."

The magnitude of letters Ona scripted was Brobdingnagian (one of Jonathan's favorite adjectives). As I explored her boxes of letters (separated by the decade) I was flabbergasted at the amount and variety. She especially wrote her sister Clare voluminously and Clare, as well, wrote back just as often. Both sisters loved to write not just to each other, but to all family members. Opinionated and accomplished, their letters both illuminated what was happening in their own lives as well as in the lives of family members and both sisters included anecdotes, witticisms, and personal philosophies. It did not take Ona long to jot another missive from Oakland. "Sunday night, June 27- Jonathan David, Tonight the Chausson piece tried to reach the location of my thoughts - I hope it succeeded. Three Berkeleyans who had been asked in for tea had long since departed. Their interest in the sculpture exhibit was, on the whole, pleasing. Two missed *The Sea*." [Author's note: *The Sea* is one of Jonathan's sculptures]. "During the day I read some from *Jean Christophe* and others - Then I reviewed some of your letters and drawings.

"Arriving from Carmel very late on Friday night, (and one feels so lost in parting from that loveliness) it was so comforting to find your letter there in the box just as I had promised myself. The faces of the various tenants". Tenants was a reference to Jonathan's sculptures stowed in her apartment] "waiting about in the midnight stillness of my room seemed to turn joyfully toward me as I read, sometimes aloud, the soft song of winds long-blowing.

"Each time the telephone rings now the sculptured people wear an expression of veiled alertness. *Only Young Earth* remains tranquil, and somewhat scornful of our forgetful faster pulses.

"Your notes about the poet and the sculptress" [he wrote her of the Eversons] "also of the records (even mutilated!) make the sojourn sound a bit more promising "Joyce" [author's note, that would be Joyce Lobner] "plans to give up her house and live with Oakland friends. She asked me to come over there yesterday to decide about her piano, which she would like to have me keep for awhile. How I would love that! But what do I do with the bed, the refrigerator, the books, or *Gone*? Eurydice could, of course, go on the piano, with the blue jewel vase. Too bad to live in such a cage" [Ona was referring to her apartment on Greenwood Ave.] "Now I go out in the darkness of the garden for a last look. I cannot say anymore now.

"Good night, dear Jonathan, Ona and Eurydice." She tacked postscripts from her home five days later: "Sunday letter was held for postscripts. Thursday early, July 1. An alert called us all up at 6:30 a.m. around the Bay. Your letters, Monday and yesterday are here beside me, giving the greatest joy, only that I am so concerned about this mastoid operation. I am trying to find who is the best doctor here for such work. You must have the best one because it will make some difference in the time and quality of recuperation. Is it giving much pain? We can perhaps locate a good man in Portland who can be consulted very soon. I will speak more about this in a day or so, when I know more. (Let me know just how you are).

"Much work now, two nice new people to be "trained" in our Lockwood (Knockwood!) customs." [Lockwood was the library where Ona was employed] "But I do keep the verbena from the seaside very close, and often do I go to a forest studio or see you in the ocean. Perhaps I can write on the weekend.

"This goes by airmail as Monday is a holiday for P.O.s. Did you have the two books yet?

"Eurydice sends a small Postal order for your late birthday. (Not out of the 175.) She earned it. If we can get this to office in time to buy a money order - if not, tomorrow we do so - "Behold the handmaid…. -Anna.

"Please be patient with these quick little notes. I have had a busy time since Saturday - no like."

Ona's contemporaries customarily chose marriage, husband, children. Ona, the exception, remained single well into her forties. Practical, businesslike, self-confident, her missives spoke not just of quotidian humdrum, but of countryside musings, recent readings, an occasional smidgen of mythology, of cats and nature. For Jonathan, this librarian was a breath of fresh air. For years, he had been urging Dorothy to read the great classics and he regularly procured books for her birthday presents. I am sure she may have read some, but overall, she was never the voracious reader he hoped she would become. He never dreamed a well-educated librarian with a major college degree would become his topmost champion. And she never imagined he would someday become her husband. Her expectations were to be his distinguished advocate, which apparently included sending postal money orders. If he was on the fence about leaving Dorothy when he left for Waldport, Ona's letters, luscious and delightful, certainly gave him that final push.

In her June 27 letter Ona mentioned two of Jonathan's sculptures, *Young Earth* and *The Sea*. The Sea, sculpted in 1940, was on exhibit in Carmel when Ona was on her retreat.

July 6. From Ona. "My Dear, not all of my letters go down on paper. Since you left there have been occurrences which demanded most of my time, but never the stream of thoughts of you, the stream which goes on and on, even in my sleep. At last I have overcome some obstacles preventing me from sending words to you. You will notice a difference.

"First of all, you must be sure that silence on my part is never due to lack of desire to write. I am most unhappy when I cannot. Tonight, when I read your Friday letter with the poem "The Remembrance" (to me one of the most wonderful things) there were some tears on my face. I cannot put down here the palest outline of what I felt.

"There was a little time after I went to Saratoga when I suffered from a kind of shock. One can go about through the usual motions of spending a holiday in the country without feeling anything but sadness. Due to the great kindness of the Lundblad's this melancholy finally transformed itself into a certain attempt to communicate with you in thought. When your letters came it seemed that you had received the messages I had spoken in my mind.

"Then, after I wrote the first two letters on paper, there came a long letter from my sister. Before I had opened it I guessed the contents. Something I had been expecting for two years. She has been much dissatisfied with her environment and has at last resolved to start a new life. She appealed to me for help. Certain legal proceedings have been set in motion which will give her freedom. I had to help with that. She is afraid my father will not approve and she knows that her move is to bring upon her some severe criticism and much opposition." [Author's note: Ona's sister Clare started her life as an ardent Catholic; after her holy vows she decided the nunnery was not for her, so she flew the convent coop. Her strongly active Catholic parents would surely disapprove, causing some worry.] "She will start in now to earn her living as a teacher, being of swift mind and possessing the necessary college degrees. She will leave all behind except a small legacy given to her by one of our uncles. I am expecting her to stay with me at first, after which I shall send her on a holiday to some lovely spot where she will find the essential beauty to comfort souls like hers. Then she will leave for a locality where she can teach.

"All of this necessitated a sudden trip to Palo Alto over the last weekend. A doctor who is a valued friend of my sister is also helping her to move. (He is going to find out right away about ear specialists for me.) You can imagine how this affair has occupied my spare time. I will find a room nearby or else borrow a little folding bed and have her at the apartment. She was like a child on Christmas Eve when I said that she must come to me as soon as free. She knows that I want to do everything to make her happy." [Author's note: the ear specialist was for Jonathan, not Ona].

"Enclosed is Eurydice's delayed birthday greeting for present or future needs. We wonder if you are painting a series of the Great Green Grandeur. All the flowers and leaves you send we keep in *Peter Ibbetson.* Our ferns from Oakland hills are thriving gracefully. And some immortelles from Joyce's garden are in the tall vase of wavy glass beside the lady with hands so eternally manacled." [Authors note: the 'eternally manacled lady,' with hands bound, is one of Jonathan's sculptures. Why shackled? Jonathan explained it represents a woman breaking from bondage to freedom. Jonathan's imagination may also have been influenced by Donal Hord's own version of a manacled woman.]

Photograph by Deborah Waller.

I would like to take a moment to note that although the chained woman is difficult for some to look at, it is not a reflection of Jonathan's nature. The artist was ultimately a very gentle man, self-absorbed, but never brutish. Ona's letter continues: "At Palo Alto I sounded out a lovely old Parisian piano. It had been long silent. Only discord prevailed.

"There will be a little box for you presently.

"It was a certainty that you would like the Welch poems. The poem you sent on June 29th gives me a special kind of delight. It carries me into the spacious regions of a mind I love. All of your letters are here in time order, 21st, 25th, 27th, 28th, 29th, 2nd. I reread them much to help various moods. Then I can almost see you, I do see you, here, listening to the music.

"Have you written to the Service Board about the mastoid necessity? It should be emphasized that the damp climate will not be good for it. Please take every care, Jonathan. And know that you are very much loved always.

"Sleep well now, and be of good heart. It had to be typed this time as there seems so much to do. Joyce I saw for a moment on Sunday. She was so happy that you wrote to her. She is a fine person."

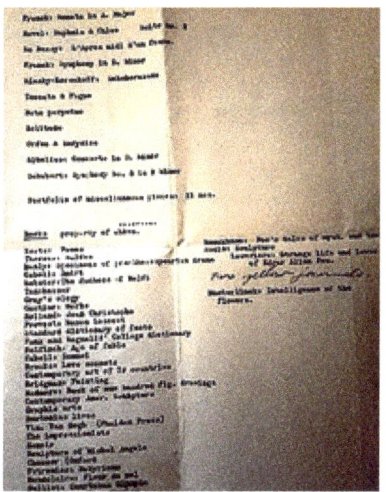
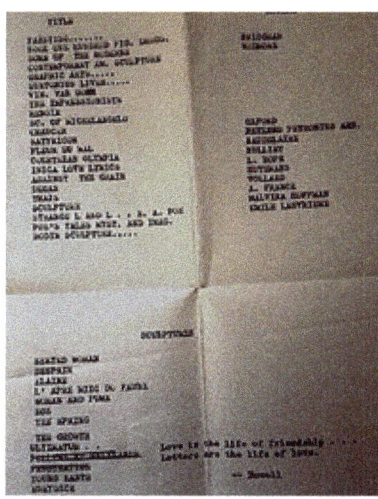

Previous page: Lists of Batchelor items stored at Ona's Greenwood Ave. apartment. It was typed in June 1943 so it could only have been dashed off by Ona. Not only was the artist still in Waldport, but I can see where she handwrote 'two yellow journals.' On the left are his records and books. On the right are his art books listed on top, his sculptures beneath. Ona added a quote: "Love is the life of friendship … Letters are the life of love." Howell.

Dichotomy is the word for Waldport. At times, Jonathan likened it to prison. When formerly jailed in California, he had pondered the injustice of it and ranted to Dorothy. He did similar tirades from Waldport, except without his former need to produce reams of rants. But he was also caught off guard and enrobed by lush Oregonian forests, lagoons, atmosphere. Despite mood swings, he was determined to make the best of it, and in a nutshell that summarizes him. By way of example, years into the future, when our old, battered Jeep Wagoneer abruptly malfunctioned amidst Oakland (mid-1980s) we spent the afternoon exploring a local duck pond while the car was patched. Likewise, at Waldport, multitudinous days were spent meandering forests, marshes, beaches.

Jonathan and I returned to Waldport in late1980s; he was hoping to find the lagoon and indeed, we found it! Big Lagoon it is called. In 1943, when exploring it, Jonathan found a fallen tree with the inside burned out; he used the log as a boat and pushed himself off with a branch. Then one day he found a real boat, a dinghy, he baptized *Nereus*. On *Nereus* there lived a chicken lizard he named Aibrich, (after an ancient Irish poem). Aibrich became Jonathan's kindred spirit on that sacred pond-voyage, sunbathing and doing little lizard 'push-ups' while being petted. Jonathan immortalized it in his log. Although that particular journal was destroyed in the house fire, one solitary page astonishingly survived. The fire marshal explained if anything survived it was sandwiched between two items. I can't help but wonder what enshrouded this page to keep it intact. Here is his pet, Aibrich in heavier ink, and one can see the skiff lightly penciled in, surrounding the saurian. Either he carried pencil and ink or inked the lizard when he returned to camp.

Aibrich the chicken lizard. Scripted on the right was the final sentence from a letter …. "up and be still. Someday you must remind me to tell you all about it."

Short poem titled "Salamander" within an unscorched journal.

> Spawn of softness
> And the watery drifts
> What cryptic doom
> Lifted you from your well
> Of darkness
> Into the sun?"

Endlessly floating, he made effective use of the new ledger Ona gave him. August in Oregon is emphatically enjoyable, but weather in the Northwest is never surefire. Apparently, 1943 had been a rainy year: "Another day of pleasure in the sun this and the lagoon my only joy. Indeed, were it not for the lagoon and the occasional days of pure sunlight and warmth I should find the time bearing far too heavily upon me. An afternoon such as this one lying in the sun, drifts by, leaving me almost completely unconscious of time; (the prolonged rain being depressing to the spirit) and these hours during which I am a sun-worshipper imbibing the delicious, penetrating substance of light and color are tending to heal the inflammation (the inflamed tissues) causing my auditory trouble. This is really something I have needed for years delay in the sun.

"But in this watery, mist-shrouded realm there actually is not enough of the sun and the periods of sunlight are becoming more frequently interspersed by the turbulent rains. The rain fascinates me, but too much of it borders upon the unpleasant and certainly I cannot go out to paint when everything is dripping as though it had just emerged from the depths of the sea.

> "Submerged September"
> From the high, shadowy trees
> The leaves fall, coloring
> The purple fog in the morning.
>
> Slow sound tolls its bell
> In the afternoons
> As I drift on the lagoon
> In the fog; and the winds,
> Which gently stir
> Deep water,
> Where saffron, aureus
> And magenta leaves
> Are floating
> Cool the blood…"

Pedantic, erudite and sometimes antiquated jargon is part and parcel of his observations: "It is late in the morning of an overcast, somewhat uncomfortable day. But I have wandered through the mists and dank gloom to the heath, and embarking on the *Nereus* set out along the narrow confines of the watery ways of the lagoon, looking with silent wonder at the luxuriant beauty crowding at all sides, beauty which, to be sure, never fails to draw me out into that half-pleasant emotional realm so important to my state of mind and spirit. Doubtlessly, if it were not for this release from the clutches of time, temporal though it is, my woe should be unmitigated beyond endurance. I have within me the powerful urge to climb into the firmament and be off to other worlds, because this one has proven to be so filled with idiocy and soilure; and were it not for this inner ken of the beautiful and the lovely which renders me so much to contemplate and understand, I should certainly do so, if it meant the need of destroying my body for of what value is this tortured coil if it serve merely to draw the attention of devils and morons who would molest one and depredate one's chances for happiness? Indeed, this latter is the case, because if one could but be invisible if to these fiends, they should be at a loss to lay their evil tentacles upon one's body: for this is precisely what they have done to me and they have hung treacherous chains about me which have a hidden power to destroy me should I seek to escape.

"But within the boundaries of the gaol into which I have been led, unbeknown st to them, I have discovered places of limited security and splendor. Of a certainty, this grandeur at times becomes little more than a contiguity, half of rapture, half of spleen, which tantalizes me most painfully yet, I reflect, if it were not within my power to seek it, nothing could prevent me, under existing circumstances, from being one of the most miserable of mortals and I should then surely wish for a speedy quietus to all this suffering.

"The voyage I have just completed has taken me far beyond the accustomed extent of my explorations. I have traversed a vast inner lagoon resembling one of those expansive, enchanted lakes one dreams about encompassed everywhere by the most amazing and variantly colored verdure, sweeping far up into a strange, Cyclopean forest, so utterly dense and so savage and frighteningly huge. I passed numerous floating isles possessing weird, phantastic [sic] beauty, some of which I visited for brief sojourns, observing that I could set them into motion upon the shadowy waters which I found I could not fathom with the fifteen-foot pole I carried. Upon one of these isles lying adjacent to land-bound logs reaching far out upon the water, covered with masses of exquisite variant vegetation, I disembarked and penetrated the boggy and reed-grown wilderness at the base of the forest, whose prodigious trees may be seen towering high into the mists from far out on the heath.

"Here, where I am resting while I write, the great sward of rich moss has engulfed gigantic roots beneath me while looming at my left and right and three-quarters to my front and at my back stand unimaginably Titanic boles of trees which have lived here exactly upon this spot for centuries, and which now form a marvelous momentary bower for me in which to recline and meditate, and look, and try to visualize vividly what you are doing" (at this point, I interject to say I believe he is thinking of Ona, and not his wife) "and to write these words, while, of course, wishing I were not here at all, but there, and utterly free to gratify the demands of my daemon who wails within me.

"I have been clambering for hours over the most magnificent terrain I ever beheld. The going is very much of a struggle even though the struggle is worth it due to the deep chasms concealed by the rank vegetation into which one is precipitated at nearly every fourth step, having, of course, again and again, to crawl and clamber out to continue one's journey. The sheer inclines are veritable walls of abundance and exotic beauty. In every direction loom the fluted columns as of some Cyclopean cathedral which mount up into the ineffable abysses of glaucous and azure and aureous growths, leaping or surging forth, or jutting like resplendent, moss-grown cliffs, from the lovely earth in tremendous strength and massiveness. Now, the sun thrusts its rays through the clouds and pours bright, flashing gold over all that it can reach as though filtering through the lofty, stained-glass windows of some stupendous fairy palace. And a great wind sweeps in from the sea to set all this into wild, rhythmical motion while I watch, completely fascinated ....

> In the night
> I go to dream
> With your lips pressing
> Like roseal petals
> In the softness
> And the sweet...."

Estuary ardor notwithstanding, his mind never strayed far from art. Philosophy morphed into ideas on art. He drafted a short essay and gave it the heading, "On Art and Nature". His classification of colors into maleness or femaleness is curiously intriguing. Strongly drawn to reds and ochres, it was reasonable he would equate those hues with femininity.

"Once again, I am happily drifting on the lagoon. I am sitting on the deck of my little boat looking at the masses of lotus covering the surface toward the flower-fringed lea which is visible through the tunnel of arching trees in this narrow stretch of the lagoon. Huge clusters of vegetation bearing bright green and russet blossoms stand over there on the fen toward which I am slowly moving. And beyond loom the tall, ever-vigilant Titan trees and the emerald mountains.

"Because the lagoon is so narrow here and trees grow so densely along the shore, hiding the lagoon on one side, sometimes on both sides, my little craft occasionally tangles with outcropping, low-lying branches. Hosts of birds have come to look at me not sure I'm an animal to trust. I have just now extricated the prow of my boat from a branch which had held it as though in affectionate embrace. Large brown and green leaves of aquatic plants flourish nearly everywhere, floating drowsily in the dark water as I pass over them.

"In this wing of the lagoon I observe large schools of fish just below the surface. They constantly splash and dart about, leaping in pursuit of winged prey swarming close to the water. Hardly anyone ever comes here. At least during the many times I have come to this lagoon I haven't seen anyone. Perhaps most folks fail to appreciate this kind of beauty.

"Here is all this loveliness lying nude and wanton before me. It is a truly magnificent wilderness and I must say, I appreciate the quiet loneliness of it, so glad that no one else comes here! It is satisfying to know that it is here and that I may return.

"Because of the frequent rains, the land along this part of the Oregon coast is very green. So much green! I am fond of green, but for me, there must be at least some reds and ochres. When I paint the human body, often placing it in a landscape, I find the humanness of life particularly in the female more than in the male. In the female I find an earthiness, an emblematic creativeness. I use the male being, though, as I might use green or blue in the landscape or in a still life. But in the female being I find the warmth of reds and ochres so satisfying to me. The male emphasizes the azure of the firmament, and the predominating shades of green in the land especially in this land. But the male principle exists, in land and sea everywhere, to balance the color of the earth and its life. For me, the avoidance of monotony is important in art, including the arts of literature and music. I find it hard to endure the tendency in some modern music where monotonous percussion is dominant!

He closed with a personal assessment. "Aside from my personal concern about art and nature, I have recently observed that it was E. Jola, not J. Ruskin, who said that art is a fragment of nature seen through a temperament. Do I agree? Perhaps I do agree, but does it matter?" Dorothy, undoubtedly unfamiliar with art history or art critics may not have understood his last paragraph. Ona would have.

It had taken nearly half the librarian's life to find a man with an intellect to match hers. Expectations are a different matter. Surely not marriage; she knew and had met Dorothy. Yet she was unconditionally entranced; her overloaded mind was exuberant with the sculptor. Prolific missives trailed one another. "July 11," she innovated. "Two people emerged from a cool, rain-like mist which half-hid every tree on the hillside. One, a tall giant, bearing on his shoulder clothing, books and travel impedimenta, pressed forward vigorously. He did not care for the journey but he knew it to be necessary. With his free hand he held firmly that of a bright-haired boy, his brother. The latter looked ever backward, entreating that he remain in the country he loved. But although the giant knew the way to be perilous, he would not allow the sensitive lad to stop at home. They must share their travels, troubles and pleasures, said the sterner brother.

"A woman, standing in her hillside garden, watched these two disappear into the mists, her heart being full of pain. The giant she loved for his great accomplishments and his design for a new world. But his young brother she thought of with a great tenderness because an expression of great magnitude and beauty often came into his eyes when he sat at her knee in silence. She wondered which one would be most absent from the hillside.

"At last came the day of jubilant return. The sun came back and out came the waiting one. The giant came up first, embracing his friend in great happiness. Looking beyond his arms, however, the woman noticed that the younger brother stood back wistfully against a eucalyptus, doubtful seemingly, that there was any love to spare for him. With a slight cry the woman ran quickly to the bright-haired brother, taking him to her heart - She knew now the one she loved best – Anna."

"July 21, The rhododendron arrived in exquisite shape - I read the letter again and again Wednesday very early. Quite a contrast between "Landslide and a Storm" and notes taken in the Lagoon two days later. I feel as though I had discovered that exquisite refuge and that you had been revisiting and recalling it to my memory - But I do remember stopping near just such a place in Oregon, almost too lovely to be real. All of your descriptions leave rather permanent pictures somewhere in the back of my head. Very conveniently I can bring them forth at will whenever it is most necessary.

"How beautiful were all the flowers and leaves in the lagoon letter! You are such a careful sender that they always arrive in unbroken shape. I wonder if you could send me some bouquet, especially leaves, in heavy cardboard with some dampened newspaper about the flowers? I have mailed flowers for overnight delivery, but of course this would be two or three-nights journey. Which reminds me I sent you a package of paper, but no cake. It was not just right. (I shall feed it to two small boys who are coming tomorrow. They like my cakes when slightly tough). But as soon as I can get more brown sugar and various fruits you will receive yours. The last was just practice.

"Bill is one of my sixteen-year-old friends at Lockwood. He has another year of high school but is working this summer at Moore's. You should see him. He is enormous, but with tin hat and heavy jacket, etc., looks huge! He carries a tin lunch box and is growing a mustache - I believe he added two or three years to his age. Yesterday I asked just what he did at Moore's. "I help everybody, but not very much," said Bill, grinning. He is reading as follows: *Low Man on Totem Pole, Let Your Mind Alone,* and *Look Who's Talking.* He asked me what salary I received, and being told it was a military secret but not so much as a shipyard might pay me, Bill said; "Even so, I'd much rather work here. Could you take me on when school starts?" You would enjoy knowing Bill. I believe he is getting interested in Geraldine, our new help, also 16, and quite likeable.

"In the evenings after nine I often look over your books as I listen to the music. You are often there, listening or drawing or reading to me. Then it is that I marvel 'that one consummate brain conceived and planned, that we were hammered by the same great hand.' Until very soon again – Anna. I wrote for you some 'poems' which later I may send. Can you really hear me?"

"One consummate brain conceived and planned, that we were hammered by the same great hand". Ona recognized they were kindred spirits, and truly they were. Their mutual adoration, the scholarship, music, education, he sending her plants and she sending him books, all manifestations of a passionate romance. Anyone who has experienced vivid passion for one love understands the churn of extraordinary emotions; Ona knew she was drawn to a wedded man, but loved him nonetheless. Jonathan may not have recognized he was in love with Ona, but he knew she was unusual and he would never find another like her (Indeed, did he even know what love was?) They savored consuming compulsions to write and missives were furiously mailed back and forth. "Monday morning. July 26th. Jonathan David, You must try very hard to forgive me. The days through this summer have been so furiously occupied, but I am hopeful of a necessity Probably from reading on the bouncing bus and streetcar. Doctor insists resting will fix them, so I do that. But it is so hard to give up w to rest more because I have had some little trouble with my eyes writing and reading except a minimum allowance. This has happened before and lasted only a short while.

"During the last days I have had much company. The Sougeys from Arizona were here, not staying with me but very close by. They come up each summer when the U. of Arizona closes the regular term. Then yesterday I had asked several musical friends to tea and listen to music. They brought Brenda and Sylvia, aged seven and eight, an elf and an angel, yet kindred spirits. Before we started "with those violins," as the elf said, we played and danced to the little French song, Boum! Brenda snatched up a Japanese parasol from my dressing room as she whirled through the apartment, ending by kicking a hole through it and landing on her head. The elf got up calmly, remarking that perhaps it could be mended with scotch tape. (Yes, beforehand I had removed much of the sculpture to boxes and shelves in clothes closet.) Sylvia, however, could be turned at large in a room crowded with crystal. Someone should paint her now. You would agree with me that she is very beautiful. Her father is a singer and is giving her lessons in voice placement. Yet Brenda, with her pigtails and dancing eyes is the one I should adopt if choice had to be made. What matters a little broken parasol or a glass or two?

"The "Wood Demon" gave me perfect pleasure. Some arrangement I would like to make of these Oregon poems and the sweet flowers and leaves I find in your letters. I mean the mss. Oh, what I could do to those imbeciles who took away your coast painting. Idiots. That made me feel ill. But never mind, you can understand what made them do it and you will go on discovering more lights to preserve with your paints. I do so look forward to seeing them. In your "Wood Demon" letter, July 21, you said to look for "a bundle" and sure enough, the mailman left a card in my box saying that a package had been returned to the post office where I might call for it. As the post office named closes at 1 p.m. on Saturday I could not get it, but will call there this morning if it is not delivered here again. If you have sent some of the blossoms and the leaves, I pray that they may not be languishing and dying in that stuffy Dimond post office. On Saturday I thought of you as I stopped to buy more of those lovely blue strawflowers for my tall vase on the floor beneath Eurydice, standing on her blue velvet carpet. Much of the time I imagine that you will be here in a day or two. Especially when the telephone calls me from the middle of a book or from some long distance where I have traveled during a concerto. You are the only one with whom I can converse at a distance, my darling.

"There is so much to be done for Clare. I must take one full day this week to go to San Francisco and attend to business affairs for her. She should be here in a short time now. I will later tell you more about this, when I see you. You will then understand why I have had to give so much of my time to her affairs. But I am happy to do so. It is an amazing and beautiful tale. Mrs. Blumenfeld was here yesterday, just home from her holidays in the Feather River Country. She tells me that next June or July (not good later) I must go to Grey Eagles Lodge. She had the most wonderful two weeks up there among the snows and pines and mountains. Horses, too. She said so much in praise that I dreamed last night I was there, running through virgin forests, following someone I love.

"What do you think! The grocer, hearing that I was in need of brown sugar, made me a present of a pound. Don't tell the OPA." [During World War II, sugar was among items that were rationed by the Office of Price Administration. That the grocer handed one pound of brown sugar to Ona was exceedingly benevolent.] "So the first opportunity I have this week I shall make the cake I promised. Brenda and company ate the last of the old one, the quasi-failure.

"In listening to music I believe that your painting principle holds good. In literature it happens also. But in his *De Poetica*,

Aristotle had a different and yet similar explanation. For the writer there are two important guides, Aristotle and Tolstoy. (Largely for the dramatic or fiction writer.) (My type errors are because I am not looking at machine at all. It is better for my eyes.)

"Away on the back shelf I have some little marmalade jars labeled J." [Author's note: Jonathan adored her orange marmalade.] "The library thinks of giving me a five-day week! That will mean that I can be free from Friday night to Monday noon. Otherwise, I cannot write much in my book. Until tomorrow, dear Jonathan, Anna. You should have had a letter from me week before last, and two last week, with package."

At that time, Jonathan must have been well into his thirties and Ona in her late forties. I met her late in her life; and when I did, she flung back her head with jubilance and elated laughter, a long, shaggy white mane framing a very youthful face. She was so happy to see Jonathan and she immediately liked me. And he, despite the years, had fallen back into his old disposition. At that moment, although I did not realize it, he sincerely needed her judgment of me. [He was not quite sure about me and wanted her opinion.] She, so much shorter than I, reached up, took my face in her hands, and exclaimed, "You will be good for him." It wasn't a command, as much as an observation. I don't know how she was able to discern I 'would be good for him' with merely a superficial glance, but in my muteness I accepted her assessment and felt rather pleased. Not one word bolted from my lips. Due to my autism, I was not speaking with human beings in those days, not because I did not want to, but because my ability to form words was stunted. I was reactive and responsive to people; a superficial greeting was controllable. But I could not create or perpetuate conversation beyond the greeting; words simply did not populate my mind. So, I did the next best thing: I stood and smiled. I never knew her well; Jonathan and I visited only infrequently and the two reminisced over wine while I observed. How I wish I could go back! I have a million questions I want to ask her, and now that I am older, and my ability to converse is finally fluent, I think I could hold my own with her.

If it was bohemianism she craved, 1940s San Francisco Bay Area certainly housed multitudes of unconventional creative folk;

it was home to a nascent counterculture of people disaffected with society in general and the war specifically. The beatnik era had not yet mushroomed, but there could be found a smattering of coffee houses with willing poets and musicians. Rabidly social and exceptionally curious, Ona was busy not just with poetry readings, but concerts, lectures, and her infrequent sojourns into the countryside. By the time she met Jonathan, she had collected any number of friends and acquaintances and did not seem to have any problem finding eccentrics. But she also had the upbringing and manners to fit in with very commonplace, traditional middle-class people. What a true social chameleon! I can only speculate how difficult it must have been, for someone of that era with her background, knowledge, culture, education, to find a partner who was not only her equal, but as unorthodox and lively.

Her unchecked warmth and enthusiasm for the artist/ illustrator abounded with letter after letter. On July 28 she wrote, "Wednesday, early morning. Jonathan, dear Jonathan, have you any idea of just how I felt on unwrapping that "bundle" on Monday? As it is a busy workday, I could but take a brief look before leaving, but all the day I thought of nothing else. No words will come for the rapture I experienced. At last eight o' clock released me. When I came in I placed them in a row against the pillows, sitting a long time before them, immovably on the floor. The portrait is so magnificent, so subtle, that at first I could not approach it at all. But later I took it carefully in my arms, where it began to speak to me. While I write to you it is standing here on the desk. I cannot look away from it very long. All four of these works seem to me so rich and so great that they will be among the future's prizes. Or am I partial? I do not think so. The coloring of figures and background in the people of the earth made me marvel at such a creator. But when the portrait is placed where the world may see it I will always remember that the things I see in it are even a little more. I will remember where, and why and how. Oh, Jonathan!

"These, with your other possessions, shall be kept with care until you can take them. But do you not think it would be good to have some gallery managers (S.F.) see some of these soon, perhaps to display this fall? I would be glad to try this (very discreetly, of course). If you give permission. We are having a sculpture exhibit to August first at Oak Art. G." [Oakland Art Gallery] "rather amateur in character since exhibitors are the wounded service men only - some artists among them no doubt. Yes, you did send me "The Idol" on July 13. "Fate hangs like carven chain about his throat" …right? I am especially blessed with it.

"Please do not go to much trouble about sending flowers and leaves, much as I desire them - But if so, early in week is the best time, so that they are not long imprisoned in post office.

"Sometimes I feel that your stay up there is about over. One thing you are escaping now. The sordidness, the sadness of seeing all these blind thousands, mostly mongrel types" [Ona was referring to uneducated, non-cultured humans. The bay area population proliferated with shipyard employees from all walks of life. Some may have been ignorant but that did not preclude them from raising strong families who became the backbone of the next generation.] "who have invaded our bay cities for war work. Come back soon - Anna.

"The naiads I do envy - But please take care in little boat -

"Rudi and Erna are camping in Yosemite. Happy people!" [Rudi and Erna Halbe were friends of Ona's. In turn, they became good friends with Jonathan. More on the Halbes later.] "Joyce went to live with a good friend, where she is very comfortable. I am to meet her tonight at a children's club near my library. She is to tell them about marionette theaters.

"It is necessary - as part of my work - to read a great deal. And listening to the music is essential to my well-being. And writing is my inner being. Otherwise I could write to you so much more. My workday is so long, also. But I speak with you during all the occupations."

Ona's spirited daydreams suffused her soul with musings of the beguiling illustrator/journalist; emotional bouquets enclosed her heart. She knew many artists but their work paled next to Jonathan's. Truly, she must have recognized how outstanding he was; by the time he passed from this planet, one can only stack the number of hats he wore. Artist, sculptor, draftsman, sailor, carpenter, mechanic, playwright, journalist, composer, storyteller, binge drinker, you name it, he did it. He was a self-educated polymath, endlessly inquisitive, never ceasing discoveries. From cradle to winter of life, he never lost his examining mind. Early in our friendship, after hanging around Canyon for a day or so, he asked me to inspect a drop of his spring-dispatched drinking water which he placed on the observation plate of his microscope. Reflective of that moment, I know he was searching for some kind of reaction from me, but my autistic deficiencies left him a bit baffled. My silence was not due to lack of examination; the microscopic water creatures were fascinating. But my mind was a blank slate: I didn't know what to say or ask. At that time, I did not know I was autistic; gradual awareness of my flaws would not happen for another ten years, and I had not yet developed what I call a "vocabulary of life."

Ona had the same creative, analytical mind-set as Jonathan; the only difference between the two was her pragmatism. She had good business sense, he did not. Mailing enjoyable letters, she stepped up to his plate, and became a much needed outside connection from Camp 56. Cheerfully, she continued with this expressive thank you message: "July 30, Friday evening. This is being written in the San Francisco main P.O. where I had to come on a business errand. This week you should have had two letters before this one. This will have to be confined to a brief, faint expression of my rapture over the huge box of leaves, flowers, berries - It came yesterday and I opened it about 6:30, when I arrived home from L." [Lockwood] "I sat on the floor and looked and laughed - and cried a bit, I'm afraid. Then I rushed about, to rescue the faint and to awaken the sleeping. Every flower container and a large basket (holding fruit jars of water) soon stood waiting - Many items arrived in beautiful condition, notably the ferns. The berries had a white fungus veil in some cases, but I thought them very wonderful. What colors and what vigor! Some gay leaves I placed in your blue bowl. There are cattails everywhere in the kitchen also. A little snail sat up and rubbed his eyes. "Greetings," said he sleepily, "From the mayor of Waldport." "And who is this generous mayor?" asked I. "Jonathan David," said the small traveler.

"How wonderful of you to take all of that care for me, Jonathan. But you must not so humor my wishes. Receiving that box is just something that I shall never forget, so beautiful it was.

Especially the vision of you selecting the chosen.

"Hope, and all will be well. I feel certain of the outcome of the Salem visit. Yes, I know what is going on inside - But never give way, Jonathan - You have a future of greatness. I have read your last letters many times - Something will be done. Now I must rush to take care of matters for the coming Clare - I will write to you a little each day hereafter, if possible. You will be with me all the time. Anna. I had to scratch this off standing -- I hope you can read it."

To quote Ona, "But never give way, Jonathan, you have a future of greatness." The myth of the 'great artist' has been recycled for hundreds of years. Indeed, there is something very mysterious about the slogan, begging contemplation. Who designated artists to be great? Seems that human beings have a need to believe there is something grander than they are, but an artist? I suppose my bewilderment stems from my own artistic inclinations. I cannot conclude most artists are 'great', not even the ones who seem to be ground breakers. Craftspeople live in dimensions of giftedness and follow compulsions to create, but what makes them great? They certainly have remarkable abilities but despite the marvels they produce, they all have their flaws and come up short in diverse realms. Ona was raised in a generation when the concept of the 'great' artist was profuse in classical literature and admiration of 'great' artists a given.

It did not take her long to send a further dispatch. "Sunday - August 1. Jonathan dear, I took your Wednesday letter from the box on my way to the library yesterday morning. The day was so busy that I could not enjoy it nor could I treasure the delicate blue flowers and the ferns until nightfall. But how happy it was to live for a little in your green retreat. On the map there is a creek near Waldport called Drift. That is where I wander, wade and float so often. I must see that country. There are no retreats nearby. I go to the roof for a solitary sunning, but others collect there and I am not pleased. If one could only have a little wilderness of one's own! I shall keep on searching. This evening I will walk up to the hills anyhow. During the day I have occupation, as you know.

"At either side of the desk tall, luxuriant exiles of Oregon bend toward me. They are doing excellently in such a cage as this.

The leaves on desk also.

> "Near the snow, near the sun, in the highest fields,
> See how these names are feted …
> The names of those who in their lives fought for life
> Who wore at their hearts the fire's center" - S. Spender

"Watch out for the cake, soon. And some fruits. Later today, as in the early morning I write some more. This Sunday mail collection (the only one out here) is about due. The time is not long now. Anna. I could not write very much because Clare has me quite anxious. She has sent me no recent message and does not appear, as we had planned. I hope to hear her voice on telephone soon. When there is no one here I take out the self-portrait and play some music for you."

Ona's affect upon Jonathan's mind packed a punch; he became fervidly experimental. The left painting is titled *The Lovers*. After he met Ona, he began experimenting with broken shapes, lines, and color as can be seen with *The Lovers*. After trying current fashionable artistic styles, he decided he preferred the 'old school' and never advanced far afield from impressionism. The second painting, *Forbidden Fruit*, is adapted from Christian mythology. Both paintings are, or were, small sized oil on panel. The whereabouts of these paintings is unknown, and they may have perished in the fire.

"Aug. 3, Tuesday morning," she brooded. "For you, but time is still another. Time is the headstrong, unbroken horse, maddened by the bridle rein, carrying me onward through the roaring darkness. At times I lean forward desperately, clinging to the rough, whipping mane, my arms about the taut, huge neck. At other times, when the pace intimates a smooth stretch of road, I dare all, rising on tiptoe, one hand still at the end of the tightened rein. Again I slip down to a crouching position, sensing the coming leap over the gap between us and destiny. After aeons of this breathless clash with winds, dark, and the animal of restlessness, the slow, faint marks of light appear, apprising me of a disheartening fact all the effort has been in error all of this plunging and leaping has been done without any progress forward. So, I free my horse to pasture and take to counting all the stars visible above the eucalyptus trees. Anna." [Authors note: As seen below, Ona has drawn the stick figure of a Muni bus driver on a steamroller going to Lockwood. The stick figure is yelling "Gangway for a late commuter, everybody!"]

The postscript reads: "Blueprint (with apologies to Munro Leaf) for a device (patent pending) to propel me from home to labors without pain. I have tried everything owned by Key System" [local Oakland Muni system] "with rather poor results."

"Tonight I do that baking if at all possible. I hope so for success of Salem trip. Found another Thomas Wolfe book - The Hills Beyond."

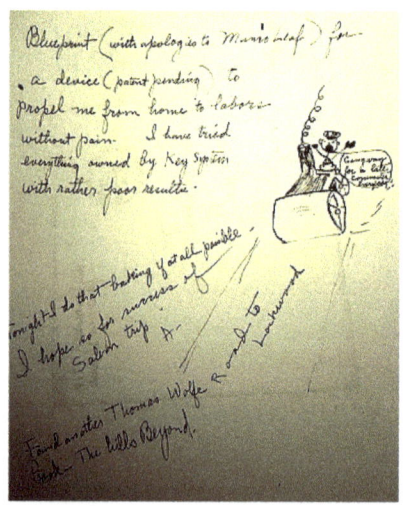

Two days later she scribbled "August 5th, Thursday morning. Just now, Jonathan, I finished wrapping for you some fruit and some of my culinary adventuring. I cut a little from one side to make it fit the box and to see what flavor it had. If you do not mind chewing valiantly I believe you will like it. The hard upper crust will help it to travel well. Some companions may help you with it, or maybe the birds, little snakes, pet lizards. You will scent the bit of orange marmalade inside. Please take some for a lunch in the studio." [Jonathan was fond of Ona's homemade orange marmalade and spoke of it longingly. I was not so adventurous with food. He had to settle for store bought with me].

"Two whole days and no brown ink in mail box! Last night I lay awake imagining the ear trouble. But on my way out today the two missing letters and some flowers! I hope by now came Salem news.

"This has to do for the moment because I have just learned that I must entertain a mob of children at another library today emergency. So, I will come up for breath later. Your letters are to me as wonderful as you are – Anna. Oh, just for more time! After this week, however, I shall have Saturday all day!"

With the arrival of Clare, the librarian's life turned abruptly hectic, and she ceased jotting or typing until August 12. Borrowing library stationery, she addressed: "For J.D. Morning notes. Very forlorn was she, for there was no letter in the box yesterday. This is not logical, but very forlorn she was. Then, upstairs and for a few minutes alone. Over again I read some of the last letters, as a prelude to some words spoken to you before dropping off to sleep. How many things have been left unanswered in your letters! But I shall not forget, and there is the wistful hope that very soon they will be given in speech, not writing.

"So much has happened this week. Clare has had so much to solve and needs much help. She will be leaving soon, however. We were apart so much since childhood that we are strangers, almost. It is slightly difficult, but I am trying to give her much love and understanding and some financial help. She has had to live a narrow life. I have been showing her some few of your pictures and the self-portrait especially. She has sensed my feeling for you, I suppose.

She asked a strange question: "But is he not too temperamental and impractical?" I answered that all of my friends, my real friends were almost as temperamental and impractical as I. That closed the conversation. Tonight I shall write the thoughts I must not put down in a machine. On borrowed time, too. Anna."

Ona's compulsion to compose letters was nearly as fanatical as Jonathan's. She finally found a stretch to execute a decent missive: "August 16, Sunday morning on the roof. On my way to San Francisco yesterday the news in the airmail was singing in my head. I don't know anything Clare was saying, nor what happened through our day across the bay. It was something I could not share, and my joy left me completely alone, merely going through the motions of living with the others.

"Somehow, as soon as I had your Corvallis and Salem letters there was the expectation, the knowledge that all would be well. It will be difficult to wait through the days until I see you, but the thought that you are really coming soon leaves me walking on clouds indeed.

"This last week has been somewhat strenuous and unpleasant and a little sad. Clare is just now in a rather irritable, demanding mental condition. Realizing her past struggles and the physical deficiencies with which she has always been burdened, I have been making a special effort at patience and help. She has been a week with me now, and improvements are discernible. She is beginning to understand and to find the adjustment necessary. In a few days she will have decided where she is to teach and then she leaves for a vacation trip and her new location. Probably near Los Angeles. Her money was not immediately available but I was able to tide over present needs. Today I feel so hopeful that all will yet be very well with her. You see, she is very dear to me. I can easily forgive all her little whims. (And no doubt she finds me hard to comprehend, especially since her life has been circumscribed with people who are my opposites).

"How rich in coloring were the Salem rose petals! They are here, still in the folds of your letter on my knee. As I sit here, looking out over the partly misty morning, I can see you struggling with your intense anxiety, strolling through the night among the apple trees and the Oregon roses. And then, too, I see your chipmunk friend in the retreat, analyzing according to the sum of his previous experiences, the flavors of your offering.

"Last night I played the Chausson concerto, with a few others of our choice. I became completely lost and happy again. But with my companion it was not possible to bring forth the portrait or to be as gloriously alone with you as before. You will understand. Later on, though, I felt nearer, even hearing your voice.

"This is being scratched off on the roof floor as I take a little sun. There is to be symphony at Woodminster today. I go there with friends while Clare has a dinner engagement across the bay.

"Whatever I can do to help with your return, I wish very much to do. P.O. order? Whatever you may need. Today the garden puts forth new blossoms and feels a new pleasure, now that you will soon be walking in the terraces below. I have such hopes that now life will be very fortunate for you. All will be well for my darling.

"Please forgive me for unburdening myself in re family troubles. But it does help me so to tell you things. I feel your kindness and your thorough understanding of me, an enormously consoling feeling. Your friendship is my joy! With my love - Anna."

The artist and the librarian. Striking, how alike they were, driven by passions for art, literature, mythology, classical music, nature. Moreover, how many people enjoy sunning themselves on the roof? For a significant chunk of his life, the sun-worshipping artist, who believed our daystar vital to his health, spent copious hours sunning on his Canyon home roof. I find myself wondering if the idea was Ona's? Or, was it derived from Jonathan? If any two people could be said to be like-minded, none could be more similar than this breathtaking artist and this brainy self-determined librarian.

But what of Dorothy? Dorothy may have enjoyed some of the intellectualism ushered into her life, but she was no match for the college-educated bookworm. In 1991, as the artist perused some of his Waldport journals, he came across a very short poem titled "Portraits", written decades ago, for Dorothy on her birthday in 1943. In 1991 he sent the poem to Dorothy who was by then living in Diamond Springs, California. "To Nutmeg and Teaney" he wrote, including Dorothy's longtime friend, Vivian Teaney, in the greeting. "Among some old papers I discovered this: 'Waldport, Oregon. Tuesday, August 24, 1943. To little Dorothy on her birthday". [The poem was presented earlier in the book.] "Perhaps you do not recall receiving this writing. I found it jotted on a sheet of stationary I occasionally used in those days."

Dorothy, of course, had also written to Jonathan at Camp 56, sent him food, supplies and goodies, and was a vital contact for him. He accepted all she had to offer gratefully, but he was also trying to break up with her through a wrangling of words and missives.

His intermittent uneasiness and anguish regarding Dorothy was surely momentarily forgotten with this August 23 letter from the Selective Service System. In our government's own amusing and capricious way, Mr. Jon David Batchelor was sent a second notice by the folks with too much time on their hands who needed to track down meal and lodging tickets handed to Mr. Batchelor prior to his journey north. "On August 6, 1943, we wrote you as follows: Before you left Oakland, California, to Waldport, Oregon, you were given Meal Tickets for the following: breakfast, lunch, dinner, and breakfast. Through an oversight you were not given a Lodging Ticket. In place of the Lodging Ticket your tickets for breakfast and lunch were used as the Lodging Ticket.

"Will you please let us know what you did for breakfast and lunch while you were en route from Oakland to Marshfield? If you paid for your own breakfast and lunch, will you so state in your reply? Please tell us exactly what you did for every meal and for what you used each Meal Ticket.

"We dislike annoying you with this matter again, but it is the only way we have of straightening it up once and for all. An early reply from you is requested. The enclosed envelope is for your convenience. Won't you please answer this letter? Your cooperation in this matter is appreciated. Very truly yours, Local Board No. 72, Emeryville, 8, California."

I can only imagine how absurd and irrational this letter must have appeared to the artist. How does one take our government seriously when administrators turn circles over meal tickets?

Using a Camp 56 typewriter, August 26 he replied: "Before giving you the requested information regarding what I did for breakfast and lunch during the journey from Oakland to Marshfield, permit me to assert that, to my recollection, no previous letter such as you describe has come into my hands. This seems to be another manifestation of someone's inadvertence – possible of that enigmatic nature with which few of us are acquainted.

"I recall having examined the tickets which were supposed to provide for my meals and lodging while enroute, observing with, I fear, a slight concern that they were all designated "for meals." I naturally assumed that they could be used, through their accumulate sum, for both requisites. I took no meals between Oakland and Marshfield, preferring to fast until I had reached a more convenient situation.

"The evening I arrived at Marshfield I broke my fast on a meal which provided both breakfast and supper. Upon finding a night's lodging, costing $1.50, I merely used two of the $.75 tickets. Before leaving in the morning I had breakfast, using another ticket. This accounts for four tickets. It seems there were five. If there were, the fifth was left unused.

"I hope this complies satisfactorily with your request. I further hope that I may hear nothing more about this "ticket" affair. Sincerely yours, Jonathan Batchelor."

The quest for the missing tickets certainly must have provided a slight diversion from the artist's everyday problems. Cushioning his anxieties about Dorothy was Ona's passionate adulation. Incorrigible, she continued her flurry of love letters, typed on Lockwood notepaper: "Aug. 26, Thursday morning, Tonight I go home to solitude and time for writing to you. This is just to say that the enchanting paintings arrived and that I look forward to tomorrow because it will be a full holiday in which I shall be able to contemplate their grandeur. Oh, that package did make me so happy! More about it tonight.

"This morning I rose at 5:30 to take Clare to the train. She is going to stay with my father for a little. I hope you will forgive all the silences this week. I sent the check all by itself because it had to be written in such a hurry. No time for a postal order. But perhaps you can be identified easily. If not, let me know. Anna."

August 31. "Tuesday evening. Letters for August 25, 26, and 27 came yesterday, so I had a lovely time reading them in the late evening. Please do forgive me for the letterless check. Of course, I can always read your writing, but last week when there was no time to write to you I began to wonder if perhaps you might not be having some unforeseen expense in relation to preparation for the homeward voyage. This is to be posted as I run out for lunch. In the morning (tomorrow) I hope to send more. It seems now that I have so much more time. Eurydice wears a most expectant look these long days. Anna"

Friday, Sept. 3. All of the music now seems charged with a great jubilee, and yet there are errant moments when I doubt all joyful tidings. And yet the hours are tiptoeing past, whispering of good. And there is a force at work which will guard the destinies of a few needed ones.

"Erna and Joyce will be with me tomorrow evening. The paintings and some of the sculpture I shall keep in seclusion. You will display them for us later, in a gallery of your own. Joyce came out to our library and presented us with her puppets and marionettes in a joyful children's hour. Every seat was taken Sunday!

"In the library I commenced as above, but so many book seekers demanded my time that it was impossible to speak to you more. And since Clare's departure it has seemed that all relatives, friends from distant ports, etc., arranged to use up every minute. Also, I have been engaged in trying to solve a problem connected with my work. All desire to write, even to you, did, for the time, disappear. The only joy and consolation I felt came to me in your letters. Taking some of the older ones from their seclusion (they are arranged by date) I found much the original rapture in reading again my favorites. Sometime soon you may be willing to read aloud from them, especially the poems; I find poetry in all of them, you must know, yet some there are to produce a special enchantment. The flower petals and the leaves live in a little box, giving out their own pure chants to a listening ear.

"Dear Jonathan, this evening I walked swiftly over the dark avenue of the Glen finishing the ideas upon which I had been weaving a most disturbing and yet beguiling pattern through the solitary day. I had been wondering about the influence for good and evil of mind on mind. There was nothing personal about these thoughts. It was the attempted solution of the fates of three characters resurrected from my school days, all of whom were, in reality, soon lost to my small world. Finally I came to the consideration that perhaps we are influenced less by those with whom we spend our "formative period" than by those minds contacted only indirectly through a certain book, an artist's work, or one concert performance.

"When I think of your hours in the sun (despite those frequent torrents) I am somewhat philosophical about this unwanted sojourn of yours. If you can continue to take intervals of sunlight, and surely such a program can be arranged, those ears must improve. When I go sailing on the Lagoon in the paintings, I can feel the approach of an overpowering Oregon rain. Once I stood under a tree for I know not how long, lost in the wistful glory of a downfall which shut off the rest of the world. All I could see were trees and white roses.

"Spending one day in solitude gave me a demonstration of the efficacy and necessity of an occasional "delay in the sun" - or at least a delay. It is anything but a waste to spend a few hours speaking with the inner voice. I hope to live at some time away, far away from all city influences. Wishing for this so consistently, perhaps I shall achieve it. But in the meantime one can always go to the "realm within the realm."

"My benedictions cannot equal that of the sun which finds you there in your wilderness. Good night to Jonathan David – Anna. Monday, Thursday and Saturday are holidays for me this week. Don't you love the little boy with the snake necklace? I do!"

His impending departure from Camp 56 brought the following short note: "September 12, Sunday morning. Dear Jonathan, this may arrive after your departure. I am almost certain that will be the case. Each day of this week past seemed already too late to write to you. Your Tuesday letter arrived only yesterday, so I know not yet when you are leaving. When the phone rings I expect your voice and an arrival as unheralded as lightning. Will you send a message when leaving?

"The Melody, Trajectory, etc., are ample compensation for brevity. I know quite a bit about the difficulties of letters during a period of anxiety.

"This month the Fine Arts Museum in Golden Gate Park has assembled many self-portraits of American artists. I did not know of this until this week, or I should have been tempted to take over the two (three!) in my keeping. Perhaps I could still find a time to have an appointment with Mr. Heil, the director. These exhibits have a way of continuing after the dates set.

"... 'Ah, many flowering islands lie in the waters of wide agony '... Anna, with love." [Quote is from "Lines Written among the Euganean Hills" by Percy Bysshe Shelley.]

Lockwood Library where Ona worked

Sept. 14. Jonathan's continuing absenteeism inflamed her motivation to correspond. "Your Wednesday 8th and Thursday 9th letters were waiting when I arrived at nine last night, my Jonathan. It is somewhat as I had suspected, for I had been lying awake much in the last few nights, distressed by an insistent suggestion that you were still in difficulties. I know something of your psychic strain, under these circumstances, because of my own reaction to those events which war against your welfare. These agencies are often slow and sometimes in error. You will be very patient and keep out in the sun as much as possible. And when the rains come (and oh, how they can come there!) perhaps you will make some further pen and ink sketches for you and for me. I do love the Aibric." [Ink drawing of Jonathan's lizard companion] "How carefully I did open the envelope with the warning: 'Aibric inside!' Not knowing just who or what might have been so named, I was cautious.

"One thing I would suggest: that it may be as well not to mention release and return elsewhere until official signal is given. Something has come to my attention recently which makes me see the wisdom of this - I will explain later.

"Did I tell you that on Thursday last I was over your loved trail in Oakland hills - where we went that misty afternoon in the spring? Two friends came from Berkeley with car, and bent on a long walk, so I took them there. It was wonderful under the trees but much dustier on the trail now, of course. How much I wished for you and missed you, even more than on the other days!

"On Saturday I think of going over to the deYoung Museum or perhaps to Legion d'Honneur.

"Be of good heart, my dear one. This time will soon be over and your life will be free in all respects. You have taught me so much. Whatever comes now I shall be always comforted by the thought that there is one to whom I can speak when I need to speak.

"The beautiful sketches I studied this morning until I was a bit late. Anna with love."

Two days later, another: "Sept. 16th, Wednesday night.

Jonathan David, Tchaikovsky's *Pathetique* symphony has been playing on and on, while I have been sitting here, very still, by the blue vase of friendly flowers. I have been looking at the meditations from your Sunday, September 12th. I have been clambering for hours with you over that wildly beautiful fairyland. I am as one whose sight has just been restored, breathless over the beauties you interpret.

"Sometimes the world seems to delight in breaking all of its promises to its most promising children. Then does the desperate mind recoil with the "speedy quietus" suggestion. Once, when I believed that I had cause to lose faith in all mankind and the stars above, a dear college tutor who sensed my agony led me away from unspoken plan of escape with his understanding and his words both stern and compassionate. I can still hear his kindly voice saying that I had a purpose in living, one I should understand better as time went along. Not only must I live to give to the world, he said, but to one special person who would seem most worthwhile I must give the utmost in love and understanding. This would partially make amends for a certain failure (due to childish attitude), which had just led to tragedy.

"So, though I am profoundly disturbed on the thoughts of this same urge born of your sufferings, there seems every reason to believe that you will lift a glad face skyward, you who are so richly endowed with love of life. With your soul aflame within its precious hermitage, the remainder of the exile will go quickly.

"Forgive me, my darling, if I have not been of any great comfort in your isolation. I wished to be, and I love you.

"Goodnight once more. This is the hour when you seem nearby - Anna.

"The future world will be kind. Put your trust in it."

Her concluding communication dated September 17, was returned to the Bay Area. The mailman had written Jonathan's Goss Street address on top of 'Camp 56'. It must have been returned to Dorothy who still occupied the house. When Dorothy discovered her husband and Ona had exchanged letters, I can only speculate 'Nutmeg' was aflame with emotions. She declined delivery; the postal service further changed it to the correct return address: 4188 Greenwood Avenue, Apartment 17 (Ona's place).

"Friday early morning" it opened. "The chief trouble may be that most men are idiotic enough to forget past carnage. Just a few, sometimes those who have not taken part in it physically (such as you and the author of *Red Badge of Courage*) can see it as it is and can struggle to waken the multitude to the danger involved. All that each thinking individual can do is attempt to keep his sanity, while with his talents, chiefly the written word, he can strive to make those yet to come to maturity aware of their brutal tyrants' designs. As you know, I have the opportunity of talking with a number of "the people" all the time. These often give me confidential opinions. So I am not altogether pessimistic except when I consider the difficulties of achieving unity and solidarity against the forces which kill and maim. Perhaps I have told you about the family who gave up defense work (highly paid, here) to take up the hazards of living in Alaska's interior? This man had three small children. He and his wife read and spoke very intelligently. They stopped at library to say goodbye as they went northward. They simply could not stand having their children grow in this atmosphere. Of course, they realize that they cannot escape completely, but still they will be somewhat separated from the sight of all this degradation.

"The time is almost past. The rest will leave us soon. With love to a courageous one, in whom I am well pleased. Anna"

September 20 was the final day for CPS Worker 000429. Batchelor, Jonathan David was sent home via bus and given hotel and meal passes. One would think he would be pleased returning to Oakland. He couldn't wait to embrace Ona, but he was also dreading and anxious about Dorothy. His heart was in his mouth as he pictured facing Dorothy and untangling his very complicated life. He cared for his Nutmeg, and would continue to correspond with her for decades, but also felt deceived and upset by her verbal scorn to mutual friends. Ona's intelligent letters, her little gifts, the sent art supplies, the extraordinary similarities of their educations and reflections, all left him concluding he wanted Ona in his life. Yet he wanted Dorothy in his life as a friend. How to approach her about a divorce? Dorothy was just a wee bit thing but quite capable of heated anger, as I witnessed when years into the future we visited her in Diamond Springs and she lit into Jonathan. She never forgave him for leaving her, even all those years later. If she could so easily pick on him in the 1980s, I can imagine the bickering of the 1940s and I'm sure there were plenty of moments when the artist had to rapidly flee a verbose tidal wave.

He never returned to Goss St. to live, although he did visit, sometimes for business and sometimes on a bender. One inebriated evening the plastered artist somehow made his way to Goss St. Determined to crash he did just that. He may not have made preset arrangements; of that I am not clear. According to Cheryl Parent, Dorothy and Teaney cooked up a prank. With the artist out like a light; the two women folded sheets over him and stitched the edges with him inside. I suppose the following morning he awakened them with his kicking, hollering and bellowing.

He 'dropped anchor' at the Greenwood Avenue apartments, used the address for mail, and found a room to let. As a backup, he still had his carriage house art studio and boat; both were spacious. Oddly, for a man with patently ambiguous relationship boundaries, he refused to share residency with Ona as long as he was married to Dorothy. Visiting Ona was OK and he welcomed her to his art studio. And although he believed he loved Ona, he wanted his life to continue as he was accustomed: work when he could find it (he did not want to return to the shipyard), sculpting in the carriage house, sailing. He steadfastly believed a man must have his own domicile without relying on womanly support. Yet as if to make up for a younger lifetime devoid of female relationships, he continued to date interesting women despite his reverence for Ona. Or perhaps, I do believe, he used the diversity of women to mask his darker side of despondency, self-abasement, and feelings of depression. His despair was seldom viewed by anyone, even those closest to him. Ona was one of the few who noted his heightened mishmash of anxieties.

The artist's self-torment was compounded by his imagination. "My dejection," he wrote after his return from Waldport in September, "is assuredly not confined to my own inner frustration --my crushed inner demands and desires --but owes itself to an amazing multiplicity of woes compounded out of the nefarious and soul-shattering discords of an unfortunate world. For, despite profound endeavor to the contrary, half of my brain is consistently beaten raw by the complete realization of what is transpiring upon the far-flung, hell-sullied periphery of the earth. Concurrent to each word that I write, a human being is eviscerated, or simply shot to death, somewhere out there. One can only visualize the lurid hideousness of it if an attempt is made to observe what can happen under the influence of extreme sudden demolition exerted by the diverse unstable nitrogenous substances which modern chemistry has concocted for this fool's paradise. Within an infinitesimal wink of time a hundred healthy young men may be strewn bizarrely over a sundered soul, spurting their lives into the red, incinerated dust, their clothes disintegrated, raw splintered bones protruding from bubbling ensanguined pulp, half recognizable, or worse disrupted anatomies mingling in ironical semblances still clutching avidly at the last vestiges of twisted life."

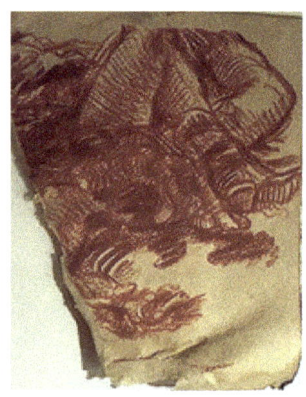

Previous page, Remnant, *Scourge of War*, sanguine conte on paper. Jonathan's inner turmoil included images of decapitated and disemboweled human beings. As long as the war persisted, the moody artist easily imagined such visions.

Wrestling with His Demons, black conte crayon on paper.

His journals were jam-packed with mind wanderings, his sketchpads sometimes a dwelling place for dark thoughts. When angst thrummed, he buried himself in pencil and paper. Letting his hands work he oft times allowed his mind to get lost in bizarre, unplanned sketches. *Halloween*. Black conte crayon on paper.

The Tomb of the Spiders, sepia conte crayon on paper, 1944. The artist was partial to bees and certain kinds of ants, but he cherished spiders.

His post-Waldport jottings continued: "Words have their stark limitations imagery moves only so far, then stops, or frays out into nebulous babbling. But the real horror of the blood-blobbed carnage goes on not the calm, painful death to which most of us are inured, but the grim menace of a nightmarish and incredibly grotesque massacre of youth and beauty, inundating three-quarters of the earth.

"In the face of these cruel facts, can any conscious man or woman be of light heart? Unfortunately, by far the greater part of the populace is either totally unconscious or absolutely and loathsomely insane. This fact, in turn, and in addition to the other horrors, is anything but negligible. The knowledge that I have set foot upon a land inhabited by puling idiots is, alone, enough to sadden me to distraction. To save me, I cannot fancy anyone, in their right mind, deliberately bringing forth offspring in this miasmic desert of despair."

Offsetting this gloomy view of his world, the last paragraph of this essay expresses a flicker of optimism: "Yet, I cannot veraciously say that I am sorry to be alive and this chiefly because I have a grasp upon what is sweet in this world. I cannot say, despite all exterior signs of disaster, that the land is lacking beauty for those who can perceive it who are not blind to it or that it wants in joy for those who seek it in the right pastures. Much lies within one's own power of locomotion if shackles are not clamped about one's flesh, or if somatic wisdom has not been set up for worship in a temple separate from that of the sacred. For me, at least, there is an awareness of bliss higher than which no mortal has risen and for which there can be no fulfillment, since there exist no trammels to hold it…."

His journal entries became short at times, sometimes only one line. This indicates to me he must have been busy working, painting or, I presume, involved with wine and poetry readings, his second great love outside of art. "You have got to watch Time … if you don't, Time will watch you…." he noted, and with humor, "There is tragedy in human affairs. Amongst the children are the many who pretend to be grown-up; while amongst the grown-up are those who think they are grown-up. Childhood is sweet. There is never enough of it. Let us all be little children who want nothing better." That is a great sentiment on childhood, coming from a man who wanted nothing to do with children.

Refusing to spend money for a haircut, the artist learned to cut his own thick locks. When he didn't cut them in a timely manner, they grew over his collar, in those days considered long hair. That brought on scrutiny. "Someone once asked me why," he penned, "I allow my hair to grow longer than the male of the species is usually permitted, according to current style and custom. I did not respond to the query. But were I to be so obliging I should inform my fine quizzical friend that nothing is so meaningless and idiotic as style and custom. People should do as they like to be happy. But it is really the most effortless form to open revolt against the blind tyranny of style and custom and politics that I know of. I permit myself access to a natural prerogative which is actually a natural law simply because I have an interest in things which to me are vastly more important."

Jonathan standing with wind tousled hair. Photographer
unknown.

End of Part I

APPENDIX

A Compendious History of the Batchelor Family Descended from Captain John.

By Jonathan Batchelor

Now I begin the writing of that section of the family history that stems from my grandfather Captain John Thomas Batchelor. This writing, which will be recorded in the computer, is set down in narrative form based on accounts presented to me during many years by my father Thomas Leon Batchelor. The accounts were given to me as he said according to extensive information he received directly from his parents. My father was very close to his parents, particularly his mother Blanca Mende de Merez. In truth, it is doubtful that either of his two siblings his older brother John and his still older sister Maude ever got so much first-hand biography therefore, I feel privileged to have been the recipient of so much of the family's history. Being the youngest child, I suppose my father had ample opportunity to observe at close hand the tribulations of his family, and thereby to gain in-depth knowledge of life's imperfections. I suspect that this account will be enjoyed and appreciated by all members of the Batchelor clan, including their in-laws and associates....

(In the following account some dates are approximate.)

During the early nineteenth century a certain British sea captain by the same of John Thomas Batchelor, was commissioned by an English shipping firm to command shipping between London, England, and Boston in the United States. On one of his crossings, arriving in Boston, he requested permission from his firm to be temporarily relieved of his duties as captain in order to take residence there. His second in command was granted captaincy, relieving him from the need to return to London for an indefinite period.

Shortly thereafter, Captain John was joined by his younger brother Leon Edgar, from Liverpool, England, a swashbuckling, hard-drinking fellow whose life's ambition seemed to be women and raising hell. Leon had worked his way around on English Merchantmen, and had come to Boston on one of the many brigs that exchanged cargo at the docks. Though he was just twenty-three, he had been a jack-tar on many voyages since the age of fourteen, had seen much of the world, and could quite easily become an officer if he'd only settle into the business of navigation and quit petty fogging around. The captain's love for his brother prompted his tolerance of all the ruckus he created at the waterfront.

One night Leon delivered a blow to a sailor's jaw that bowled him over a low bulwark into the murky water of Boston harbor, whereupon he dove into the water to save the unlucky man from drowning. Fellow tars rolled up a small crane and proceeded to haul them out with a block and tackle. Lamentably, incidents of this sort, involving rough-and-tumble fights between Leon and sailors, including burly stevedores and beachcombers, were annoyingly frequent.

The captain had taken lodging at a fine Victorian house located a few blocks from the harbor, where he boarded with the Stimsons, a middle-class English family. Happy to see his brother Leon, he invited him to share his rooms on the second floor, facing the sea. Large windows presented a wide view of the harbor where ships large and small sailed in and out daily. There were two spacious bedrooms, divided by a fine bathroom. Leon was given the extra bedroom. There was even a private entrance, reached by a stairway, which led from a garden pathway to a small balcony.

One afternoon, the captain was having tea with the Stimsons on the veranda. It was an excellent day in early June, with a gentle, rather warm breeze wafting the earthy fragrance of a recent spring shower out of the southwest. The family father James Stimson, mother Alice, and their adolescent daughter, Ellen enjoyed the captain's salty yarns of his many voyages, especially to the orient. Thus, he was amidst one of his tales when a boisterous halloo heralded someone's approach on the pathway below. The captain recognized Leon's voice and braced himself, hoping his brother was on good behavior. Although he knew that the Stimson's were long-time residents and were aware of the rough ways of some seafaring men, the captain wished to avoid the chance that Leon might get out of line and embarrass the family.

"Well, hello, everyone!" exclaimed Leon. "Thought I'd drop by this fine Saturday afternoon."

"Have a chair, Leon," said Mr. Stimson, gesturing to an empty chair next to young Ellen, who blushed noticeably as Leon sat down.

"Leon, this is our daughter, Ellen. Ellen, please pour Mr. Batchelor a cup of tea." Leon grinned broadly as he watched the pretty child's hand tremble as she filled his cup.

"Mr. Stimson" commented Leon, "please know that I appreciate your letting me stay here. It's so much better than residence in one of those bloody rat houses on the docks!"

"Oh, I fancy it is," laughed Alice Stimson.

By then, Leon Edgar was leering at the "sweet young thing" at his side. Just turned seventeen, she was home from school. Leon, of course, had not seen her before, had not known that the Stimson's had a daughter.

Though he was just twenty-three, Leon had been a jack-tar on many voyages since the age of fourteen, had pretty-well seen much of the world, and could quite well become an officer, at least a mate or captain, if he would quit pettifogging around and settle into navigation. So, here was Leon Edgar, in his full, sailor's habit even wearing his well-varnished tarpaulin hat, which he now removed and put into his lap.

The captain noticed the sort of interest Leon was giving the young woman, and wasn't surprised, but he was prepared to take his wayward brother to task. Of course, he sensed that Mr. Stimson might also be aware of it.

"You know, Captain, we are used to this," commented Mr. Stimson. "It is something to be expected when one is so fortunate…" He didn't complete his sentence. Leon had caught the hint and had stopped staring at Ellen, who laughed lightly and said "Daddy, you needn't be so subtle, you know. Besides, I rather like Leon. He's far better-looking than most of the sailors I see in town. And, after all, at least he notices me!"

Mr. Stimson looked at his wife's face. Alice Stimson beamed back at him, full of the warm humor of a parent who wisely faces the inevitable progression of life. The captain remained taciturn, knowing full-well the wild state of his brother's mind, praying to himself that matters might go no further. He was deeply relieved when Leon finished his tea and rose to apologize that he must take care of some business at the harbor.

"Well, folks," he said, "this has been a rare pleasure." He glanced at Ellen, who was smiling up at him. "I must say, I certainly enjoyed meeting you, Ellen. Perhaps there'll be another time." Leon paused for a trice, looked at the captain. "Found an agency for a big new company, John. Maybe sign-up soon. Talk about it later." He walked off to the stairway. "Another time, soon?"

"We'll be here, having tea on most fine days, Leon," smiled Alice Stimson. "You're always welcome, you know."

Miss Ellen got up and ran over to Leon, holding out her hand. "I certainly hope you're not going to ship out again, before I even get to know you. Please come back soon."

Leon held her small hand in both of his burly paws, grinning happily. "Glad you feel this way," he said. "Good-bye for now."

The captain was quite surprised by this pleasant turn of events. Perhaps there was still a bit of the gentleman in his brother, after all, he thought. But he was relieved to see his brother sauntering down the pathway. Leon turned to vigorously wave an arm before disappearing into the village. Well, thought the captain, at least he didn't hang on, or ask for something "stronger" than tea!

Events during the days that followed were trivial enough--even pleasant. The Stimsons sometimes had guests on weekends, among who were illustrious persons ship owners, merchants and an occasional sea captain. Captain Batchelor always enjoyed these gatherings. Now and then some ship owner, learning that he was a captain, admonished him that he ought to look into shipping out on one of the new clippers, "The best vessels ever to sail the sea!" Indeed, he learned that there was a swiftly growing demand for experienced men to command shipping in the Far East.

"What about westward, around South America?" he once asked of a ship owner.

"Well, sir, I must say, Captain Blaine here can answer that better than I. Captain Blaine, would you mind sir?"

He was introduced to a remarkable gentleman standing close by, who extended a huge, gnarled hand that had known the rigors of much rough usage, whose voice resembled the base notes of a foghorn.

"Overheard the question, Captain. Just come in from my

fourth trip nearly lost a ship once. It's a bad one, Captain. Yes, of course, California looks good, but so far, the best we get is cowhide in that wild country. Mostly Indians and a few Mexicans. Nothin' much north of Santa Barbara. Even the Sandwich Islands don't make the extra time worthwhile. But, Captain, it's Europe or the Far East for me from now on. Thinkin' of shippin' out soon?"

This Captain Blaine was a grizzled, burly giant of a man, who looked every bit the sort who had been at sea all his life.

"Just biding my time, Captain Blaine. Thought I'd look around a bit, though."

"Say, Captain," said the gruff old seafarer, "understand you've been sailin' brigs and brigantines same as I've been doin'. Seen the clippers down their, yet?"

"Sure have, Captain Blaine. Not been aboard yet, though."

Such dialogues were typical of the socials at Stimson's. There was scant discussion of matters other than maritime and shipbuilding enterprise. Indeed, among the guests there were often shipbuilders and marine architects, including such notables as the designer and builder of the greatest ships that ever sailed the sea - the clippers. His name is history in the shipbuilding industry, the Nova Scotian Donald McKay, whose triumph was probably the magnificent Flying Cloud, "Queen of the Clippers." Of course, to inspire all this conviviality, to delight the more venturesome guests, there was a well-appointed bar, where an amplitude of beverages ranging from potent to light, including sarsaparilla, not to mention a large, beautifully embellished punchbowl containing liquids of mysterious potency.

Subsequent weeks passed pleasantly, with rare incident involving the captain's prankish brother Leon. But one of those incidents was notable enough, even amusing, to those whose humor verged on the ribald.

That Saturday in August had been an exceptionally warm day. Captain John had spent the afternoon wandering on the docks, meeting fellow seafarers and studying some of the newer vessels. He had even visited McKay's shipyard where the huge clipper hulls were in progress. Evening with the Stimsons was enjoyed in their large dining room, having supper and casual conversation.

The captain had retired rather late and was fast asleep when he was aroused by the noise and voices of persons on the small balcony at the entrance to his quarters. Lighting his bedside lamp, he put on a dressing gown and was about to call out when the door burst open and his eyes were greeted by the sight of two very pretty young women, whom he could easily see were a bit inebrious, followed by brother Leon, ostensibly well-oiled, who rather ceremoniously set a bottle on a small table near the door.

"Best Jamaica rum in Boston!" declared Leon.

"Well, come in and make yourselves comfortable," said Captain John. "Leon, please shut the door...and please don't bump around too much. I'm sure the Stimsons are all asleep below."

"Hey, John, excuse the intrusion, but it seemed to me time for you to know some of the sweeties in town. Beat some of the best ones in Liverpool, you know."

"Leon, damn it, you know I don't need any of this sort of thing. Have you forgotten? There's Maggie, and--"

"Don't wish to spoil your dreams, John," interrupted Leon solicitously. "Maggie's past tense now. Tired of waiting, I say. That little strawberry blonde, Yorkshire pudding has gone and married a farmer back in her homeland. But don't cry, Captain. See who I brought you!"

Leon gently pushed forth a flashing, red-haired young woman. Her hair was an amazing mass of tiny curls stranding like a bonfire over and around her very pretty face.

"Meet Katie, John. She's Katherine MacIver, says her folks are fresh from Scotland. Ball of fire, she is!"

"Quite pleased to meet you, Captain. Leon tells me you've been at sea too long. Sorry about your little Yorkshire lassie!"

Katie's voice resembled the wintry song of sleigh bells. Indeed, the captain was a bit titillated. He studied Katie's fine features, allowing his critical gaze to flip down the well-made garb she wore. French design, he surmised to himself.

"And this is Angie. Mine, John, if you don't mind!"

Also well dressed, Angie wore a flowered bonnet, slightly tilted on a wild cascade of golden hair. She smiled curtly at the captain, but said nothing. Surely, Captain John had rarely seen more charming young ladies. Of course, he was thoroughly impressed.

He propitiously drew chairs from an alcove and bade them sit. Leon brought forth his bottle of rum and asked if there were glasses handy.

"This is English Navy rum, John," said Leon. "I'm sure you're familiar with it." Glasses were produced from a cabinet and Leon filled them, grinning mischievously. The captain settled in his reading chair and Katie MacIver quickly drew her chair close by him.

A bit precocious for a young Scottish lass, observed Captain John to himself. Doubtlessly, she'd been primed with something from a flask he knew was always somewhere under his brother's blouse! Certainly, quite what he might expect of this wild, but much-loved brother of his! (The captain's sense of moral decorum was certainly far more acute than brother Leon's. He felt keenly compunctions permitting activity which clearly intimated raunchy behavior in the respected Stimson household…particularly, since it was their graciousness to provide him with this excellent board and lodging.)

Katie had moved so close to the captain that the disturbing scents of her stole into his brain like the fumes of some exotic drug.

"For a sea captain you seem a bit shy, Sir," Katie commented. "Please, no offence, Sir but it would be wonderful to me if perhaps we could be friends."

Gad, thought Captain John, this one positively has her way with men! But what am I to do? She's the prettiest girl I've seen in Boston…and she's making matters quite obvious…none of the usual barriers! Brother Leon really knows how to pick them! And he could easily see that these girls weren't prostitutes. He had long concluded that prostitutes, as a rule, don't really like men.

He noticed that Leon and Angie were sipping their rum and chatting merrily. Indeed, it appeared to him that they had known each other for some time. It occurred to him that they were deliberately keeping to themselves to encourage Katie…all part of Leon's sly, mischievous plan to get his big brother back in circulation!

After all, the captain had been at sea more than a year always determined to remain faithful to his beloved Maggie, whom he'd left in London and hadn't seen for nearly two years. Yes, of course, he'd written to her, had received a couple of replies, but it had now been over a year since her last letter…And now he was startled to realize that Katie had pushed a knee against his leg and was smiling winsomely while looking squarely at him…as though expecting some sort of response! Surreptitiously, he glanced at the chronometer a valued instrument he kept in his quarters whether on land or sea noting that it was 0225.

"I saw you checking the time, Sir," said Katie. She put a hand on his shoulder. "I think you'd like company tonight, Sir. Please allow me the privilege." She gently pushed back the hair from his face and caressed his ear with her tongue.

Egad! He thought. I shan't escape this time. This Katie's a real driver…the veritable Sea Witch! Siren or Nereid…her power is a full-rigged ship; a fair wind in tropical seas. Check the compass, Captain John which of the four points south, west, east, or north? You're in unchartered tropical waters now. The fair winds of chance, change, or certainty, are yours to choose!

Leon Edgar drew back from Angie long enough to take a sip of his rum. "I say, time to hit the bunk, John. Mind if Angie and I repair to our quarters? Not leaving you alone this time, eh John! Cheerio. See you on deck at about 0900?"

Might even be later, thought the captain, as he put both strong arms around Katie's slender waist and kissed her warmly on her neck, cheeks and mouth…Then, with astonishing skill, Katie unfastened her blouse and revealed the loveliest bosom and the finest, most buoyant pair of titties he'd ever had the pleasure of seeing. Perfectly matched and gravity defying, the two exquisite mammas stood out proudly in the quiet air disturbingly erotic, allaying all vestige of the restraint he had been trying to maintain.

Leon Edgar was delighted to observe how well his plan progressed. To say that true love grew from that single night's camaraderie in the aerie (an eagle's lofty nest as Leon called it) might be considered purely simplistic. Whether Captain John could feel so profound a state of mind for Katie MacIver, for him at least, would be a bit premature. The captain had, since adolescence, learned that the intrinsic sentiments of Eros could not grow from the soil of mere sexual encounter, gratifying though it might be. Even from casual analysis of the human psyche concerning love, he had concluded that it was far more than purely physical charm titillating enough, but demanding more thorough awareness than mere familiarity could provide. To Captain John Thomas, the common concept of "love at first sight" smelled of simple vulgarity, and could hardly provide the time and care to put a great ship in thorough order for life's tempestuous voyage. However, this Scottish Katie MacIver did become the happy means of easing some of the troublous wonderment which afflicts an honest man when he finds himself adrift in life's ocean without anchor and rudder. She certainly remained thus for all the months he would stay in that swiftly growing Boston seaport. Nevertheless, might this relationship betwixt the captain and the beautiful young Katie MacIver be at least a small stone or a bit of the mortar that played its part in love's edifice? Or might it not have been a symbolic figure in the building of the captain's ultimate need for love symbolical as perhaps the small though indispensable martingale of a seafaring vessel?

So, the weeks and months passed happily by for Captain John Thomas. Indeed, Katie often accompanied him on his numerous wanderings about town, and even cultivated a fair knowledge and understanding of maritime affairs. She could often identify the various types of rigging and vessels that crowded the Boston harbor; and occasionally went with him to visit shipyards. (To be sure, the captain became a bit concerned that his lovely companion might be contemplating marriage!)

Brother Leon, of course, had frequently managed to get himself into tavern and dockside brawls. Though the captain loved his brother, it often became a chore to keep him out of jail, and to temper his womanizing. The final blow came when he learned that Leon's womanizing got him into such a fix that he was obliged to sign up to ship out. He had struck up a torrid affair with some Boston belle and got her pregnant. So, of course, the captain was warmly relieved the night in late August when his fractious brother shouldered his sea bag and waved goodbye as he climbed aboard one of the many brigs bound for the Orient. There were a few letters exchanged, but he soon lost track of Leon Edgar. There were matters of greater consequence in store for Captain John Thomas Batchelor....

During the following weeks the captain, who occasionally whiled away evenings at one of the numerous waterfront taverns, became acquainted with a certain Cyril Connors, a purser who had for many years been commissioned on one of the American clipper ships plying the seas far and wide. He was to learn that there were openings for good captains to command these great ships. (Katie, who otherwise was his constant companion, never joined him in these moments. In those days it was considered quite unseemly for a woman to be seen in a tavern!)

One blustery, cold Saturday in November the captain had joined Connors in one of the better taverns that stood hard by the dock where several giant three-masters were moored. It had been snowing heavily, with flurries of stinging bits of ice sweeping along the rows of warehouses and pubs. The two sailors were having some of the bartender's warming draughts, enjoyed by weatherworn men who had often been at sea for years. There was a stiff gale wind knocking at the gates and windows, and if one stood on the dock a raging sea could be seen smashing at the sea wall a thousand yards across the harbor basin.

"But I've heard that there is a bit of prejudice against the hiring of British men."

"John", interrupted Connors, "there are exceptions. Good sailors are much in need to man these giants. Why, I've known some Dutchmen who are excellent mates who've handled the toughest assignments. I know of a Frenchman who started as a tar; he's now a captain aboard the Angela, a ship that regularly sails to India and China rounding the cape each voyage...and you know what that is!"

The captain took a sip from his steaming mug, searching Connor's eyes.

"Yes, John...in this rough business there's no room for prejudice. I could tell you about Danes and Norwegians, and not a few Scots. And John, look at me--I'm a bloody Irishman!" Connors chuckled heavily and ordered a refill. "And what do you think these Americans are, anyway. They're mostly immigrant European stock!"

"All right, Connors," said the captain. "You've convinced me." He grew silent, casually observing the busy bartender. "I understand that there's a commissioning office for one of the shipping companies next door."

"Not that one," said Connors. "Try a big one. What say we go together. Meet me out front of this tavern at 0500 Monday morning?"

"I shall be here."

That morning the weather had gentled down. Connors was standing at the dock peering out at sea through a space between the ships. Sailors were making ready one of the huge vessels. Some were climbing a gangway to the gunwale, bearing sea bags and chests. A crane had been rolled up and cargo was being hoisted into the ship's hold.

"Going out, I suppose?" commented Captain John as he strode to the purser's side.

"Just a short one, John. She's bound for Jamaica and New Orleans. Probably lay over at Havana. The men love these short voyages, you know. There'll even be time for fun ashore. She leaves in the morning."

"I've heard New Orleans is quite a town," said the captain.

"You've heard right, John. You doubtlessly also know that it was originally a Spanish colony…until the French took over. But the populace there is still mostly Spanish. Do you speak Español, John?"

"Fairly well. One doesn't do business in Spanish ports without some knowledge of it."

Minutes later, they were walking briskly along the broad wharf to an imposing structure housing a hotel and maritime offices.

"Good morning Connors," said a portly gentleman at the counter. He opened a ledger and dipped a pen into an inkwell. "Want a ship for your friend there?"

"Anders, this is Captain John Batchelor. Been resting a bit in town…ready for the best you have."

Anders peered critically at the captain for a moment, then turned a few pages. "The North Aurora. She's a new clipper, been out twice. Far eastern ports. You board tomorrow, 0900, sail next Monday, 0500. Owner, Hyde and Engles. Come in tomorrow, 0800, for itinerary. Sign on?" Anders pushed a double page of printed matter toward the captain, who took a pen from an inkwell and quickly scribbled his name and office on the legal forms.

"Hyde and Engles, you probably know, is a big company, Captain. It's a tough outfit, but I think you'll like them. They'll treat you well if you know the ropes."

The captain smiled and reached to shake hands with Anders.

"Ouch!" exclaimed Anders. "Watch that grip, captain. Someday you're going to break something."

Connors was chuckling as the two friends strode out of the office. "What say we have a couple, John."

"Thanks, Cyril, not today. Tomorrow at Randall's…1900?"

"See you there, John, 1900 sharp."

Connors sauntered off up the wharf as Captain John walked home to the aerie at Stimson's. He found Katie still in bed….

So, the captain had just a week to get acquainted with his three mates, the cook, the steward, those of the crew who had remained with the ship, and move his gear into the capacious cabin aboard the North Aurora. Then, of course, he had Katie to deal with. She even begged to sail with him. "Well, not yet, little one. Maybe next trip. Never commanded one of these rigs, you know." And when Katie broke down and wept, he gathered her in his arms and tossed her on the bed. It was getting late, anyhow.

(Later, the Stimson's were to invite Katie to stay on with them during the captain's absence. This was a source of wonder to the captain, who considered his hosts a bit conservative in their views on love and sex.)

Of course, the Stimsons were not surprised when Captain John announced his intention to ship out. "I presume you'll jolly well be gone from us for awhile," said William Stimson. "Trust you'll join us in a bit of well-wishing before you shove off, eh captain!" Alice put her arms around the captain. "Please come home to us when you return to port, captain. Bill and I shall be looking forward to it, you may be sure. I'm certain Ellen will miss you. Please write to us. I shall personally reply."

Captain John was deeply moved by the Stimson's display of affection They'd not had a son, he reflected, and he had sensed the strong parental attachment that had developed during the year he'd lived so close to them. At twenty-six, and because he appeared younger, he could easily be Ellen's big brother.

Speaking of Ellen, who had joined some of her school chums that day; often she had accompanied him and Katie on walks along the wharf. She once begged to go aboard the fine clipper ship, which desire, of course, the captain granted. As Ellen looked around in the cabin at the excellent woodwork and cabinets, the beautiful varnished mahogany paneling, the teak floor, the roomy bunks, the brilliantly polished brass chandlery, she commented, "Goodness, Captain John, this is so comfortable and luxurious! Oh, I'd so love to sail with you!"

Katie, who stood by and had been observing the girl's enthusiasm, laughed as she said, "Now, Ellen, I'll have you know, the captain is mine. Hands off, dear girl!" Ellen then burst into tears, protesting Katie's inference.

"Captain John is my big brother," she cried, "and--and I love him!" The pretty girl looked up into the captain's face. "Please hurry home to us. I--I need you. We all need you, Captain John. I shall personally tend your quarters while you're away. You can be assured we won't rent it to anyone else."

(It must be remembered that, in those days, most ships leaving port were often gone at least a year. A leave-taking was therefore sometimes a sad event, for it was well known that on some occasions the ship was lost at sea, and all hands lost with it. Also, it is well to bear in mind that, at that time, most people felt and expressed sentimental emotions quite freely and without hypocrisy.)

Well, Captain John was so warmed by all this that he knelt and put his arms about her. "Yes, dear girl, I shall be your big brother. When I get back to Boston I shall have something special for you. And never forget it, I love you too." Then he stood up and went to a cabinet where he drew forth a sheaf of papers. "Ellen, while we are on this love subject, knowing how much love means to us, here's the latest letter from Leon. In it he writes that he will return in a couple of years and will want to see you. So, here, you may have it. He says quite a lot about you, which I feel sure it is well for you to know. I suspect that you will be hearing more from him, Ellen."

The beautiful girl was grinning happily as she reached both hands to take the envelope. She saw that it was enclosed in a kind of oilcloth and that the postage indicated the port of Singapore.

"Take it home, darling. Read it when you are alone."

It had been a very cold and rather stormy day, such heavy rain, threatening snow, typical for late November in Boston. Captain John was given the honor of celebrating Thanksgiving at the Stimsons, along with much well wishing for a safe and prosperous voyage.

Katie, of course had been invited by the Stimsons to enjoy this happy occasion. (The captain was astonished--and a bit amused--by the fact that Katie was so well received by them!) He was particularly pleased when he found Connors among the guests. Before the evening was over, when some of the guests had gone home, Connors assured the captain that he would be at the gangway of the North Aurora Sunday at 1800 sharp. (It, of course, was customary for a captain to bunk aboard his ship the night before departure.)

Sunday evening, shortly before 1800 o'clock, the captain and Cyril Connors strode down the wharf toward the North Aurora. They had enjoyed a few scintillating glasses of Randall's best Irish and were in high spirits. About a block away, they discerned several people gathered about the gangway.

"Well," chuckled Connors. "Appears we have a boarding committee!"

A well-clad young woman was presently seen to break from the little crowd and come running up to them. Throwing herself into Captain John's arms, Katie MacIver began planting wild kisses on his face and even his ears. Her blue eyes welled with tears that streamed down her cheeks.

"Oh please take me with you," she implored.

"Not so fast, Katie. Maybe next trip. I've got to sail this amazing rig at least once. And besides, you know what they say about having a woman aboard ship!"

"Old wives' tale," taunted Katie, plastering a broad kiss on his mouth, so he couldn't say any more. "All right," she conceded, "Promise you will write soon as you can."

The 'committee' was, of course, the Stimsons, including pretty Ellen. But the captain was particularly delighted to see the grand old Captain James Blaine towering discreetly in back of them. Ellen came forth holding something bejeweled and sparkling in her hand. Holding it aloft, he saw that it was a very unusual pendent or necklace of some sort.

"Captain, I was told by a very old woman that this Egyptian amulet can protect its wearer from harm. You can wear it under your shirt so the men won't think you're a sissy! Katie was seen to restrain her humor as the captain accepted it and held it up to the morning light.

"You can be sure I shall wear it," said Captain John, trying hard to appear quite serious.

Ellen looked up at him, standing on her toes. "Now, Captain, you may kiss me. And promise me you'll wear the amulet. And--and, do you really think Leon likes me?"

"I certainly do, dear girl. I know you'll be getting a letter from him soon."

Katie MacIver had been standing by, indulgently smiling during this pleasant display, feeling somehow sisterly toward the charming youngster.

Captain John's two voyages to the Orient netted him ample opportunity to master the challenging mechanics of sailing a clipper ship. Aside from a few beastly weather incidents, including a savage gale, during the first voyage, off Cape of Good Hope as he left Cape Town enroute to the Indian Ocean, during which a man fell into the sea from a top-gallant yard and was lost, the trips were successful and quite profitable.

After much nagging and coercion, Katie MacIver was taken aboard to accompany him on the second voyage. She had gone on numerous short voyages aboard the sleek packets that frequented the waters between Boston, New York and Baltimore, and had made a round-trip aboard a bark from New York to Savannah, Cuba. So she was fairly adapted to the pleasures and perils of seafaring. But Captain John was pleased with her excellent demeanor aboard the great new vessel. Indeed, she proved to be a comfort to him in the cabin, lavishing attentions he might expect from a good wife. (To be sure, there were those moments when he wavered on the verge of considering the wisdom of marriage to this intensely desirable young woman!) Katie particularly enjoyed the layover in London. The captain took her to visit his folks north of town while unloading several tons of China tea and Indian spices at the port of London. (He had three tons of tea and spices, plus much more, such as fine oriental works of art and huge bolts of silk to take home to Boston, where the profits would be appreciably greater.)

After more than two years, the trips to the Orient were finished. The company had been aroused by interesting developments on the west coast of North America. It was rumored that, in addition to the wealth of cowhide and much desired fur pelts, rich sources of silver and other rare minerals had been found in Nevada, near the California border. So now the scene was set for Captain John Batchelor's grandest adventure…the often hazardous though fascinating voyages westward.

The worse hazards were the wildly treacherous passages around the "Horn!" the sea-blasted, uncharted extreme southern tip of South America. Within miles of the Horn, vicious, unpredictable currents running between the Atlantic and Pacific oceans, and scourging, immanent icebergs, often invisible in dense fog, made navigation all but impossible. But the seemingly endless, ship-straining, man-crushing beat into fierce winds and currents northward along the western coast of South America was bad enough to dishearten even the dauntless sailor. The captain sea-consciously kept a wide berth between his ship and the irregular coast. A help to the captain on these difficult voyages was two of his three mates, who had sailed this route not long before.

Katie, of course, was not to be taken on these voyages. The captain could never forget, during the rest of his life, the tear-drenched day he left her on the Boston wharf to sail away on a trip that would absent him from her for more than two years.

The year was 1861. California and other ports west had become an important objective for many ship owners. The captain's cargo often consisted of coal, sugar, wheat, whiskey and rum from Boston; tobacco, rice, cornmeal, cotton and kerosene (called coal oil in those days) from New Orleans. Coffee was to be taken aboard at a South American port in exchange for part of the kerosene, a profitable trade, for coffee was in great demand in California!

One of the several ports of call enroute to the west coast of North America was Nouvelle-Orleans (New Orleans) in Louisiana, at the Caribbean end of the Mississippi River. Established by a French company during the early eighteenth-century Nouvelle-Orleans and the Louisiana Territory was ceded to Spain during the last half of the eighteenth century. Once regarded by the French a mere trans-shipment center, under Spanish influence it developed into a respected and fairly prosperous shipping center for Mississippi cargo being floated down river by enterprising American farmers and ranchers. It remained a Spanish colony until the early nineteenth century, when it was returned to France. Napoleon, the French Emperor, promptly negotiated sale of the entire Louisiana Territory to the swiftly growing United States (the historic Louisiana Purchase).

During the infamous Spanish Inquisition, many Spanish Jews, called Sephardim, who had inhabited the Iberian Peninsula since the time of the Diaspora (dispersion of the Jews after the second Babylonian exile, about 135 C.E.) were made victims of religious and economic scourge. The Diaspora has remained a continuous state of the Jewish people for many centuries up to the present time. A certain portion of these ancient people had wandered into the lands that later became France, Spain and Portugal, long before the expansion of Christianity in Europe, and before the Moorish invasion.

To escape the horrors of the Inquisition, many Jews moved to Holland and England; some managed to reach the Atlantic coast of North America, settling in the young towns that later became cities of the United States. A few of the Sephardic families settled in Nouvelle Orleans when it was a Spanish colony.

One of these families, the Mende de Merez-descended from those Sephardim who for centuries had lived in that part of Spain called Castile had found safe residence in a hidden quarter of what subsequently became the Vieux Carre. (Most Jews, of course, changed their original names to fit into the communities and nations where they lived.) Even then, the inveterate fear of persecution prompted the family to carefully hide and disguise any appearance of Jewishness- -a practice deeply resented by some younger members of the family, who considered it cowardly and hypocritical. These young people wished to ignore the hideous tales of horror, told by elders of the family who could not forget the hellish years of the Inquisition.

But the abominable living conditions in the colony were very hard to bear. Mosquito-infested swamplands nearly surrounding the place brought attacks of malaria and yellow fever, which were often fatal. The almost total lack of a sewage system, the general squalor along the primitive, unpaved streets and alleys, resulted in occasional epidemics of cholera and typhoid fever.

By the time in 1858, when Captain John sailed into the busy

New Orleans harbor, living conditions in the fast-growing city had been somewhat improved. In fact, New Orleans, since the historic Louisiana Purchase in the enterprising hands of American engineers had become an important seaport, rated fourth in the world. One of the chief items of cargo was cotton and cotton fabric including sailcloth.

The de Merez family soon took advantage of this, becoming fairly successful cotton merchants. A few members of the family had grown wealthy enough to move into the best districts. New Orleans, however, had not been able to overcome the serous health hazards; the absence of a sewage system and contaminated drinking water, lack of adequate drainage, flooding after frequent heavy rains, resulted in sporadic epidemics of yellow fever and cholera.

While he conducted business in town, Captain John inevitably contacted the de Merez family. He dealt directly with an astute gentleman whose name was Juan Castillo de Merez. Señor de Merez's secretary sat discreetly and quietly at her desk, notating transactions. The captain had occasion to talk to her and was soon quite impressed by her decorous demeanor. She spoke English well, with a charming accent, and although she recorded her notations in Spanish, when requested to write a receipt in English, the captain was delighted to see the beautiful script.

"Would the Señorita mind writing a note of approval of the transaction on a separate sheet of paper? And please sign your name."

Señor Juan Castillo de Merez cast a quick glance at the captain and, smiling visibly, resumed conversing in Spanish with men at a backroom entrance. It had apparently occurred to Señor de Merez that, were it not for the modest role of business secretary he had assigned to her, his exceptionally attractive young niece might well become the village belle!

Back in Boston for a month's stay, after an absence of more than two years, proved of decisive significance. During an evening at Randall's tavern, he learned that Connors was off to the Orient--had been gone for nearly a year. Resuming residence at the Stimson's was pleasant for Captain Batchelor. The family was more than hospitable toward him, graciously accepting him as a much-revered son. He was pleased to learn that Ellen had indeed received several letters from Leon, including some fine oriental jewelry and a box of silk clothing, some of which of particular delight to the young woman, now nearly twenty well-designed lingerie.

Katie MacIver had gone to visit her parents. The captain didn't see her until a few days before his departure for another voyage around the Horn and west. Of course, she was very happy to see him, still hoping he'd take her with him to California. After all, many people in the east had heard glowing rumors which true or not convinced them that California was a wonderland, the fabulous El Dorado…to be reached somehow at any cost and with whatever effort.

The captain left Katie at the Stimson's, needing to make certain all was in order aboard the North Aurora; Boston cargo properly stowed, all officers, the cook, steward, sail maker, carpenter, were accounted for and shipshape. The port and starboard crew were assigned to their quarters in the forecastle. The ship was ready to sail.

Returning to his rooms at the Stimsons, late that afternoon, the captain was astonished to find Katie standing amid items of luggage.

"I'm going!" she announced emphatically. "And please don't worry. You won't regret taking me. Now, just help me get this stuff aboard the North Aurora."

Captain Batchelor stood just within the doorway quite impressed by Katie's determination.

Why not? he thought. "But what about your parents? How will they take this? You may be gone as long as three years this time. It's the fall of '64; you might not be back until sometime in '65, or even '67! Possibly later."

"Oh, John, look at me. I'm surely no child. And, you know, Sir, I might not ever wish to return."

The captain peered searchingly into her eyes, now glowing with an intense blue flame. Like sapphires on fire, he thought.

"All right!" he exclaimed, almost shouting, a humorous smile stealing into his countenance. "We'll get you aboard tomorrow at twenty hundred. I'm sure the Stimsons will want to know about this."

"I've already informed them. Oh, John, please, let's get me aboard now. I adore the aroma of that grand ship. The Stimsons have assured me they will have a fine dinner for us this evening."

The captain quickly acquiesced. He grabbed two of her leather bags and headed for the door.

"They're so light," he said. "Is that one you're carrying heavier?"

"I'm taking mostly things to wear," she said. "Oh, let's go. I'm so eager to get back into that fine cabin!"

A fair, offshore breeze from the beautiful coast of North Carolina bellied the cloud of sails, well set and neat, as the great ship plied southeastward, knifing through the Gulf Stream with the ease of a racing vessel. Every sail had been bent including moonrakers and studding sails. All was well, and Captain Batchelor had relaxed on the quarterdeck, breathing deeply the early sea air and profoundly relishing the ineffable blaze of gold as the sun rose slowly across the expanse of gently undulating ocean. The night-watch bell had sounded and the watch crew were turning-in to their bunks in the forecastle, while sailors busied themselves on deck, coiling lines, scraping and tarring rigging, swabbing, scrubbing and holystoning decks, etc., etc. (All labors of course were conducted under the watchful supervision of the mates in this case, the second and third mates. No man could stand, lean, or sit idle except Sunday and late Saturday, unless an emergency arose; even then a sailor was often busy tending his personal gear.)

The captain had been leisurely watching the man at the helm for a moment, and was about to retire to the cabin when--

"Like some company?" The voice of windbells heard on a cool morning in April sounded so near he felt her breath on his neck.

"Katie, you'll have us a shipload of jealous brutes, you little witch."

"They're not seeing me, captain. I'm well hidden behind you. Anyway, I wanted to come out and enjoy the morning gold." She walked to the rail and gazed out toward the sunrise. "Looks exactly like a sea of molten gold, does it not? And that exquisite breeze! Where is it blowing from?"

"Some of it's the sea out there, but there's a healthy blend of the earthy redolence of forests and meadows of North Carolina which lie about twenty leagues west."

"Well, for me," mused Katie, "there's something disturbingly erotic about it."

The captain had joined Katie at the rail and was savoring the splendor of morning light at sea. "You know, Katie, I don't wish to alarm you, but an important part of our cargo is a sizable shipment of gunpowder, dynamite and firearms." He turned aside, and in a moment of wry humor he added, "And Katie, take care not to lose that fiery temper of yours; it would surely ignite the huge store of blasting powder that's also down there in the hold, and blow us all to the other world!"

"Now, Captain, just what do you mean by 'the other world?'"

"Oh, don't let it worry you. Just be careful. And while we're indulging in this persiflage, please quit the captain bit. Just call me John. It sounds better!"

"I like that…John." She moved quite close to him and nuzzled his ear. "Please know that I deeply appreciate you're taking me. I don't think I've ever enjoyed anything more in my life--although I'm hardly forgetting the voyage to the Orient and that exhilarating stay in England!"

New Orleans hadn't changed much. A few homes were now equipped with a semblance of plumbing. Riverboats were doing business delivering demijohns of drinking water. In fact, the town had begun to assume all the attributes of a major shipping center. Captain Batchelor was greatly moved by the improvements in the old colony, now becoming a bustling, even beautiful young city-- with much of the original French influence still intact. But for him, of course, it was business as usual, ordering the commodities needed for barter in the west. Perhaps the most prominent item was cotton and cotton fabrics.

Katie often accompanied the captain on his tours about town. She was adept at making friends and was occasionally urged to join them at the various festivals that occurred weekly and sometimes daily. She was off at one of these events the day the captain did business at the de Merez warehouse. Juan Castillo was his customary efficient self, advising the captain that he now had in stock particularly excellent sailcloth and other cotton fabrics, including a variety of material for clothing manufacture. His niece still sat at her desk busy with accounting and billing. The captain noticed that she wore an exceptionally fine blouse and skirt, richly embroidered in tasteful colors. He approached the desk and stood silently observing her for a moment. He remembered well the name she had written on the requested business approval note of his former transaction.

"Buenos Dias, Señorita Blanca Mende. I trust you won't mind my saying that it is a special pleasure to see you again!"

"Ah, Captain Batchelor, so you have been to San Francisco? And now I see in the accounting that most of the cargo is to be traded there! Is the city so beautiful as they say?"

The captain smiled thoughtfully, tactfully studying the young woman's fine features and remarking once more to himself how strongly he was attracted to her. He reflected that it was an affinity, which he realized exceeded mere physical attraction. Indeed, he was suddenly quite disturbed as he considered the far-reaching implications. And he was just a trifle unnerved by the thought of how Katie might feel if she knew what was happening to him!

"Well, Blanca Mende, San Francisco is not quite yet a city. It is rather a rough-and-ready town, full of sailors and vagabonds. But, just the same, it is a splendid place, a magnificent harbor for ships." He paused for a moment, contemplating the lacteal tone of her complexion rather like the color of fresh cream not much trace of the olive tint so often characteristic of Spanish women. Her name...yes, the name meant white. Doubtlessly, as a child she had been so pale she'd been given the name 'Blanca.'

"Now, Blanca Mende, you certainly must be aware that you give the impression that you'd like some day to go to San Francisco. Is this true?"

"You know, Captain Batchelor, your appraisal of San Francisco hardly frightens me. But yes, indeed, I should like some day to go there. Do you suppose that this might be possible?"

Juan Castillo de Merez dropped his hand holding the notebook, in which he'd been jotting orders, to his side and stared at the floor. He had heard his niece's comment and it troubled him. He certainly did not relish the thought of losing his fine secretary. She would be hard to replace! However, he reflected, he had expected eventually to lose her. But San Francisco...it was so far away He might never even see her again!

A week later, the North Aurora sailed out of Jamaica harbor, where a store of sugar and rum had been lowered into the hold. A few stops along the eastern coast of South America, and then a steady, hard drive southward to Cape Horn. Always a hazardous maneuver, the captain reduced sail as the ship approached the wild currents and unpredictable seas. He alerted the mates to be prepared for inclement weather and watch for icebergs. Sailors, of course, were kept in constant readiness to reduce more sail.

In fact, foul weather a high gale was encountered off the coast of Tierra del Fuego, which required all hands-on deck to deal with halyards and climbing aloft to the yards to furl sail. The captain was always amused by Katie's behavior in stormy weather. Far from intimidated by the storm, not content to watch the scene through the port lights in the cabin, she had to be restrained while trying to get out on deck half naked to feel the stinging fury of wind-lashed sea spray. To be sure, as Leon Edgar had said, this vivacious young woman was a "ball of fire!"

Not much had changed in San Francisco. There appeared an increase in the number and variety of ships in the harbor, and perhaps the population had grown a bit. Riverboats were also bringing a larger assortment of goods from the interior. But, aside from a few more warehouses along the embarcadero, new building and general development of properties seemed almost non-existent; indeed, the most prominent structure was a large church on one of the hills surrounding the town. The busiest places appeared to be the numerous saloons that crowded any space not taken by warehouses. (Out west all taverns were called saloons.) Fortunately, there were plenty of hotels, and the captain quickly located the best of them.

It was a rainy, rather cool day in April 1861. Katie MacIver and the captain stood on the dock looking up into the town of San Francisco.

"So, this is the wonder city we've heard so much about!" said Katie morosely.

"Yes, dear lady, it's a bit primitive, but, so far, it's the most promising shipping center on the coast. Now, I think you ought to climb back aboard while I scout around to find us a good hotel, and maybe."

"Please, John, none of that. You're going to take me with you. There's something about this place that fascinates me."

Wending along the unpaved, but fairly well-maintained streets, less than an hour later the captain decided upon the best structure they had seen. It stood on one of the low hills a bit out of town, encompassed by beautifully landscaped gardens and young trees.

"Looks expensive, John, but I love it."

"Nothing's expensive here yet, Katie. This town is still little more than a rather quaint village."

A few minutes later, the captain left Katie in her room to return to the North Aurora to see that all went well with unloading cargo and dealing with the several agents who had come out to evaluate the merchandise.

"I must say, Captain," commented one of the agents, "that your vessel is the finest I've seen yet. I understand this is your second trip here. Am I correct?"

"You are correct, Sir, and I intend to return."

"I trust you do not think me naïve if I say that I believe you will do quite well. Perhaps you are aware, Sir, that California is now declared a United States possession. Believe me, from what I've observed, there are some excellent possibilities for future development. I must say, Sir, this country is bound to become very important."

By late afternoon, all business had been transacted. The captain left future lading to be handled later. He would return to the hotel and see how Katie was faring.

The lamplights were glowing merrily among crystal chandeliers as Captain Batchelor entered the hotel lobby. A few gentlemen sat around, reading newspapers. The quietly ticking clock over the reception desk told him that it was nearly six p.m. Upstairs, he knocked at Katie's door.

"Come in, John. I'm in the tub."

Katie's voice was once again the happy holiday bells and warbling of birds. It was spring, of course, and Katie sounded like spring. The captain realized he was quite pleased that this charming young woman had made the voyage with him. Then, a sudden wave of remorse swept over him. His thoughts carried him back to New Orleans and the vision of Blanca de Merez, her beautiful, exotic face turned questioningly up at him as she sat at her desk. She had said of San Francisco, "I should like to go there some day. Do you suppose that this might be possible?" He also realized that this feeling about Blanca was totally unfamiliar to him. Why had this woman taken such a hold on him? He could not recall ever feeling this way about a woman. In fact, he could not remember ever being in love!

Oh come now, John, he said to himself. Perish the thought! This simply cannot be. He entered the apartment and, instead of yielding to the urge to go into the lavatory and help Katie dry herself--as he usually did he went to a chair and sat down, but not before he noticed a silver ice bucket with a bottle of champagne buried in it and two fine crystal goblets on a rosewood table nearby. The door to the lavatory, of course, was wide open and he could see Katie standing by the tub, giving her shapely body a brisk rubdown with a large towel.

"Captain John," she said plaintively, "you've disappointed me! Why weren't you in here helping me with my rubdown?"

That evening they had gone into the rather well-appointed dining room and were waiting for the maître d'. They presently saw him approaching when...

"Well, well, well, so you are Katherine MacIver. My goodness...what in the world! And you, Sir, are Captain John Batchelor, just sailed that magnificent North Aurora into our fine harbor!"

A bit surprised, both the captain and Katie turned to see a rather large, well-dressed, red-haired, mustachioed gentleman, a little taller than John, smiling warmly at them.

"Oh please forgive me. Certainly, I've committed a flagrant faux pas, but, you know, I was afraid you'd take me for the maître d'!" He laughed the deep, hearty laugh of those who are quite wont to having their own way. "And please, allow me, I am Gregor MacIver; friends call me Greg. And you won't be requiring the service of the maître d'. I shall personally take you to the best table in the house!"

The captain and Katie, of course, quickly overcame their astonishment and silently followed Mr. MacIver to a table in an elevated section of the dining hall, set off by a carved-wood bannister.

"This area is reserved for my personal guests. Indeed, you are both my special guests, and from now on, for you everything is on the house!"

A waiter stood at the table and drew a chair for Katie, making sure she was seated comfortably.

"May I please join you at dinner? That is, if you'd not rather dine alone, and I wouldn't be intruding?" asked Gregor MacIver humorously.

The captain, who was still standing, happily accepted the situation.

"Why yes, of course, Mr. MacIver, assuming that it is agreeable to Katie."

"Oh John, stop the nonsense," laughed Katie. "You know I shall be honored to have Greg dine with us."

"But Mr. MacIver," said the captain, "you must know that I, for one, am just a trifle amazed by all this."

"Oh, don't let it seem at all strange. Please sit down, Sir, and we shall talk out a few matters. Now, would you have a cocktail or perhaps our best wine?"

"Wine will do, Sir."

Turning to the waiter, Greg said quietly, "August, will you please bring us a bottle of our finest Barsac Sauternes, and a bottle of the Chateaux Lafite I'm so fond of. You know the vintage. And, August, make sure the bread is warm."

Mr. MacIver then sat down. "Now, I am sure you are both wondering. Katherine, when I last saw you, you were fresh out of grammar school. Perhaps you've since heard that your father had two brothers. I'm the elder three years your father's senior. Our other, younger brother is still back in Aberdeen, caring for our aging grandparents." He sat back for a moment, looking with an affectionate smile at his niece, who boldly stared him back squarely in the face, grinning with what seemed to the captain rather brazen humor.

"Well," continued Mr. MacIver, "after leaving Boston, I decided to carry on the family's business dealing in Scottish wool. Fortunately, it proved to be quite lucrative."

The wine and bread had arrived. The waiter was starting to uncork the bottles, but MacIver stopped him. "August, I shall do the honors this time," he said with a chuckle.

"As you wish, Mr. MacIver."

"So, you wonder how I came to end up in this blossoming little village. I had done some business in Baltimore where, one evening relaxing at a tavern, I met an enterprising Yankee captain who spun some titillating yarns about California and a tiny seaport called San Francisco. He concluded his story, telling me that he was shipping out in a few days on his third voyage around Cape Horn. Well, I'd had a few of the best whiskey in the house, and was feeling a bit wildly adventurous. Would there be room for a passenger aboard ship?

"Uhah! So ya liked my tale of wonder, did yer! Sure, come aboard at bark Angela. She's moored at dock not more than five minutes away. She'll be headin' out in three days. Say, let's have a stroll over that now. We'll hunker down in at cabin an' have another. Are ya game?' I've quoted the man as closely as I can recall his lingo.

"Well, I was game all right. That's how I got here. But, believe me, there were moments during that voyage aboard the Angela when I felt certain we'd not even get around the Horn! So, I've been here for three years now. Within a week after arrival, I stumbled on this hotel. It was a bit dilapidated and was owned by an elderly British couple who were relieved to get out of it. The rest, you may easily surmise. Now, let's enjoy some of this wine. Katherine, which do you prefer, red or white?"

"Oh, Uncle Greg, I enjoyed your story about how you came to San Francisco, and I'm sure there is much more you could tell, but just now I'd love some of that Sauternes. I've heard it's delicious. And please call me Katie. But I must say, this is all so absolutely magical! Moments ago, I wasn't sure I might not be dreaming."

"And you, Captain?"

"Red for me, Greg. And since we're your personal guests, please, just call me John." The captain had noticed and enjoyed the strong, Scottish burr in MacIver's voice.

Nearly two weeks of pleasant relaxation passed by. The captain was obliged to get back to Boston with the ample lading garnered in San Francisco, much of it with Gregor MacIver's influence on merchants dealing with trappers, ranchers and farmers from the heart of California and elsewhere.

It was well into May, 1861. A fair northwesterly bore the ship down the coast, to round the Horn during the southern autumn.

The captain hoped to land in Boston by the end of summer. He had suggested to Katie that she pack her gear and prepare for departure in the following morning. But, reflecting that she had seemed rather taciturn as he left her that day after breakfast, still sitting at the table chatting with Greg MacIver, he suspected that Katie might well be reluctant to leave all of the good life she was having with her affluent uncle. So, of course, that evening he found that she hadn't packed a thing.

"Well, Katie dear, something's troubling you?"

"No trouble, John, but I just cannot bear to go back to stuffy old Boston. Oh please know how much I appreciate your bringing me to San Francisco! Of course, I shall be looking forward to your return to this wonderful and fascinating country." She stood on her toes and planted a rousing kiss squarely on his mouth as they turned to go downstairs to dinner. "Uncle Greg has promised something special for us tonight. Oh John, do try to delay one more day before departure? I shall be terribly sad if you don't."

Adverse weather and dense fog near Cape Horn delayed sailing into the Atlantic for nearly two weeks. Icebergs, of course, were a constant hazard. It was the middle of September at two a.m. when the North Aurora entered the Boston harbor to be escorted to a mooring at the dock. No one left the ship. All hands were retired to their quarters and the captain rested in his cabin until daybreak. It was good weather that greeted them, and putting the ship in order was easily done as the sun climbed in the eastern sky. Disgorging cargo could wait until the next day.

It was mid afternoon when Captain Batchelor climbed down the gangway to the wharf, where he was surprised to be greeted by Ellen and Mr. Stimson. Miss Ellen threw herself into his arms, effusing sincere enthusiasm, kissing his ruddy face and pulling his beard, grown full and long during the voyage to Boston. Ellen was excited about the captain's beard. Usually kept trim and neat, it was now grown wild and showed more than ever the red of a Norseman.

"You know, Captain John, but for your fine captain's habit, you resemble the dreadful Vikings I've seen depicted in illustrations! In fact, I suspect, Sir, that beneath the fine veneer of the gentleman, I'll just bet that's exactly what you are! But that is why I love you,

Sir!"

"Well, Captain," said Mr. Stimson, "are you free to go home now? You could probably do with a warm bath and a bit of regale. Alice Stimson has been at work preparing a grand supper for us. And Sir, don't bother with stopping at Randall's, we have all that sort of thing in the cabinet at home, you know." Mr. Stimson looked up at the gangway. "I assume Miss MacIver is still aboard, Sir?"

"Katie has remained in San Francisco, Mr. Stimson," said the captain. "She simply refused to leave." From an inside pocket, he withdrew two envelopes. "One of these is for you, the other is for Katie's parents. They are letters from Katie." He discerned a bit of alarm in Mr. Stimson's face, and added, "Oh don't be disturbed. All is quite well with Katie in fact, she's in very good hands and is probably having the happiest time of her life!"

The captain had extensive business with Hyde and Engles.

He also stopped in at the maritime office to visit Anders. He was told that Cyril Connors was enroute to Boston from Ireland, where he had stayed some time with his aging parents and family. "We expect him here any day now, Captain. I'm sure he'll want to see you. He is making the trip aboard the English bark Mary Doone out of Bristol. You're not shipping out for awhile, are you, Sir?"

"No, Anders. The North Aurora must lie in Boston for a few months. The ship will want a bit of refurbishing, and I shall be tending to that. Besides, there are some matters I need to attend here in Boston. And, as you know, the firm has some bright new ideas about California. Meanwhile, I shall stand by, looking forward to seeing Connors."

During the evening at the Stimson's, the captain learned that Leon Edgar had been in Boston, had remained a month and had shipped out again to Europe where his ship took in ladings at France, England, Holland and Germany, trading wheat, corn, cotton and furs. But best of all, he had proposed to Ellen. Indeed, brother Leon returned shortly before the captain left once more for California. He and Ellen were married within a week after his arrival.

Captain John left Boston feeling that his brother had at last earned the warm respect he'd yearned for years to give him. The young couple was to take a small house not more than a mile from the Stimson ménage. Leon Edgar, of course, was to continue work as a jack-tar. But before the year was out, during a stay in Boston, he was granted a mate's rating.

When Cyril Connors met Captain John at the dock where the Mary Doone was moored the two friends strolled over to Randall's tavern. "Understand you've been doing some sailing west. Well, when next you ship out mind if I go along?"

"Bravo Cyril! Anyway you'd like: jack-tar, first mate, or just passenger first class."

"I'll take the latter," rejoined Connors. "Perhaps I can help with business transactions all that sort of thing." He took a sip of his whiskey and turned to face the captain. "Incidentally, since gold was found in the hills, I suppose the state is booming…something of a population explosion?"

"Quite so Cyril. A bit on the wild side, it is."

The North Aurora left Boston toward the end of December 1862, landing in New Orleans the first important port of call by early January. All general matters of lading were swiftly consummated. Connors wished to pay a visit to an old friend, leaving the captain free to walk into the de Merez warehouse office for his final and perhaps most significant transaction of the day. Cotton and cotton goods were now a matter of priority in San Francisco. Looking at Blanca's desk, he was deeply troubled to see that she was not there.

"Oh, Captain, don't fret," placated Juan Castillo. "Your dismay is quite apparent, Sir. My niece had to do some shopping for her mother. We expect her back at her desk in perhaps an hour. Allow me to say, Sir, Blanca has been harping about you and will be pleased if you stand by for her, Sir. I'm sure she'll be back by the time we put your merchandise aboard ship."

And so it was. The captain returned to the office within two hours. Señorita Blanca was visibly delighted to see him. She stood up before him, her eyes brimming with tears. For moments she said nothing, looking alternately into his face and at the floor.

Egad! Said the captain to himself, these Spanish girls are an emotional lot!

(It is not clear to this writer whether Captain Batchelor and Blanca de Merez were married in New Orleans or in San Francisco.

To be sure, there is conflicting opinion as to how soon they were married after the incident in the de Merez warehouse office. That they were soon completely enamored of each other, there is no question. It is known, however, that Blanca was taken aboard the North Aurora enroute to California, and that the arrival in San Francisco occurred about June or July, 1862. Nevertheless, the writer assumes that because there could hardly have been sufficient time and preparation for the wedding to occur in New Orleans, it follows that the marriage was probably consummated in San Francisco).

At latitude thirty-eight the beautiful North Aurora began shortening sail as it approached the entrance to San Francisco Bay, a fair westerly driving her steadily onward. It was late afternoon and the rich red-gold of a setting sun painted the tree-fringed rocky escarpments towering on either side with the blazing colors that would give the entrance its name the glorious portals of gold that for all time would be to mariners and landlubbers alike that memorable golden gate!

Thought Captain John as he stood on the quarterdeck, it is the ineffable gold of a gateway to an enchanted land! He stood gazing out across the emerald, gently rolling waters at the hills of the bay's eastern shore. Señorita Blanca Mende had come out to watch too. She commented, "Oh Captain Batchelor, Sir, it is all so very, very magnificent. What a grand thing of magic it is! I have never felt such happiness in all my life!"

The captain turned and stepped over to her. Not yet daring to embrace her, as he had the urge to, he said softly, "Well, Señorita Blanca, now you see why so many have come back to us in the east with tales about this land that stir the imagination and beguile so many to sail to these shores…for it is indeed a golden state!"

Cyril Connors had joined the first mate, Matthews, standing amidships, calmly scrutinizing the majestic pylon to a land lying, virgin and vulnerable to this most predacious creature on earth… called human. So this is the fabled El Dorado, he thought. What next shall mankind do to enslave and exploit the sweet woman Earth? And when finished here with this lovely planet, shall this human creature set forth to pillage and rape the teeming worlds of the skies? Connors, the philosopher, glanced at Matthews; "What say you, Sir? You've seen it all before; does it still not seem the pristine land, awaiting mankind's inevitable grasp?"

"Hah!" exclaimed Matthews laconically. "So, you know my mind so well! Are you a scholar, Mr. Connors?

"No. Not quite, Sir. But it has been my business to observe perhaps more intimately than most people the enterprising activity of us humans. And this remarkable introduction to our most recent acquisition does stir the mind to further wonderment."

Matthews could say nothing to this of course. Being of necessity a rather pragmatic sort, he accepted civilization, as it seemed to be, without question, finding no cause for alarm in any of mankind's demeanor. After all, it was his business to simply keep men hard at work sailing ships...even though, as Hesiod the Ancient Greek farmer advised us, "Keep away from the bitter sea!"

Early the following morning the captain, Blanca Mende and Connors descended the gangway to the wharf. Mr. MacIver and Katie greeted them. Beyond them were several vehicles hitched to well-groomed horses, among which were broughams, cabriolets, surreys and buckboards. Katie of course ran immediately to Captain John and threw her arms around his shoulders. She raised herself and kissed him noisily. The captain expected this sort of display, but found that he was somewhat embarrassed, even annoyed. He moved away and stood calmly gazing at her, feeling confronted by a rather difficult situation.

"Oh, Captain, it's so wonderful to see you again. And who may I ask are your two friends?"

"Katie, this is Señorita Blanca de Merez from New Orleans, and the gentleman is my dear friend Cyril Connors from Boston." The captain turned to Greg MacIver. "I trust I'm not presumptuous to ask if perhaps there is a vehicle available to us? We have some luggage"

"You have your choice of anything you see over there," said Mr. MacIver. "May I suggest a brougham for the Señorita and Mr. Connors? Perhaps you and Katie can go in one of the other broughams. I shall have Choy care for your luggage...anything"

"Mr. MacIver, please, Sir, perhaps Mr. Connors would like to accompany Katie. You see, Greg, Señorita Blanca is with me." The captain hesitated for a moment, recovering from his annoyance with Katie's affectionate onslaught. "You see Greg, the Señorita and I are going to be married!"

At this sudden proclamation for which Katie MacIver was totally unprepared everyone except Connors who was quietly smiling at the captain, stood open-mouthed, transfixed with astonishment. Señorita Blanca de Merez of course was ostensibly affected by the captain's abruptness, but quickly regained her composure as she realized the captain's need to clear an otherwise awkward predicament. If during the long voyage she had grown to love Captain Batchelor, the strength of his statement aroused all the ardor and passion that she had decorously controlled...especially whenever she caught his eyes penetrating the mask of polite civility that concealed the fires within.

There was an agonizing minute when Katie stood staring in shocked alarm at Captain John and Blanca de Merez. In truth, the captain felt the electric tension growing in the uninhibited young woman whose emotions he knew might be rising to the explosive point. Then to his relief she turned to Greg MacIver, raising her arms about his shoulders, sobbing wildly with her face pressed against his chest. Cyril Connors understood how Katie must have been suffering. He slowly stepped over close by her, saying, "Well, Katie, I hope you won't mind joining me in a bit of a spin in that fine brougham your Uncle Gregor has so propitiously offered us? Indeed, I'd be quite pleased if you will. Do you suppose I could have this pleasure Dear Katie?"

The North Aurora was due back in Boston, so the captain was hard-pressed to consummate his marriage to Blanca Mende and tend to business with Hyde and Engles. The company had built a warehouse and office on the San Francisco waterfront, which simplified ladings; by then the cargo included shipments of gold which necessitated installation of small artillery and other weaponry and trained militia-personnel as defense against piracy. During the early eighteen-sixties, Confederate attacks complicated this situation.

While Captain Batchelor was away on the first voyage after his marriage to Blanca, their first child, Maude, was born. Blanca had been urged to remain at Gregor MacIver's fine hotel where she received the care and attention she needed to ease parturition. Katie had quickly overcome the loss of her beloved Captain. (It is known that Cyril Connors facilitated this transition!) Katie had even begun a sororal relationship with her former rival, Blanca de Merez. She refused, however, to call Blanca 'Mrs. Batchelor' indubitably because the utterance was painful to her. Mrs. Batchelor indeed! She would say to herself. She is just Señorita Blanca de Merez so far as I am concerned....

Upon his return to San Francisco, after the second voyage, the captain decided that he should move his family to Sacramento. Indeed, Blanca had begun complaining that her Captain-husband was often gone too long to be a satisfactory father! This sort of thing commenced to be more difficult to bear after their second child, John, was born.

So it came to pass that upon his return to their home in Sacramento, the captain requested leave of his duties with Hyde and Engles. The year was 1866 and steam vessels were challenging the grand old sailing ships contemptuously called windjammers by the "weaklings who sailed those horrid steam-driven stinkpots" as the "real sailors" often retorted! To be sure, Captain John was frequently heard to express his disgust for "these smoking, clangorous, dirty coffins!" Certainly, it was not the mere fact that the steamships were swiftly replacing sail-driven ships. As he said, "I cannot tolerate the noise they make; but it is the hellish stench that is most unbearable!"

Meanwhile, Katie MacIver was beginning to think seriously about the captain's best friend, Cyril Connors. They were finally married in San Francisco during the captain's final stay there a source of particular pleasure to him. Connors had been best man at his wedding to Blanca and now he had the chance to return the favor. So he was drawn willy-nilly into the job of captaining riverboats between San Francisco and Sacramento. To say the least, this was a job he detested, but alas! fate had now begun to bear down upon him! "The slings and arrows of outrageous fortune..." He was aware that he had no choice. Blanca and the children needed him, and this job allowed him more time at home.

But life in Sacramento during the last days of the mad and often violent rush for gold in the Sierra hills was hardly to remain stable for the little family. Maude had become ill and needed a doctor's care. When she seemed improved the captain and Blanca had to find a house in Woodland, a tiny village northwest of Sacramento in Yolo County. There, in 1871, the second son, Thomas Leon was born.

But grave misfortune was in store. A few years after the birth of Thomas Leon, while serving on a posse in a wilderness area northwest of Sacramento, the posse was ambushed and several of the men were shot off their horses. Captain Batchelor was one of them. The renegades were soon apprehended. All were summarily hung the swift judgment of the Old West! (No expensive criminal defense lawyers out west in those days!)

Grim and whimsical irony! Here was a man who had been captain aboard sailing ships, during some of the world's toughest years of shipping commerce. He had commanded those ships amidst the worst storms and hazards the sea could throw at the sailors of those days and had come out unscathed only to be shot to death in the back while riding a horse on land by a gang of worthless louts.

But the loss of their father meant that the two boys, John and Thomas, would need to find small jobs to help their mother.

Gregor MacIver and Connors teamed up to send a stipend to Blanca; but the pall of sadness that had settled on the little family could not be so easily lifted. Maude, who had loved and adored her father probably more than anyone else, soon fell terminally ill and died. Thomas had found a job starting the early-morning fire in the schoolhouse, while John went to work in a saloon, keeping the place clean and washing bottles.

Several years before all this, a certain gentleman by the name of Jacob Olhahn (pronounced Olhan), had set up keeping store in town where Blanca often purchased groceries. Mr. Olhahn, who was a widower, had noticed the interesting Mrs. Batchelor and had been quite taken with her. When he learned of the captain's death, he refused payment for anything Blanca needed, and often gave her special treats for herself and the two boys. He soon offered to put the boys to work in the store. John happily accepted, but Thomas wished to keep his job at the schoolhouse. It seems he had developed a fondness for young Miss Baxter, the schoolteacher, with whom he often conversed at length after school. Thomas was particularly intrigued when he found that she loved music. Her father had been a trombonist who was an instrumentalist in opera and symphonic orchestras in the east. Thomas was overjoyed when she told him that her father had left her his trombone when he died, and asked if he would like to see it.

One day Miss Baxter brought the trombone to school. It was a very cold, wintry day in February. Thomas of course had been at school an hour earlier and had set a roaring fire in the big stove. When Miss Baxter opened the leather-bound case, there it lay--a shimmering, magical thing of shining gold! Young Thomas, who had freshly turned the ripe age of eight, was deeply enchanted by the sight of the beautiful instrument. "May I touch it?" he asked timorously.

"Are your hands clean, Tom?"

"I shall wash them," said Thomas.

"If you promise to be very careful, you may hold it."

"Oh Miss Baxter, I don't dare hold it, not yet anyway. Do you have a book I can read about it? I have never even seen a trombone before, you know, and I would be scared I might do something wrong."

"Tom, you are a dear! Yes, I have some literature about music and musical instruments."

And so, the next day Miss Baxter brought everything about trombones she could find that her father had left her which included a quantity of music. "You may take all this home, Tom. I am sure you will want to read every bit of it, but do not neglect your homework!"

So this was how Thomas Leon became a musician. Miss Baxter had him learn to play simple exercises for trombone--when the other children were not around. She wasn't satisfied until Thomas evinced genuine and unfailing interest in learning to play the trombone. Of course, Miss Baxter finally gave Tom the instrument. And we know that Thomas Leon ultimately became an accomplished professional trombonist.

Blanca and Jacob Olhahn eventually married in Woodland, and the family moved into a large house near the store. Mr. Olhahn revealed to Blanca that he owned a sheep ranch in Eastern Washington. Later, when the boys were well into adolescence the family moved to the ranch where John and Thomas were given the task of keeping wolves, coyotes, bears and mountain lions from harassing the sheep, which often meant night vigilance. They were provided with rifles that they often fired into the air to frighten the predators. The boys of course found the job fascinating…this was real excitement!

Years later both boys, now young men, left Eastern Washington. Olhahn had died, leaving them to run the ranch. But Blanca grew weary of the grueling work of keeping the big ranch house in order. The family sold the ranch and moved to Cle Elum, a town in central Washington. Thomas, who was closest to his mother, told John he could leave, that there was no need for both to care for Blanca. When Blanca died and was buried in the village cemetery, Thomas moved to Tacoma, Washington.

In 1894, while playing trombone in an orchestra at a town celebration, Thomas met Katherine Gano, whom he soon married. Katherine had a son, Ralph Elliot, by her first marriage. When their first child, Leon Edgar, was born Thomas moved the family to Bandon, a small lumbering town on the coast of Oregon. There, Thomas moved his family into a large home overlooking the sea a place he dearly loved. They had two more children a girl, Blanche Demeris, and a boy, Jonathan David.

John had gone back to California, to the San Francisco Bay Area. He had cultivated skill as a house painter while at Olhahn's ranch. Continuing this line of work in Berkeley, California, he developed a prosperous business as a painting contractor. He dealt with a small paint company owned by the Swanson family. It was while conducting business at their Berkeley store on Telegraph Avenue that he met Selma Swanson, whom he subsequently married. John eventually purchased a large Victorian house on Harper Street in Berkeley, where the family raised three boys and a girl Lester, Clarence, Frank and Esther.

EPILOGUE

The last events mentioned in this writing bring the story to a close. What occurred afterward may be classified as well-known statistics. The writer feels that it is pointless to bother with the delineation of the several descendants of Captain Batchelor and Blanca de Merez, whose progeny are presently, in this late twentieth century tending their separate gardens of life.

Lamentably, some of these descendants hardly know each other, and might even be regarded as strangers. The writer also feels that Captain John and Blanca Mende would be saddened by this and would find it hard to understand. But surely they might be expected to know that the offspring of even the best-organized families are often of such disparity that they seem alien to each other; siblings sometimes spend a lifetime of alienation from one another.

So, we will leave it at that, for the question of how better life might be if disparity amongst individuals, religions, politics, nations and races weren't the root of so much misfortune in our world, remains interesting, though idle speculation. Once again, granting that the thing we call civilization meant that we would all have the opportunity of working together for the common good (if we even knew its definition!), perhaps then we should know as the ancient Greeks knew--that men shall come and go like the generations of leaves in the forest; that men will continue to be weak even when they know better; that the quality of a man matters more than his achievements; that violence and recklessness will still lead to disaster, and that this will fall upon the innocent as well as upon the guilty.... (In these last lines we are reminded of Ecclesiastes of the Holy Scriptures, a name which is derived from the Greek word Ecclesia.)

If indeed we are strong enough to admire that this is true, we realize that it is not a source of solace to the millions of us who need the comforting love, the protection from our own follies, of an omniscient Father God, or the embrace of an all-powerful Earth Mother. Deplorably, the majority of us are hardly capable of searching ourselves to find strength and security within. We wonder how many of us have ever been able to do this!

Perhaps, for the sake of honesty, I should acknowledge the

quasi-historical nature of this writing. What we have here is the mass of raw material derived from tales related to me during the many years of close relationship with my father, Thomas Leon which has been made into a structure rather different from dull statistical recording. In truth, most of it is of my own devising, mind you. I have avoided the tedious jotting of facts whatever they really were. Who can possibly know? Since none of us who are descendants of Captain John Thomas and Blanca was there to bear witness! Nevertheless, it is clearly a tale I expect to win credence among the members of the Batchelor clan.

In conclusion, I wish to say something of personal concern. Whenever I write, there is a kind of compunction that creeps over me spawned from the awareness that I speak well above the minds of the "madding multitude," to quote A.E. Poe. I habitually assume of course that most if not all Americans are an educated and intelligent lot, and that therefore I am not communicating to ignoramuses. It has always been my personal contention that one should not talk down to people but compel them to rise to higher human levels. Are we not all supposed to be equally intelligent? Judging by the sad state of our world, this appears not to be so.

I think it interesting if not important to note that Captain John, while generally a temperate and thoughtful man, was no saint. He certainly lived a full life, replete with adventures that most men, either being timorous or thinking it unpropitious, would comfortably avoid. Of course, we ought to know, he lived in a time when men consumed strong drink and were expected to shun emotional display.

It is perhaps amusing that my father who, during our many years "batching" it together and while I was married to Dorothy Dickinson, in the 1930s, related the many tales that are the essence of this brief history, occasionally commented that he regarded his father with something bordering awe.

"How's that?" I once asked. "Did he intimidate you, or something?"

"No, Jonnie, but he did seem rather overwhelming at times. I suppose it's because it was hard for him to suddenly stop being Captain of his ship. I must say, though, he showed deep respect for my mother often hugged and kissed her in the presence of us children."

"But Dad," I persisted, "why haven't you written down all this stuff you tell me? You tell the stories so beautifully. It seems to me you could write them at least as well. Why not?"

"Jonnie telling a story is not the same as writing it. You know, I've read some of your school papers. I thought they were pretty good. And that's it...you're the one to write it. I hope someday you'll do it!"

Could anyone who has perused these pages even remotely conjecture what the outcome of this extraordinary bond between the cool, rather pragmatic Captain John Thomas Batchelor and the intensely warm, romantic Blanca Mende de Merez? When one studies such a union through the penetrating scientific eye, this blending of genes geographically so divided by remoteness, divided by the passage of countless millennia, this fascinating miscegenation, this marriage between the far-northern Celt and the hot, emotional blood of the southern Semite, one is smitten by the awareness of profound, biological forces that might aptly evoke consequences defying banal reasoning! Here was this mariner, long inured to the exacting, behavior-compelling rigors of the sea, in the days of the most difficult sailing ships in maritime history, and this lovely, passionate young woman whose commanding purpose in life was to know and express the full meaning of love? Who could foretell what almost magical, miraculous wonder might arise from their union?

Jonathan Batchelor
Canyon, 1995

About the Author

Julia Rosenstein painting *Nez Perce*, as photographed by her father, Max Rosenstein.

Julia Antoinette Rosenstein is an award-winning artist and author. She has art in her DNA. Her great-grandfather and grandmother were painters. Her mother was an artist. So are several of her siblings. She lived in the Bay Area for 18 years with artist Jonathan David Batchelor. He is the subject of her debut book, ***Last Bohemian: The Life and times of Jonathan David Batchelor.***

She attended Mills College in Oakland, CA. She held various jobs, ranging from hot dog stand worker and security guard, to cocktail waitress, pretzel maker, and corporate call center work. She found her calling as an artist but was unable to make a living by painting.

A former member of North West Oil Painters Guild, she won a ribbon for the drawing of a mare and foal at The Society of Washington Artists. A few years later, in 2010, she won a Judge's Choice Award for an oil painting she did of a friend and her daughter.

Born in Adrian, Michigan, her family moved when she was 10 to Moraga, California. She left California in 2005 after her house burned down, and now resides in Vancouver, Washington. For more information, please see: www.wildhorseart.com

Not diagnosed until she was in her 40s, Rosenstein is on the spectrum for Autism.

www.ingramcontent.com/pod-product-compliance
Lightning Source LLC
Chambersburg PA
CBHW051136120626
46547CB00012B/820